THE
PLAYMAKER'S
ADVANTAGE

THE
PLAYMAKER'S
ADVANTAGE

HOW TO RAISE YOUR MENTAL
GAME TO THE NEXT LEVEL

LEONARD ZAICHKOWSKY
AND DANIEL PETERSON

Gallery Books

JETER PUBLISHING

New York   London   Toronto   Sydney   New Delhi

Gallery Books / Jeter Publishing
An Imprint of Simon & Schuster, Inc.
1230 Avenue of the Americas
New York, NY 10020

First Gallery Books trade paperback edition January 2019

GALLERY BOOKS and colophon are registered
trademarks of Simon & Schuster, Inc.

For information about special discounts for bulk purchases,
please contact Simon & Schuster Special Sales at
1-866-506-1949 or business@simonandschuster.com.

The Simon & Schuster Speakers Bureau can bring authors to your
live event. For more information or to book an event, contact the
Simon & Schuster Speakers Bureau at 1-866-248-3049 or visit
our website at www.simonspeakers.com.

Design by Renato Stanisic

Manufactured in the United States of America

10   9   8   7   6   5   4   3   2   1

Library of Congress Cataloging-in-Publication Data is available.

ISBN 978-1-5011-8186-3
ISBN 978-1-5011-8187-0 (pbk)
ISBN 978-1-5011-8188-7 (ebook)

For Linda, a lifetime of unconditional support,
sons Justin and Bryan and their families, Tamara, Tracy, May,
Talia, Greyson, and Benjamin—you are the best!

LZ

For Kyle, Matt, and Steve, who give me pride,
and for Shirley, who gives me joy.

DP

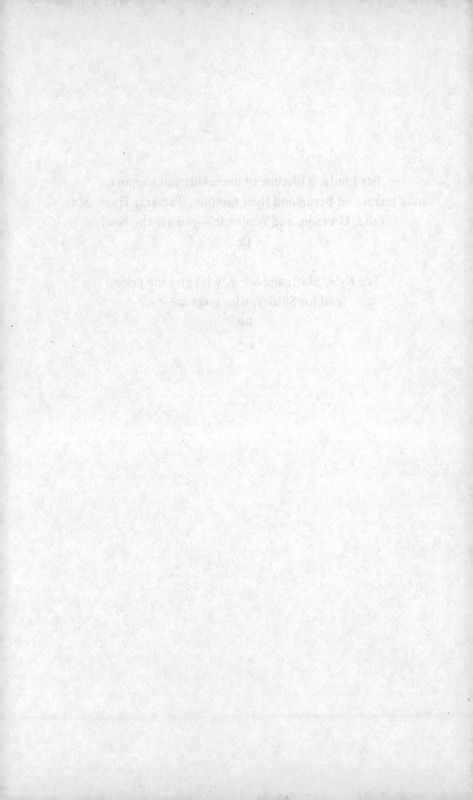

CONTENTS

FOREWORD

Mike Sullivan, Head Coach, Pittsburgh Penguins

Back when I was a college student and hockey player at Boston University (BU), my father was coaching my younger brother in a youth league in the Boston area. In the summertime Dad asked me to go on the ice and run practices with some skill sessions for the kids. I was trying to find certain drills and activities that would be best for their overall development. The first thing that dawned on me was that if I was going to be an effective teacher—in essence, what a coach is—I'd better have an understanding, at least on an elementary level, of how people learn. Otherwise, how could I effectively put together strategies and methodologies that would maximize the opportunity to teach these kids?

So that's really where it all started for me. That's why I began learning about the cognitive side of sports. I was trying to better understand how people learn at their respective age groups, because I've always been a big believer in age appropriateness when you're coaching sports. If I'm coaching a group of eight-year-olds or nine-year-olds, I can't go out and run the same practice that I'm running with the Pittsburgh Penguins. Cognitively, they're at a very different stage than grown men. I need an understanding of what their limitations are, where their potentialities lie, so that I can focus on certain things that can leverage that knowledge.

The reality is that kids are not miniature adults. Their brains are different. They're not fully developed. I listen to parents in the stands around the rink and hear comments like "Little Johnny doesn't pass to my son because I think his father gives him ten bucks for every goal he scores." Well, maybe little Johnny's peripheral vision isn't fully developed, so he doesn't see your son on the back door.

When I was playing in college in the late 1980s, the new frontier was in physical fitness and training. That's when players started to get into the weight room to work on strength and conditioning with plyometrics, developing power in the neuromuscular system. That was cutting-edge back then.

Now we have a pretty good understanding of how to train athletes physiologically. The next frontier is how to get players to better understand anticipation skills, recognition skills, and decision-making. How to deal with high-stakes environments. How to handle pressure. In my generation, there's always been an assumption around the rinks that "hockey sense" is something that you're born with: you either have it or you don't, but you can't teach it. The reality is that hockey sense or game sense is not unlike learning how to skate or learning how to stick handle. This new capability is, as this book's title says, "the playmaker's advantage."

For me, the simplest definition of "playmaker" is someone who makes the players around him better. Playmakers' understanding of how to create competitive advantages by utilizing their teammates is what sets them apart.

During my NHL playing days, it was Gretzky and Lemieux. It was Steve Yzerman, Joe Sakic, Peter Forsberg, and Doug Gilmour, to name a few. All of these playmakers were one step ahead of the game. They saw plays develop in their brains before those plays actually happened. They took advantage of windows of opportunity because of their ability to see the big picture.

Today's best example of a playmaker is our captain, Sidney Crosby. He not only makes his teammates better, he makes the coaches better. I enjoy so many of our conversations because he thinks the game on a different level. What separates those types of players, the elite players, from the others is how they see the game and how they think the game. As a coaching staff, we're always fascinated by the comments, observations, and insights that players like Sid have when we have team meetings. Even during games, Sid will come back to the bench and he'll have an observation about what our opponents are doing and how we should think about countering. I've probably learned more from Sid than he's learned from me in the years that we've been together.

With every player, there is a floor and ceiling. But each one can get better if we put them in certain activities that give them the opportunity to develop and train the decision-making components of anticipation, recognition, and awareness. Part of the issue is that most coaches don't know how to do that. In hockey we have a much better understanding of how to improve a player's skating ability, for example. We can help a player learn how to stick handle, or work on catch and release, or improve the velocity of his or her shot. But as coaches and parents, we also need to ask how can we help this player with anticipation skills and recognition skills and decision-making skills.

For me, these are our next challenges. As a professional coach at the NHL level, I try to learn as much as I can about how people learn. By learning about the brain, I can use activities in practice that can help us train our guys to get better at the intellectual side of the game, which is every bit as important as the physical aspect.

When I sit in meetings with our scouts to talk about drafting players, I often hear "He's six foot four, 220 pounds, strong as an ox, and can stick handle in a phone booth." And I always respond with "Okay, but can he play the game?" Give me guys that have high compete levels and have a high hockey IQ, and they'll figure out the rest. Whatever deficiencies they may have in the physical aspects of the game, whether it's puck handling, skating, shooting—whatever—their competitiveness and their intellect will find ways to overcome it.

The challenge for this generation of coaches is to figure out the best ways to make that happen. Again, we have to understand how athletes learn. If we can answer that question, we've got a much better chance to develop those essential skills that we look for in our athletes.

In youth sports, we have a tendency to want to create false environments. We stage situations that might not accurately simulate the resistance that they're going to see in a game. If you want to practice or train decision-making, awareness, anticipation, and those types of intellectual skills, you have to create activities in practice that closely resemble the demands of the game itself.

The counterargument to that would be: Why don't we just play five-on-five games all the time in practice? The issue is that if you start tracking touches or the amount of times a player has the opportunity to receive a pass and give a pass, it's very limited. Instead, you can create a practice environment where you can organize activities that replicate the demands of the sport from a pressure standpoint, so that you're practicing the intellectual skills. That way the players get opportunities to possess the puck, protect the puck, pass and receive, shoot the puck, and work on one-timers, combining both the physical and intellectual aspects that are so important.

Unfortunately, this also leads to a place where we often falter, especially at the younger ages. We never graduate beyond this false environment where all we do is isolate skills, never graduate to the point where we start to train the skills within activities that reflect how the game is really played.

When you think about how kids grow up today, it is in a very structured environment. For the most part, they're told what to do from the time they get up in the morning and brush their teeth until the time they go to bed at night. Almost every activity that today's kids participate in includes some sort of parental involvement or oversight.

When I was a kid, we grew up in an environment away from the analytical eyes of adults. With both of my parents working, I would come home to my grandmother each night after school. She would say, "Just be home for dinner," and we went off to have a street hockey game or baseball game or whatever, with no parents around. I think those experiences shaped me as an athlete because they allowed me the opportunity to explore the game—not just the game we were playing, but different sports. I've always been a strong believer that there are certain sports that are developmental in nature, and there's a lot of carryover and crossover.

I first met Len Zaichkowsky—or "Doc Z," as we like to call him—when I was a player at BU and he was our sports psychologist and a professor. When I became a young coach in the NHL, he often invited me over to speak to one of his classes, which I always enjoyed. I have so much respect and admiration for his passion for hockey and all sports, helping so many of us young athletes to be our very best.

Doc Z was ahead of his time in studying and promoting the intellectual and emotional aspects of sport. I am very grateful to him, both as a former player for helping me become a pro and as a young coach trying to get better.

That's why I am so excited about this book, *The Playmaker's Advantage.* Any coach who isn't tuned in to this stuff, in my opinion, is going to fall behind. There just aren't that many books out there that address these topics. Some are on the brain and learning, others are on coaching and youth sports, but there aren't very many that connect the dots. That's where the sweet spot is, where a lot of us are trying to learn and improve. Enjoy this journey into the next frontier of sports performance.

INTRODUCTION

How hard could it be? I was an adult, a dad no less, with a reasonable understanding of the game despite never having played soccer. They were a pack of nine-year-olds, veterans of at least two to three seasons of battle on fields with reduced dimensions and shrunken goals. Besides the color of their jerseys and shoes, they were open to nearly any of my suggestions as to our strategy, tactics, drills, and motivations to get the Saturday-morning win and the red Gatorade that would follow.

As a rookie volunteer coach, I researched and debated the best formation, attacking style, and starting lineups. Just feed my plans and knowledge into their curious heads, and we would surely hoist seven-inch-tall plastic trophies at the end of the season. Armed with a clipboard detailing each drill with its allotted time, I blew the whistle to start my first team practice.

An hour and a half later I realized that young brains vary from adult brains on many levels. So many concepts, so many skills, and so many rules were like foreign language lessons to my future superstars. Explaining to one of them that "you were in an offside position when the ball was kicked" only resulted in a blank stare. My coaching advice to another that "we should not all chase the ball" was similar to saying, "Don't chase the man handing out free ice cream."

Putting down my clipboard, I knew the practice had to be redesigned on the fly. I was trying to teach them calculus before they had mastered addition and subtraction. Despite the seemingly logical explanations and directions from me, they kept making the same mistakes. The mental workload was evident in real time on their faces as they struggled to transition from instructions while standing still to decision-making in motion.

Yet, when I rolled out the ball and just let them play, out came flashes of athletic genius. What seemed to be innate skills of anticipation, elusiveness, creativity, and goal scoring suddenly appeared in a few players, but not all. This talent continuum looked much like a bell curve: some kids clearly got it and some didn't, with the rest somewhere in the middle.

For those who played effortlessly, the game flowed through them. They were at ease on the ball, almost toying with those trying to stop them. Movements were smooth, passes were crisp, decisions were advanced for their age. Athletes like these are the playmakers, the ones that teams are built around. Coaches search for them like lost lottery tickets. Parents dream that their offspring have this sixth sense.

For me, it triggered a lot of questions. What is going on in the brain of each young athlete—especially in the playmakers? How do they learn the thinking, movements, and emotional skills required to succeed in and enjoy their sports at such an early age? How does that body of knowledge grow over time? Why do most kids stay at an average performance level while a few excel to the highest levels of a sport?

Over the last decade, several theories have emerged to explain the elite-versus-novice difference; genetics, ten thousand hours of practice, unequal access to opportunities, and the sheer "luck" of getting an outstanding coach at the right time—these are just a few. While these variables may combine to contribute to an athlete's growth, more detail is needed to understand why they work. Inherited abilities can provide the gifts of speed, power, and size but do they also offer learning efficiency, better working memory, and perceptual-cognitive maturity? Years of brute-force drills will improve skills, yet there are exceptions on both sides of the equation. Environmental advantages set the table for a rapid rise, but not all privileged kids excel.

As you might have guessed, I believe it all starts with the brain, as does my coauthor, Dr. Leonard (Len) Zaichkowsky. As a professor, researcher, and consultant for almost four decades at Boston University, Len pioneered performance psychology as an interdisciplinary science, integrating the study of the brain with observed behavior. While my curiosity originated as a parent and coach interested in the workings of my players' growing minds, Len has been asking similar but more rigorous and researched questions across three hundred published academic papers and speeches. Together, we wanted to create a resource, founded in science, that was accessible to millions of athletes, parents, and coaches. We partnered up as a writer and a professor to search, read, and summarize dozens of research studies, interview the scientists who wrote those papers, then validate those findings with today's best coaches to be sure theory can survive at practice. At the beginning of every interview for this book, we would ask our expert scientist, author, or coach for their definition of "playmaker." While there were similarities in their answers, each adds a unique context that we knew we had to share with you. We picked a cross section of these definitions and added them to the ends of several chapters.

While you will find our collective voice throughout the chapters, Len will provide his unique perspective based on his lifetime of research and consulting on these topics, in the sections affectionately named "Doc Z's Brain Waves."

So, What's Going On?

Every action we take on the playing field, court, or rink originates with an instruction handed down through the central nervous system to the individual muscles. Millions of signals happen effortlessly and mostly unconsciously until something goes wrong. A bad pass, a missed tackle, or a forgotten assignment triggers instant awareness within us, no doubt because of the immediate reaction from our coach and negative reinforcement from our fans.

A sporting competition comes down to the sum of our neural decisions stacked up against our opponent's overall total. Assuming physical preparation is equal, if we make correct choices to pass, shoot, and defend, then we will prevail. If they consistently outthink us, it won't matter if we can bench-press more weight or run a faster forty-yard dash: we may win the battle of conditioning but lose the war on the field.

Moreover, there is a difference between raw physical readiness and expert motor skills. A finely tuned world-class physique cannot weave a puck through four defenders or place a ball in the top corner of the goal without the intricate set of commands needed from the brain. Yet, we spend a disproportionate amount of time trying to grow muscle and increase speed when the payoff would be much greater by focusing on cognitive instructions and decision-making quickness.

Of course, the science of strength and conditioning is well researched and documented. However, the science of the brain is still at a fundamental level insofar as how we learn skills, how we perceive our environment, and how we make fast decisions. We are still learning why some of us can't master a move, why we miss obvious cues, and why we end up making poor choices on the field. To be blunt, the cognitive side of sports is hard.

This book is our attempt to dig deeper into this unfamiliar territory between the ears. To limit the possible universe, we will focus on team-based sports even though individual sports have similar questions. And while these concepts can help all athletes, much of our discussion will be centered on aspiring playmakers ages ten to twenty-two. Their natural development within the mega youth sports machine provides a useful observatory to assess different paths and approaches.

As coaches and parents, we are primarily teachers. But before we can teach, it would help to understand our students as learning creatures whose web of neural connections is forming and fragile. Once understood better, this cognitive domain offers the next big leap in training, as it is the emerging athlete's only remaining unconquered curriculum. To borrow from the title of the book by Swen Nater and Ronald Gallimore about UCLA basketball coach John Wooden, "You haven't taught until they have learned."

Our journey through this material answers two fundamental questions:

- What does it take to become a playmaker and why don't current coaching methods, thousands of hours of practice, and inherited abilities always produce the necessary underlying skills?
- What is "athlete cognition" and how can it be identified, measured, and improved?

Part One: The Playmaker's Foundation
Despite research that identifies the perceptual-cognitive tiebreakers of athletic skill, not all youth sports organizations have rec-

ognized this advantage and the age-appropriate education that is required to keep kids engaged. While the trend of kids' participation is down, a few innovative sports have reinvented their long-term player development models and coaching education to add cognitive development as a key component. We'll take a look at how these changes have boosted their participation numbers while other sports decline.

To get to a new level of elite performance, we must first be clear on what being an "elite" playmaker means. While we don't all aspire to be world-class, we need to understand in greater depth what specific advantages a playmaker has over the average player. In individual, time-based sports like swimming, track, and cycling, the fastest person wins. Winning enough races of increasing quality sets a clear path to world-class. However, in team sports, our teammates, our opponents, and even the officials can dictate overall team success that may lead to individual glory. Teasing out the qualities of a playmaker requires clever comparison studies. We'll take a look at two approaches, named "expert performance" and "component skills," that put experts and novices side by side in sport-specific and everyday life tasks, to see where the differences lie.

Once we have defined our target of high performance, there are still limits to current preparation techniques. Physical training is necessary and often makes the difference between athletes. Strength, endurance, speed, and agility provide the foundation layer on which sport-specific skills are built. Yet, the diminutive Lionel Messi is as good if not better than the Adonis-like Cristiano Ronaldo. Stephen Curry can win MVP awards alongside LeBron James despite giving up six inches and sixty pounds.

Faster and stronger are important in team sports but not always required. And in spite of the advanced science of conditioning, nutrition, and recovery, there are few athletes in the top leagues of football, basketball, or hockey who play the entire game. Preparation of the body is essential, but there are physiological limits to improvements. Despite overflowing rivers of data analytics and physical metrics, there is still a need to measure cognitive competitiveness that, at the end of the day, contributes the most to winning.

Unless it's the brain that is ultimately holding us back. Research from Samuele Marcora and others blames our mental self-preservation as the limiting factor to new standards of physical achievement. This circuit breaker in our heads protects us from ourselves before our bodies completely shut down. However, Marcora contends that this thermostat could be slowly adjusted upward to reach beyond any current plateau.

Part Two: The Playmaker's Cognition

Whether it be through acquired skills or inherited abilities, there must be something more—intelligence that weaves together rules, tactics, emotions, and actions during real-time competition. Often described as a sixth sense, field vision, automaticity, or even intuition, we can't quite get a grip on this collection of actionable knowledge. When young players jump up to the next level, they can be overwhelmed with the speed of the game. But over time and after many mistakes, things begin to "slow down," a sure sign that their awareness, familiarity, and decision-making have sped up to the new normal of competition.

Bridging the gap between declarative sports knowledge (what to do) and procedural knowledge (how to do it), athlete cognition provides a self-awareness, or metacognition, of an athlete's relative sports knowledge and expertise. Deconstructing athlete cognition is the goal of Part Two, where we will dive into the three actions of search, decide, and execute to describe perception, decision-making, and skill acquisition.

Of course, if coaches could bottle athlete cognition, they would mix it in with their team's pregame sports drink. It is often labeled a "gift": being able to consistently find the "right" pass by "reading" the action and staying just a few steps ahead of the opponent. When it works well, everyone recognizes it. This mysterious vision has to start somewhere in the brain, relying on instant access to the memories of thousands of strangely similar situations.

Collectively known as perception, being able to constantly monitor the locations and motions of both teammates and opponents requires trained eyes, including peripheral vision, multiple object tracking, near-far focus, and depth perception. While vision provides about 70 percent of the data we use for analysis, the brain also uses hearing and touch to fill in the blanks that our eyes can't provide. Listening for an approaching defender or sensing pressure from behind requires proprioceptive awareness gained over many seasons.

Pulling off the perfect pass or technically proficient tackle is preceded by the split-second decision to act. How did the player find and choose that particular teammate for the pass? What mental processes anticipated and recognized the path of a ball carrier before the go/no-go decision to make the tackle? How did the tennis player know where to place the ball, and at what speed, so the other team could not return it?

Leading up to each of the thousands of decisions during a game, an athlete needs to cycle through a repeating analysis of hundreds of past situations. This starts with anticipation and pattern recognition to be one step ahead of the play by correctly guessing opponent intentions and movements. Of course, these guesses are quickly confirmed as the senses feed visual, auditory, and tactile data to the brain.

This repeated perception-action loop always ends with a decision, good or bad. Some choices are easy for athletes to pick, while the vast majority lies in gray areas. What is the "right" decision in an intricate sequence of passes or volleys? If it leads to a goal, the player is praised for being part of the buildup. If it stops with an interception, the pass is graded as a mistake. If our job is to improve decision-making during the game, we need decision-making statistics to measure progress. We'll take a look at the current research in sports and other fast-paced environments requiring multiple quick judgments.

We will then enter the murky waters of motor skill acquisition, which often requires years of practice to perfect. Despite each sport's specific demands, they frequently share common, generalized skills. Passing a football, kicking a soccer ball, pitching a baseball, shooting a basketball, hitting a tennis ball—all involve aiming and propelling an object at a target, whether the target is stationary or in motion. Tending a goal in soccer, hockey, and lacrosse has a common objective of blocking that object from its intended path. Eluding a defender and chasing a ball carrier are two sides of the same coin.

When athletes have weaknesses in any of these skills, we can blame the motor commands from the brain. Muscles, ligaments, and bones follow directions just as computer hardware follows instructions from software. Of course, the human brain is more complex than a computer, but the metaphor still holds.

Coaches often focus on the tactical elements of their sports, correcting just the obvious flaws they see in motor skill form. Still, some players shoot and pass more accurately, while others are better at avoiding defenders in the open field. Understanding the learning processes involved in executing these skills should provide training opportunities to elevate the level of above average players to elite performance. Playing multiple sports provides opportunities for the brain to merge and generalize these motor skills to adapt to varied environments, and serves as an argument against early single-sport specialization.

Part Three: The Playmaker's Commitment

Athletes, particularly young ones, are not soulless robots. They have feelings, egos, pride, and emotions that constantly influence their actions. Why do most players give up when others persevere during critical game situations? Do the best performers have a different attitude that pushes them through the long, frustrating years of practice? Psychological research on adolescents is pointing to behavioral traits as keys to success. Would it serve coaches to watch for and train these personality features just as intently as physical performance metrics?

Just as they are not robots, developing athletes—whether in grade school, high school, or college—also don't live in a vacuum. Parents, coaches, teammates, and opponents put enormous pressure and influence on an athlete's identity and will to succeed. Well-intentioned "encouragement" from the sidelines, be it positive or negative, disrupts a player's automated sport cognition flow, creating just enough hesitation to lose the moment. Coaches even have a label of a "good practice player" for those whom they cannot count on in important game situations.

Parents are being bombarded with new neuropsychological concepts such as mindset, grit, flow, and choking that define the underlying commitment to prevail in tough times and the fortitude to thrive in the big moments of competition. We will look at how these ideas mesh with athlete cognition to describe the complete profile of a playmaker.

The playmaker is made on the training ground. But there is confusion among parents and coaches as to the best format and quantity of the hours and hours of practice that young athletes endure. We'll talk to researchers and coaches about what the latest science says about the right learning environment. Then it's time to compete with all of the pressure that game time brings. Will a playmaker deliver a clutch performance or a choking nightmare?

Research in both areas, influenced by the concept of flow and automaticity, can tell us how to manage players in the heat of battle.

Even an adequate amount of practice can't always explain greatness. Elite status can be reached by some athletes years before the population average, while a lifetime of effort does not guarantee reaching the top of the performance pyramid. In fact, recent research by David Z. ("Zach") Hambrick and others has shown that the number of hours in training explains part of an athlete's expertise but not all of it.

Traditional coaching styles can also limit individual progression. The curse of "hand-me-down" coaching (repeating what has always been done) may gain acceptable team results but rarely wins championships. To be sure, the brain of a twelve-year-old differs from that of a seventeen-year-old, which differs from an adult's. Understanding the cognitive development of emerging athletes helps coaches better organize age-appropriate practices to realize the biggest return at each training. The learning needs of a U10 soccer team are drastically different from those of a high school varsity team, yet many U10 coaches model what and how high school coaches teach.

In the same way, teaching kids the many details of a sport requires unique methods to match their learning styles. Just lining them up for redundant drills and yelling at their mistakes may not get the results we're looking for. Without understanding what's going on in their brains, it is hard to practice "cognitive coaching" to make lessons stick.

If there is a better way to teach skills or embed tactics into a player's brain, why don't coaches use these techniques? Might it be as simple as a lack of coach education? Just as evidence-based medicine helps physicians apply the latest research-driven protocols into their practices, evidence-based coaching provides new and more efficient ways to educate athletes using brain-based learning methods.

Still, inertia and the underlying aversion to embarrassment are the most likely dampers on a coach's use of creative ideas and technology. Ignorance or a simple lack of awareness of a better way may also play a role. Being able to copy successful pioneering coaches is often enough to arrive at the tipping point of a paradigm shift. Given that bias, we'll take a look at some of the coaching mavericks out there who bravely experiment with new methods that get results.

Who Is This Book For?

This book isn't necessarily for the athlete who already makes the "A" team. Rather, it's meant for all the "B" players whose dreams are just as big. They can hopefully learn to speed up their skill acquisition and deepen their athlete cognition. And for coaches with a bench full of B players, we are confident you will find ideas to get inside their heads so they, too, can enjoy and succeed in the game.

To our fellow parents: We are all too familiar with your desire to give your young athlete every opportunity to improve. We all want our kids to succeed, even if it is partly for our own ego. The ideas in this book aren't necessarily shortcuts but rather guideposts to finding the most efficient routes to improvement. There's no sense in putting your son or daughter through hundreds of hours of drills, or telling them to "go practice," or sending them to yet another expensive sport camp, without understanding their learning process at the highest and lowest levels of cognition.

Our ultimate goal is that youth sports teams don't have to give up on the potential of nine-year-old athletes, labeling them B players, creating a self-fulfilling path of mediocrity. Instead, coaches and parents will have a new understanding of why those kids currently perform the way they do and have tools and techniques to increase their athlete cognition, their in-game performance, their enjoyment of the sport, and the development of a lifelong appreciation for healthy physical activity. It is our hope that you will be better able to understand whether you as a parent or coach are providing what stress guru Dr. Hans Selye called "eustress" (good, healthy, challenging pressure) or "distress" (negative stress, unhappiness, and lack of motivation).

Our focus has been on team sports for young athletes. But, in addition, if you the parent are a B-level weekend warrior and want to up your own game, athlete cognition will serve you well, too. And athlete cognition even transcends sports altogether. The cognitive skills learned by young athletes can cross over to their daily academic and social lives as well. This is no small thing. Faster perception and information processing in the brain translates across any learning domain. The cognitive skills that allow your child to win on the field can help him ace his test, make friends more easily, and make decisions more clearly. Parents will learn through research examples that the power of athlete cognition will help on the field as well as at home and school.

WHAT IS A PLAYMAKER?

David Epstein, New York Times *bestselling author of* The Sports Gene: Inside the Science of Extraordinary Athletic Performance *and investigative reporter for ProPublica:*

I guess it's subjective, but I think of "playmaker" as different from any other sort of term for excellence. To me, that brings to mind two main things. One is someone who maybe has a more comprehensive view of what's going on, such that they set up opportunities for not just themselves but also their teammates or set up situations where their teammates are going to be more productive. I think there's a reason why in an individual sport we wouldn't call someone a playmaker.

I also think that it suggests to me that it's also someone who gets better or at least doesn't deteriorate as the pressure goes up, which I think is very difficult. One of the playmakers I think about is former Chicago Bulls player Dennis Rodman. Aside from whatever people think about his antics off the court, I've found him to be an incredibly interesting player. When Dennis Rodman got inducted into the Basketball Hall of Fame, there was a lot of sports talk about whether he deserved it or not because they were saying he wasn't a well-rounded player. He just didn't score as much as most of the guys in the Hall of Fame. There were other guys in the Hall of Fame who were less dimensional than he was but scored a lot. Ben Morris did this amazing analysis on him. Rodman grabbed the highest proportion of available rebounds for his era by a lot. Rodman's a clear outlier.

When he was in the game, even if he wasn't accumulating stats, he would neutralize the other team's best rebounder and often their best scorer, and guys on his team would end up scoring a lot closer to the basket. Whatever he was doing, even when he wasn't scoring, was often in some cases neutralizing one of the other team's best scorers and rebounders and somehow either distracting them or being annoying so that his own teammates were better able to get into the lane.

So there was a case of a guy where I think you could call him a playmaker, even when he wasn't the star—when he obviously wasn't Michael Jordan or Scottie Pippen. To me, it has that connotation of both not deteriorating under pressure but also setting up situations that cause things to happen—for yourself, but also for your teammates.

PART ONE

THE PLAYMAKER'S FOUNDATION

CHAPTER 1

Setting the Playmaker's Foundation

K ids have a way of sending messages, especially to coaches and parents. Between 2009 and 2014, over 300,000 kids aged six to seventeen stopped playing baseball in the U.S., and roughly 700,000 quit each of basketball, soccer, and football. According to the 2015 Sports and Fitness Industry Association (SFIA) report[1] on participation across seventeen team sports in those five years, total participation in youth sports declined from 50.2 million to 45.7 million kids, a 9 percent decline. In addition to the double-digit percentage losses in these four core sports, others were even more dramatic. Track and field was down 10.4 percent, court volleyball declined 21.6 percent, and wrestling dropped a whopping 41.9 percent.

Part of the explanation for this dramatic dip across eleven of the seventeen sports is that multi-sport kids are becoming rarer. The average number of sports played by a young athlete went down by almost 6 percent, with most kids only playing an average of two. Having a sport for every season throughout the year is no longer the norm, as more coaches and parents believe that single-sport specialization is the correct path to elite status.

Quitting a sport is the most dramatic sign that a young athlete is not happy with the quantity and quality of time spent pursuing an elusive, ill-defined goal. Playing the game is one thing. Constant preparation, practice, and pressure to be the best on the team, the best in an age group, the best at ever-higher levels of the sport, can become too much for a developing adolescent.

Yet, that was only half the message in the SFIA report. Beach volleyball participation jumped up 22.6 percent, lacrosse soared by 28.8 percent, and ice hockey exploded by 43.7 percent in the same five years. Even rugby doubled its U.S. youth players from 150,000 to 300,000, not to mention 300,000 new gymnasts. Granted, these sports had a smaller number of participants to start with, but they apparently have found a formula that resonates with kids.

National governing bodies in sport are starting to hear the message loud and clear. Those that listened have added a "player-first" philosophy based on age-appropriate physical and cognitive development paths.

"We're like a lot of the other [national governing bodies], in that we can see what's going on from the 30,000-foot level, but it's hard to get to ice level and have an influence," Ken Martel, technical director of USA Hockey, told *SportsBusiness Daily*.[2] "The average parent looks around and they go, 'What we're doing doesn't seem right.' In their gut, they know it's not right. Why should my 9-year-old in Chicago have to travel to Boston to play in this tournament? All they hear is the loud voice of the youth coach who wants his piece of the glory or the business operation that's going to take their money because they can convince you that your kid is the next coming."

So, in 2010, Martel and his USA Hockey peers created the American Development Model[3] (ADM), a seven-stage long-term player development plan that identifies goals at each age level. Based on the adage of "Play, Love, and Excel," the model builds on a progression of participation for all, learning to love the game, then beginning to compete. But the emphasis on games, tournaments, and winning doesn't begin until later, with no goalies or competitive games until age nine. Playing and loving the sport must come before excelling at it.

Certainly, the long-term objective of the ADM is to keep the most kids in the game until their true talent emerges. Doubling or tripling the sport's pool of potential stars will only increase the odds of dominant national teams in the future.

"We need to get away from praising talent and start to praise effort," says an ADM brochure.[4] "Praising talent is de-motivating and not really accurate because at young ages it really may not be talent. It's crucial that, for developmental purposes, we allow kids to develop at their own pace. Kids that excel early tend to be physically more mature. Even six months can make a huge difference."

Could this focus on fun and learning be the reason for hockey's 44 percent rise in participation over five years? Probably, but let's look at another high-growth sport: lacrosse.

"All of the science, all of the data suggests that a sports experience should be tailored to the child's physical and cognitive development stage," said Steve Stenersen, CEO of US Lacrosse, in a recent interview.[5] "With respect to the [US Lacrosse] American Development Model, the feedback we're getting from players is it's fun and they love it. If we can get more youth league administrators and more parents to embrace what's best for their child and what their child most enjoys, versus 'Let's prepare my 8-year-old for his college scholarship,' that will better position the sport for growth and retention."

By not pressuring children beyond their normal maturation mile markers, they will stay engaged and excited about continuing to play. Each will have his own timeline, some faster than others, but the long-term goal is to keep more kids in the sport until they reach the later competitive stages.

"It's part science and part art to develop athletes," said Dr. Matt Robinson, director of the University of Delaware's sport management program and International Coaching Enrichment Certificate Program, funded by the USOC and International Olympic Committee.[6] "The implementation of ADM in lacrosse is that. There is a logical progression that goes along in the development of an athlete. Just like in school, you're not teaching 11th-grade math to third-graders. Unfortunately, you have coaches that are well intentioned but are going to say, 'I'm going to run my practice as we did it in high school.' It's just not right. That's not the logical progression."

Lessons from Stanley Cup Champions

In a presentation[7] at the 2015 USA Hockey High Performance Symposium, veteran NHL player and head coach Mike Sullivan, who was behind the bench for back-to-back Stanley Cup wins with the Pittsburgh Penguins in 2015–16 and 2016–17, named the four characteristics that he looks for in an elite player prospect: competitive spirit, functional intelligence, puck possession skills, and speed, both physical and mental.

In explaining functional intelligence, Sullivan believes that "players at the elite level think the game fast, in a timely fashion, faster than their peers. This might be the hardest thing to recognize in players because you're evaluating their decisions with and without the puck." And while skating speed is an obvious and often genetic quality, speed of information processing can be equally powerful. "Speed of mind is your ability to recognize situations and your awareness away from the puck."

Having identified his ideal player, Sullivan then went on to give a forty-five-minute primer on skill acquisition, including a briefing on the myelination process in the brain, and theories of decision training to a room full of hockey coaches.

"Let the game be the teacher," Sullivan advised. He encouraged training in the context of hockey in a top-down manner—rather than the often-used bottom-up approach—to better grow the neural connections for the sport as a whole, resulting in longer-term learning and higher-quality decision-making. "Instead of teaching skills in isolated, artificial drills, the athlete is placed in contexts that provide them with the 'big picture,'" Sullivan said.

Clearly, when a two-time Stanley Cup–winning head coach is studying and promoting a brain-based approach to player development, the age of athlete cognition has arrived. Of course, it helps to see it personified every day in one of his players at the PPG Arena in downtown Pittsburgh.

Since being selected first in the 2005 NHL Draft as an eighteen-year-old dubbed "the Next One," Sidney Crosby has captained the Penguins to three Stanley Cup wins, including two with Sullivan as head coach. Despite two injury-plagued seasons and one shortened by the NHL lockout, Crosby scored his 1,000th career point in 2017 in only his 757th career regular season game, making him the twelfth fastest to get to that mark in NHL history. Add in gold medals from two Olympic Games, a World Championship, a World Cup of Hockey, and a World Junior Championship playing for Team Canada, and it's no surprise why Wayne Gretzky and Mario Lemieux, two iconic Hall of Famers, agree that Crosby is the best in the game today.

"Just like Wayne was when he played, he's the hardest-working guy out there. Whether it's at practice or a three-on-three game at practice, he wants to win, he wants to be the best," said Lemieux.

"Right now, Crosby is the best player, and you have to earn your stripes," confirmed Gretzky. "Until somebody knocks him off the castle, that's the way it's going to be." [8]

A common definition of "playmakers" that you'll find throughout this book is that they are those athletes who make their teammates better. Jake Guentzel can attest to that after being on the ice with the ultimate playmaker. During the 2016–17 season, as a twenty-two-year-old, third-round-draft-pick rookie, Guentzel was tossed into the fire as one of Crosby's line mates. Called up in January of the 2016–17 season from Wilkes-Barre/Scranton, the Penguins' AHL affiliate, Guentzel's sixteen goals and seventeen assists in forty NHL games were surprising for a player coming out of the University of Nebraska Omaha, not exactly known to be a hockey hotbed.

But it was the 2017 Stanley Cup playoffs that put the Crosby mentoring magic on full display. From intentionally placing the rookie's locker next to his own to pairing up with him for pregame warm-ups, Crosby saw an opportunity to mold a young player. After they both lifted the Stanley Cup on the road in Nashville, it was the Crosby-Guentzel pairing that made the headlines. Of the thirteen goals that Guentzel scored in the playoffs, Crosby assisted on five of them. [9] The rookie returned the favor assisting on three of Crosby's goals.

Still in the afterglow of a cup-winning season, Guentzel added that Crosby's playmaking skills are just part of the complete player. "Obviously, I'm pretty lucky right now," he told us after a preseason training session. "Day in and day out, whether it's on ice or off ice, you see the work effort he has and his drive to be the best at everything he does. It's the little things you take from him. I'm benefiting from the plays he sees that most of us don't see. When you play with a guy like that, you just try to get open and he'll find you. He's got that hockey sense that not many of us have. At first you're nervous, always asking, 'Where's Sid?'—but one of the things he communicates is to not pass too much but just play your game and do what got you here." [10]

Sullivan agrees that the great ones, like Crosby, do indeed make their teammates better. "I think he's a guy that is very complementary. Regardless of who we put him with, he has the ability to adapt his game to the players that play with him," said Sullivan. "I think one of the things that allows our young kids to play with Sid is how he interacts with these guys. He's very encouraging. He's very supportive, and these guys, they so look up to him for what he's accomplished in the game and the player and the person that he is that they'll go through a wall for him." [11]

Sitting down with us in Sullivan's office between preseason workouts, Crosby reflected on what he had learned from a dozen seasons fulfilling all of the high expectations. When we asked him point-blank how he would define a playmaker, his answer showed the unselfishness that he's known for.

"I think just somebody who is able to create things, whether that's for themselves or for somebody else around them. Maybe just a subtle play that ends up turning into a play later on. I don't think it necessarily has to be the primary play. I just think a playmaker [is someone] who is able to create things in different ways." [12]

Growing up in Cole Harbour, Nova Scotia, whatever sport was in season, he was playing it. "I played tons of sports in school: basketball, volleyball, track, cross-country, everything. I played hockey in the winter, baseball in the summer. I loved it. It's pretty unique. Our hockey coach was actually our baseball coach, and we had a lot of the same guys playing hockey as we did baseball. So it was a lot of fun growing up with the same guys all the time."

He is not a fan of early, single-sport specialization and didn't go full-time in hockey until he was well into his teens. "I was only on the ice twice a week in the wintertime, usually two practices and maybe one or two games and that was it. Every day was not the thing. I think the first time I was ever on the ice every day during hockey season was when I went to Shattuck–St. Mary's School [in Faribault, Minnesota] when I was fifteen." [13]

Even if a young athlete shows promise in one sport, as Crosby clearly did with hockey, he knows that participating with multiple teams and coaches helps to round out developing personalities.

"I just think it's important to play other sports for a lot of different reasons. I think it's good for you mentally. If you're really good in one sport but maybe you're not so good in the other, you see a different perspective. You might have to be a little bit more of a better teammate or you might not play as much. You see it from a different viewpoint there. Across all the different sports, one thing translates into the other. You hear from different coaches who give a different perspective on how they teach and things like that. There's a lot to be said for it, whether you move on to play professionally or life in general. I like the discipline they create and, in the case of team sports, the comradery."

Of course, millions of kids play multiple sports, but eventually they all come to a fork in the road, deciding if they are going to pursue their dream in just one of them. Crosby knows that when that time comes, the commitment must come directly from the athlete.

"As a kid, it's important to enjoy what you are doing. If you don't have a passion for what you're doing, it's only going to be more difficult. When you genuinely enjoy a sport, it makes the tough times easier. Everyone has those times where it's not necessarily the most fun skating for a half hour after practice or dryland training, but from a kid's point of view, I think that's important. I'm glad my parents introduced me to so many different sports from the start.

"If you do commit to it, you commit to it. It's like anything in life. You make that decision. There's so many lessons you can take from sports that apply to life. If you understand that, then you're going to get something out of the sport, regardless if you end up playing professionally or not." [14]

It is during those intense training sessions that the body and brain come together, forming the command-and-response pairing that is called on when needed in a game.

"I know that I need to put myself in situations where I'm challenging my hands, challenging my feet, and ultimately that's going to challenge my mind, because I've got to make decisions while I'm doing all those things at high speeds or when I'm challenged with the stick handle to do things.

"It's an interesting conversation, because it's like we can go up there and pass the puck around, and we can feel good, but are we getting better? We can go tape to tape for an hour, but I haven't really challenged my ability to learn or I haven't gotten any better. I've just done something and felt good about it. Is that better than going out there and making five mistakes, not feeling like I did good, but maybe there is some adaptability there because I have challenged myself a little bit? So I think there's a fine line. I think there's something to be said about feeling good, but you also have to challenge yourself and find some way to improve and adapt. So it's kind of finding that difference.

"The way I look at it is pretty simple. As long as I'm learning and I'm in situations where I'm adapting, then I feel like I'm getting better. I'm challenging myself. The best time to take advantage of that is in the summer, just because during the season you're more team focused on things you're going to do structure-wise and who you're playing against." [15]

While most observers would argue that he's mastered hockey skills, there is still an elusive sports skill that requires a completely different mindset from him.

"Golf! The funny thing about golf to me is that in hockey I feel like you do all of your practice actually in practice. So, when you play, you just play. In golf I still haven't got that, because I feel like there's that preparation before you swing, a practice swing, and I don't like that. I like to either practice or play. I have a hard time combining both." [16]

Learning to Move

Even though Istvan Balyi was speaking to a golf audience at PGA Canada's 2014 annual general meeting, his analogy still translates across all sports. "I learned this from Jesuit priests in Ireland. If you want to teach Latin to Johnny, you have to know Latin and obviously, you have to know Johnny," Balyi said in a presentation launching Golf Canada's *Long-Term Player Development Guide: Version 2.0.*[17] A worldwide expert in player development, Balyi, whose ideas formed the foundation of the US Lacrosse model as well as several other international sport governing bodies, points out the development issues that arise from kids living in an adult world.

"So, instead of Latin, if you want to teach golf to Johnny, you have to know golf and you have to know Johnny. We know golf very well but we do not know Johnny or Jane from age six to sixteen," Balyi observed. "Superimposing adult programs on young developing athletes doesn't work."

When it comes to this development learning curve, we literally need to walk before we can run. Balyi and his collaborators use the term "physical literacy" to define the core neuromechanical inventory of movements that are the building blocks of athletes.

Beginning at about age six, most kids are ready to learn basic motor skills. Without those basic motor commands in their inventory, young athletes struggle to grasp the more complicated combinations of intent-driven, specialized motions of their chosen sport. By building the underlying athlete first, the sport-specific player can emerge from a solid foundation of skills including throwing, catching, jumping, and running, among others. Trying to force kids into skills above their developmental age will only frustrate and confuse them to the point of quitting.

Tom Farrey realized this disconnect after explaining to parents across the country what a mess youth sports had become. In his 2008 book, *Game On: The All-American Race to Make Champions of Our Children*,[18] Farrey, a veteran ESPN journalist, investigated the alarming stories from the front lines of the teams, leagues, academies, and camps that promote early sport specialization but often just result in early burnout.

"I did the lecture tour and at each stop, people—parents, coaches, academics, industry and sport leaders—would say, 'Thanks for telling us how we got into this mess. Now how do we get out of it?'" Farrey said[19] in an interview in the SFIA's 2016 Trends in Team Sports report. "People clearly wanted solutions."

With help from the Aspen Institute, funded by the Robert Wood Johnson Foundation, in 2013 Farrey launched Project Play, an initiative built to answer such questions. After herding more than three hundred experts, coaches, and parents across a two-year series of meetings, Farrey and Project Play released their state-of-the-playing-field report, *Sport for All, Play for Life: A Playbook to Get Every Kid in the Game*.[20]

The Project Play road map asks youth sports organizations to consider eight defining strategies for their athletes, at least up to age twelve:

- Ask kids what they want.
- Reintroduce free play.
- Encourage sports sampling.
- Revitalize in-town leagues.
- Think small.
- Design for development.
- Train all coaches.
- Emphasize prevention.

These strategies were intentionally written to be plainly obvious. Picture a small band of kids gathered at the local park, supervised but not managed by parents, playing whatever sport they choose while making up their own rules. In today's control-obsessed environment of structured drills, practice plans, and formal game structure, the fun and motivation is drained out of kids before they reach the appropriate competitive age of at least twelve.

This path forward is not counterproductive to developing the next generation of great sports stars. In fact, it increases the odds of success by keeping more kids involved in sports until their bodies and minds mature to a level where they're ready for competition.

"The fundamental flaw in our sport system is our manic desire to sort the weak from the strong well before children grow into their bodies, minds, and interests," said Farrey.[21] "One thing that needs to be made clear: A focus on participation rates is not an argument for participation trophies. We're staying out of that culture war. It's about squaring the pyramid at the base, so more youth can receive the myriad benefits that flow to those who play sports—which in turn will make the country more competitive on and off the field."

To understand young Johnny, as Balyi suggests, we must first recognize that, at six years old, he is not "a mini-adult." Depending on his age and experiences, Johnny moves through a repeating cycle: trying a new skill, struggling, losing confidence, learning, mastering, then starting again with the next step up the ladder. In the more structured world of sports, this is the essence of long-term athletic development. In the world of parenting and child development, this is the process of maturation and learning.

This trial-and-error learning process sounds nice, but if young athletes really want to make it to the pinnacles of their sports, they must get serious about it sooner than later, right? If parents or coaches were to ask, say, an NBA head coach for the best player development path, then the answer would surely be to focus exclusively on basketball, wouldn't it? We asked Brad Stevens, head coach of the Boston Celtics, who in four seasons has transformed a twenty-five-win team into a conference finalist with a rising future.

"I'm a huge believer in playing multiple sports," said Stevens.[22] "I'm not a fan of specializing early, in large part because I think that you figure out what your passion is truly for as you get older. And then, when you start to specialize once you've figured that out, it becomes something that you're even more excited to work towards."

Growing up in Zionsville, Indiana, a rural community of less than 10,000 people for most of its 165 years until Indianapolis's suburban sprawl reached it fifteen years ago, Stevens played soccer until middle school, played baseball until his freshman year in high school, ran track, and, of course, starred in basketball. "I loved every sport that I picked up," he said.

But today's youth sports culture is often focused on improbable future opportunities and a persistent fear of missing out. "The reality is this: everybody is specializing at a young age because people think they need to in order to keep up with the Joneses or play college down the road, and that stuff all separates itself out later on," Stevens explained. "There's pressure to specialize earlier. Hockey wants more time, lacrosse wants more time, basketball wants more time. Every sport wants more time, and if you see some kids around your neighborhood putting twelve months out of the year into one thing, you're worried that you're falling behind."

Now, as a parent, Stevens is seeing firsthand the struggle to keep his own kids involved in multiple activities. "My wife and I encourage our children to do a number of activities."

Stevens is not saying to never specialize but rather to hold off until a child has experienced a variety of sports and activities in order to be able to match their interests with their emerging talent.

"My point is that that just shows itself at the highest stage. Where specialization is a problem is when, you know, most kids that specialize at eight are going to run into the fact that they're not able to play on their high school team or play on their college team. Now you've done one thing instead of broaden[ing] your horizons, giving yourself more opportunity to build a passion. And I just think the opportunity to play on teams, the opportunity to compete, the opportunity to get knocked down, those are all good things."

In fact, from his perspective as an NBA head coach, he is noticing an upward trend in the base skills of young players. We asked him to compare today's players coming out of college to his playing days at DePauw University in Greencastle, Indiana, and when he started coaching at Butler University in Indianapolis back in 2001.

"You know what, I hate to say this, but I think they're way better. I know we're all supposed to argue for our generation, but I just see the players getting better and better. The bigger issue is the amount of attention and adulation some of these kids have to deal with at ages fourteen, fifteen, sixteen, seventeen, and into their first year of college. That provides some real challenges. There would be a sound argument that many kids in the United States would benefit more from the international model, where there is as much emphasis put on skill work and practice as there is on games.

"Internationally, they have a better balance of skill in games. But at the same time I hear everybody talk about skill being down and then I see guys making shots from twenty-eight feet away off the dribble like nobody's there. It's just like 'Man, these guys are good now.' Even when you watch the classic Celtics and Lakers games and then you turn on this year's NBA Finals game the next night, you just look at the difference in bodies. I mean, there's a different physical commitment from a body standpoint, from a nutrition standpoint. Science has really played a huge role in sleep habits and everything else."

Start with a Strong Foundation

As a pediatric exercise scientist, Avery Faigenbaum, EdD, professor at The College of New Jersey, in Ewing Township, knows it's not just about teaching motor skills in linear paths. Balancing the delicate psyches of children as they compare themselves to their peers drives their self-confidence and courage to continue to move forward.

In an interview with us, he recalled a surprising interaction with a physical education teacher.[23] "I was in a grade school two weeks ago and the teacher was supposed to do the push-up test. The boys and girls were standing against the wall. 'What are you doing?' I asked the teacher. 'The kids can't do push-ups,' he replied. 'Push-ups?' 'Yeah we're doing the wall push-up now.' Think back twenty to thirty years ago: it was the pull-up and then that got too hard for kids. Then it was the flexed arm hang. That got too hard. Then it was the modified pull-up. That got too hard. Then it was the push-up. Then they modified the push-up. Last week, I saw the wall push-up. This is the next generation."

Faigenbaum knows that we have to start building the physical foundation of young athletes long before the skill demands of soccer, basketball, or other sports.

"Participation in physical activity should not begin with competitive sport, but we're at the point now where the musculoskeletal system of boys and girls is simply not strong enough to handle the demands of sport," Faigenbaum said. "I argue that we have to fix all of this. You can call it preparatory training, preseason conditioning, general physical preparation—there's different words that people use for this—but the problem is these kids have what I call neuromuscular dysfunction, or, more specifically, pediatric dynapenia. In other words, they have muscle weakness that was previously limited to older adults. They can't jump, hop, and skip. These kids aren't ready for a sport. It's like building a pyramid. The pyramid is only as strong as that foundation. We need that foundation."

Without it, kids lose confidence in their physical abilities (and are more likely to suffer a sports-related injury), which they hide by being less active.

"Some ten-year-olds already know that they are not as good as their peers, and, consequently, they choose to be sedentary rather than display low levels of motor-skill competence in front of their family and friends," writes Faigenbaum in his primer for coaches and parents, the *ACE* [American Council on Exercise] *Youth Fitness Manual*.[24]

Imagine a ten-year-old with low self-esteem basically going

through the motions until she is finally allowed to quit sports. For this reason, defining physical literacy includes not just the demonstration of basic motor skills but the underlying confidence and motivation to use these skills throughout an active lifetime.

As the creator and longtime advocate of the concept, Margaret Whitehead, PhD, OBE, visiting professor at the University of Bedfordshire in the U.K., and president of the International Physical Literacy Association (IPLA), provides the de facto standard definition: "Physical literacy can be described as the motivation, confidence, physical competence, knowledge and understanding to value and take responsibility for engagement in physical activities for life."[25]

While different countries and sports organizations tweak this definition to their own taste, the core elements of Whitehead's version are universal: the skill, confidence, and motivation to stay active throughout life.

She describes this form of literacy as a journey that requires constant care and feeding even into adult life. Without all three sides of the triangle—skill, confidence, and motivation—it becomes much easier to coast into a sedentary life. In fact, Dr. Whitehead intentionally and carefully chose those two words, "physical" and "literacy," to emphasize the combination of body and brain in this early form of athlete cognition.

By using "literacy" as the action component, other terms like "skill," "competence," and "ability" are avoided. Whitehead's goal is to instill a lifelong learning pursuit rather than an end that is to be achieved and checked-off. Just as we can grow our reading literacy through decades of new and different books, we can advance our interactions with the outside world by challenging ourselves with new sports, new terrains, and new levels of achievement. Saying a twelve-year-old has "achieved" physical literacy implies there is nothing left to learn.

"While experiences at this early age are particularly important, the nature of physical literacy means that this capability should be nurtured beyond the earlier years, through maturity and old age," Whitehead wrote in the classic, *Physical Literacy: Throughout the Lifecourse*, which she edited.[26]

It is this emphasis on confidence and motivation that differentiates physical literacy from the simpler construct of fundamental movement skills (FMS), which has long been part of physical education theory. In fact, to use the literacy metaphor, FMS are the letters and words in the book of physical literacy. Understanding how to perform these skills forms the foundation for more advanced sport skills later.

Specifically, the FMS include running, jumping, balance, throwing, catching, and striking. While it may seem that each child can inherently throw an object, the FMS assessment measures the skill along a continuum from novice to expert. Compare a three-year-old throwing a toy across the room to a twelve-year-old pitching a baseball with speed and accuracy. Learning to step with the correct foot, twisting the trunk, and coordinating an entire movement sequence develop over time with practice and some instruction. While it seems inevitable that every young athlete will learn how to throw, they may develop at different speeds and reach different levels of mastery.

While children explore movement during their first four years, they typically don't have the muscle strength or brain maturity to learn the FMS. Forcing instruction at this early stage will be frustrating, as the child is just not prepared to be taught. From ages four to six, most kids are ready to start learning, so involving them in activities that get them moving and interacting without specific sport instruction begins the FMS process. Games of tag, climbing small trees, riding a bike, and playing in water are examples of ways to begin exploring how their bodies move in the world.

Playing in a sport-neutral environment builds these crucial fundamental movement skills and readies kids to advance to fundamental sport skills (FSS) from ages six to nine. In our example of throwing, a five-year-old throwing rocks, snowballs, or toys learns how to propel objects. Then, within a sports context like a game of catch, he progresses to throwing a specific object at an intended target—to a parent who is playing catch with him, for example. FMS combined with FSS are the building blocks to advance to organized sports from age ten and up.

As one of the original proponents for physical literacy in Canada, Dr. Dean Kriellaars knows he is up against a century of progress in society's leisure lifestyle. "We used to be in a culture where we moved a lot, and that means we participated with each other face to face, that means we developed social skills, we developed mental fitness skills, we developed physical fitness skills," Kriellaars told Canadian Broadcasting Corporation (CBC) Radio. "We don't value movement. Physical education is a second-rate citizen, it needs to be on equal footing. Learning to move is just as important as learning to read and write, if not more important." [27]

However, just promoting healthy behavior and activity to kids has not moved the needle on obesity and sedentary lifestyles in Canada or many other developed countries including the U.S. Kriellaars, an exercise physiologist and associate professor at the University of Manitoba, knows that the days for talking are over. "I'm all about doing things now," he said.

Dr. Faigenbaum agrees. "Physical education class in school is expendable in most parts of the country," he pointed out. "The buzz phrase we see now in the field is 'physical literacy.' Everyone's using that phrase for children to move with confidence and competence. The physical education conferences jump on their bandwagon promoting physical literacy. But I stand up and say, 'Hey, this is great, but kids in Trenton, New Jersey, have PE once every six days.' So we are creating a generation of kids who are physically illiterate." [28]

To kick-start the implementation, Kriellaars, along with a team from Canada's pioneering Sport for Life initiative, developed the Physical Literacy Assessment for Youth (PLAY) Tools. [29] These online tools allow parents, coaches, and trained physical education professionals to evaluate a child's FMS proficiency. As a collection of resources, worksheets, and videos combined with an online database and dashboard, the PLAY tools can track physical literacy across a family, classroom, or team, providing progress reports that call out areas for improvement based on age. Each of eighteen fundamental skills are performed by the child and graded by the parent or coach as Developing—Initial, Developing—Emerging, Acquired—Competent, or Acquired—Proficient.

To serve parents, coaches, and physical education professionals, the PLAY tools are available in several versions; PLAYfun and PLAYbasic are used by physical education professionals who have been trained to assess a child's FMS. PLAYself is used by children old enough to understand the material and assess themselves. PLAYparent is used by parents to assess their own children. PLAYcoach is used by coaches, trainers, and other sport leaders to assess their team. PLAYinventory is used by parents and coaches to track the daily exercise activities of a group of children.

By visiting the PLAY Tools website (http://physicalliteracy.ca /education-training/play-tools/), any parent or teacher can view the instructional videos, hosted by Dr. Kriellaars, register their individual child or group, print out evaluation forms, and track all assessment data on the website. From simple running drills to more complicated throwing and catching tests, the PLAY evaluation provides a great yardstick to compare your kids to their age-related standards.

Faigenbaum emphasizes the need for any kids' program to be fun, combining skill with challenge. His program, FUNdamental Integrative Training (FIT), offers exercises that hold the short attention span of today's kids.

"I'm teaching skills and, yes, some of the exercises are challenging, but not every exercise is hard," Faigenbaum explained. "Standing on one leg, holding a soccer ball, and twisting with your eyes open and eyes closed will not be hard from a cardiovascular point of view, but it's hard from a skill point of view.

"If you take the fun out of these programs, you take the kids out of these programs. Maybe this explains the somewhat disappointing adherence rate to some of these programs. I still want this to be fun. I tell my own coaches, 'Listen, anyone can make a kid tired, but to keep that kid engaged for fifteen minutes or sixty minutes in a program that involves some complex movements, that takes some creativity and some effective pedagogy.' " [30]

By using these resources, parents and coaches of preteen athletes can better understand the inventory of basic movement skills necessary for sports performance. Revealing any early deficiencies and providing opportunities to catch up can prevent kids from falling behind their peers. In a later chapter we will dig deeper into the science of sport skill acquisition for a more in-depth understanding of the brain-body connection beyond this core set of movements.

But next, let's take a look at how the rest of the world defines sports success so we can understand the journey that our young playmakers are about to undertake.

WHAT IS A PLAYMAKER?

Brad Stevens, Head Coach, Boston Celtics:

I would define a playmaker as one who creates opportunities for himself or others. I think there's a contagiousness to a true playmaker that benefits and impacts the entire team. In basketball, I always think about it in terms of making their teammates better just by their presence on the court and their ability to create advantages for everyone out there.

I think the best example for us this past year was when Al Horford joined our team. Our three perimeter players that started with him all had career years. I don't think that's a coincidence. I think that his ability to draw attention and make the right play was a critical component of our success. And then his unselfishness and general willingness to be a great teammate was contagious.

CHAPTER 2

The Road to Elite

We have all been there. You've probably seen it in the eyes of your fellow parents on the sidelines: that glimmer of hope as your young star leaves defenders in his dust, only to be followed by a moment of exasperation when his shot sails over the goal. As parents, we often internalize our emotions, knowing we can't play the game for them. At other times during a game, we just can't keep quiet, adding a running commentary and unconscious body contortions that we hope will somehow help. We instill the drive to get better very early. But what, exactly, are we aiming for? How do we know when we get there?

Sometimes the journey starts with a predisposition to the family sport of choice. A football, baseball glove, or hockey puck is placed in the crib, signaling their intended athletic future. "Three generations of football players are not about to end with my son" sounds similar to "Her older sisters love volleyball, so she will, too." As they grow, we see glimpses of early but sometimes imagined athletic talent that inspires us to steer our kids into a sport that we perceive can best showcase their gifts.

Other parents take a "Try it, you might like it" approach, signing up each son or daughter for a variety of sports, looking for signs of success and interest. Playing whatever sport is in season often becomes the best cross-training method for future sport specialization, which we'll see later.

In the end, we just want our children to be happy and successful, sometimes accompanied by a side helping of parental pride. For many families and athletes, the goal becomes something more: achieving so-called elite status. From starting on the high school varsity team to earning a college scholarship to playing professionally, the definition of "elite" aligns with the dream attached to it. Certainly, the skills needed to be picked for the high school homecoming game pale in comparison to being a starter for the Super Bowl champion. The dream evolves over time.

The parade of practices, games, and tournaments builds on this ever-winding path to greatness. As athletes advance to the next level, the standards are raised. The pool of all-conference athletes gets refined to all-state athletes, then winnowed to All-American stardom. With so many hours and dollars devoted to young athlete development, it would be helpful to define the final destination.

By definition, we can conclude that an expert is more knowledgeable than a novice in any field. Untrained spectators' eyes can often separate the skilled players from the newbies on any field. But along the way from PeeWees to NCAA athletics, the distinctions become subtle at each age level. Early physical dominance gets confused with long-term athlete potential. The self-fulfilling cycle that Malcolm Gladwell identified in *Outliers: The Story of Success*[1] reveals that the U8 scoring champ often gets picked for the traveling select team, benefiting from ever-better coaching and competition for the next ten years.

Many individual sports, where performance is judged by the defined metrics of time or distance, provide an objective ruler to development. Being the fastest sprinter in sixth grade means nothing four years later as a high school freshman unless that relative dominance can be maintained. Selection to an elite team is an annual scorecard of development. The best time, throw, or jump wins every time.

Team sports, however, get messy. With so many more subjective variables available, determining who is the best or the elite among a peer group becomes a coach's decision. Analytics, the aspiring stopwatch of team sports, tries to measure individual contribution to a team performance. Obvious scoring metrics like goals or assists can identify who benefited in the end from a team effort. But advanced analytics that try to capture complex team chemistry, codependence, and patterns of play struggle to rank individual player expertise.

So we're stuck between specific physiological tests (e.g., forty-yard-dash time, push-ups, agility drills) and a coach's subjective "eye" judgment to identify talent and its development over time. To be sure, coaches have been doing just fine with this combination for years and have developed sophisticated evaluation tools for this task. But this book is about what's next for young athletes and their coaches as they try to break through to a more efficient and effective method. Beyond being the fastest or strongest on a team, how can we define and then train to be the most impactful player?

The Difference Maker

With our focus here restricted to team sports, the "elite" moniker is often a perk of being selected to an elite team. While being named elite may establish a final destination, expertise may be a better variable to measure. Individual skills need to mesh within a team dynamic for a coach to pick one player over another.

Team goals, and each player's contribution to them, are all that matters. Initial screening of the talent pool may begin with physical tests of speed, endurance, and power along with body measurements of height, weight, and frame size. National talent searches may stipulate a minimum height of six feet tall or a forty-yard-dash time under five seconds just to identify core athleticism before evaluating players within the sport. But this broad filter may weed out potential stars who have a much more important attribute: perceptual intelligence.

When academic researchers study expertise, they typically define, then contrast, experts and novices in a given field. Athletics is no different, with hundreds of studies across multiple sports.[2] Study designs often looks the same: Pick the sport; define criteria for being an "expert" in that sport; choose perceptual-cognitive, sport-specific tasks for three athlete groups—expert, developing, and novice—to perform; then measure and compare the results. Predictably, the experts usually win by performing at a significantly higher level than either of the nonexpert groups. The study results try to tease out specific skills or abilities where there is a clear advantage of expert over novice.

However, across sports, competition levels, age groups, and geographic locations, the dividing line between expert and almost expert can be very fine. A U.S. college football player may rely on different cognitive skills than a Brazilian professional soccer player. "This relative approach assumes that expertise is a level of proficiency that novices can achieve . . . [T]he goal is to understand how experts become that way so that others can learn to become more skilled and knowledgeable," declares the formidable *Cambridge Handbook of Expertise and Expert Performance.*[3]

This lack of consistency was highlighted in a 2014 study by Christian Swann, Aidan Moran, and David Piggott.[4] Performing an online search of research papers between 2010 and 2013 that specifically focused on "expert" or "elite" athletes, they reduced an initial result set of 731 potential studies down to 91 that were peer-reviewed, were published in a journal with an impact factor, and described their population sample as "expert" or "elite" rather than "skilled."

Overall, the studies examined a total of 8,572 athletes across multiple individual and team sports. But when they dug into the actual definitions of "elite" and "expert" in each study, they found a wide variance. In fact, eight major categories of "elite" emerged for classification: national/international competition, experience in years or at different levels, professional status, training duration/frequency, selection in talent development programs, regional competition, sport-specific metrics, and university competition. Even within one of these categories, experience, the actual timeframes varied among "years of experience in general," "years at elite level," "years of elite training," "years at national level," and "games played for national teams."

So, even among those studying sports expertise, the defined target that developing athletes aim for included everyone from amateurs to professionals, from regional champs to Olympic gold medalists, and from rookies to experienced elite team members. Novices in some of the reviewed studies would qualify as experts in others.

"Without clear agreement about how to define and/or classify expertise objectively in sport, the future of the field is bleak because a question mark hangs over the validity and generalizability of research findings on expert novice differences," concluded researchers Swann, Moran, and Piggott.[5]

The good news is that Swann and his colleagues proposed a solution. First, divide the comparison into two groups, within the chosen sport and across sports. Expertise within a sport should be judged on participation, success, and longevity at the athlete's highest level of competition. Making the national team roster is a step above playing for a college team. In the same way, being in the starting lineup for the national team and succeeding is a notch higher than being left on the bench. Maintaining that peak position over time is the true mark of an elite, expert player.

To compare athletes across sports, we have to factor in the level of popularity of the sport both within the athlete's country and also globally. With popularity comes a larger competition pool of potential stars attracted to the game. In the U.S., a top cricket player has fewer rivals than a stud football quarterback does. Internationally, the best prep quarterback in England may not make a Texas high school football roster.

Given these five domains, the researchers provide a framework to rank expertise and provide some consistent labels. "Semi-elite" athletes have not quite reached the top tier of competition available within their countries. "Competitive-elite" athletes have a spot on the roster but really haven't had much success at that level, while "successful-elite" players see plenty of action. Finally, the label of "world-class elite" is reserved for those who have become a fixture at the highest level internationally.

With these definitions in place, we can at last venture out into the academic archives to understand how elite athletes differ from developing athletes.

What Is Elite?

Pep Guardiola is not one to dish out shallow praise on his players. Having managed some of the world's best soccer players at Barcelona and Bayern Munich, he recognizes talent at the levels of Messi, Iniesta, Robben, and Alonso. But in just two months managing Manchester City FC, the "Phil Jackson of soccer" identified the same type of genius in Kevin De Bruyne, the twenty-five-year-old Belgian sensation.

"Kevin is an outstanding player," said Guardiola. "Without the ball, he is the first fighter. With the ball, he is clear. He sees absolutely everything. He makes the right decision in the right moment every single time." [6]

Vision and decision-making, also known as perceptual-cognitive skill, is that special sauce that coaches notice and attribute greatness to. Being able to pick up cues from the environment, integrate them with a memory of learned situations, and make quick, decisive, and correct decisions separates the elite player from the masses. Even on a team full of world-class talent at Manchester City, De Bruyne has distinguished himself.

Alan Shearer, a Premier League legend, noticed the difference. "Without the ball he is very good; with the ball he is just superb," Shearer told the BBC. "He starts a lot of moves off and is so clever. He is so comfortable, so in control. He started so many good things for them. It's absolutely superb from De Bruyne. He sees a picture before everyone else, he is a second or two ahead of everyone on that pitch." [7, 8, 9, 10]

The right decision in the right moment every single time, by being a second or two ahead of everyone else: Perfection is difficult if not elusive, but it is this consistency that developing athletes hope to achieve from their training. Thousands of young Belgian soccer players—and millions around the world—dream of being the next De Bruyne. So finding the source of this rare perceptual-cognitive advantage—what we'll call athlete cognition—trumps the search for more common qualities like speed and size.

For over a decade at the University of Illinois, Arthur Kramer, PhD, has studied the link between physical activity and cognitive performance. Study after study at his Lifelong Brain and Cognition Lab [11] has demonstrated that being active has benefits not only for our hearts and muscles but also for our brains. In a landmark 2008 paper, "Be Smart, Exercise Your Heart: Exercise Effects on Brain and Cognition," [12] coauthored with Charles Hillman, PhD, and Kirk Erickson, PhD, Kramer concluded that "there is converging evidence at the molecular, cellular, behavioral and systems levels that physical activity participation is beneficial to cognition."

While this line of research showed that exercise can sharpen the brain, the more interesting question for coaches and athletes is: "Can superior cognitive skills make me a better athlete?" In other words, is there really a difference between elite athletes, developing athletes, and nonathletes in measurable brain functions across both sport-specific and general domains? If so, what is the line of causality? Are certain athletes born with superior processing abilities, or do they acquire them through dedicated training?

Over the last decade, Michelle Voss, PhD, a former grad student in Kramer's lab at Illinois and now an assistant professor with her own cognition lab at the University of Iowa,[13] triggered a series of research studies with Kramer and others to tease out these questions.

"For a long time, research on the athlete's mind focused on studying the athlete in the context of their sport," Voss wrote in *Scientific American.*[14] "For example, we know that elite athletes are faster and more accurate at remembering and later recalling meaningful play formations from their own sport. They are also quicker and more efficient at searching a visual scene containing sport-specific information, especially when the target is something relevant to their sport, such as soccer players searching for the ball in a realistic soccer scene."

This dominance *within the context of their sport* describes the expert performance approach to studying athlete expertise. Previous studies have shown that experienced athletes perform better in sport-specific attention, anticipation, memory, and decision-making tests than their novice counterparts.

Specifically, a meta-analysis of forty-two different studies by Derek Mann, A. Mark Williams, Paul Ward, and Christopher

Janelle[15] found that expert athletes performed better than non-experts in finding visual cues within their sport's environment, making faster and more accurate responses to situations. Their eyes required fewer saccades, or shifts, to the best stimuli and they held those fixations longer before making the right decision. In other words, the best athletes know when and where to look to find clues to their opponents' next moves and how to exploit them. Picture a seasoned goalkeeper with laser focus on the torso of an attacker, waiting for the telltale turn to the left or right before a shot.

So it makes intuitive sense that an athlete who has practiced for years in her sport would perform well in both declarative knowledge (what to do) and procedural knowledge (how to do it). Studying sport skills within this expert performance approach validates that the elite performer has accumulated knowledge, both implicit and explicit, physical and mental, tactical and emotional, beyond her competitors.

But what about when an athlete steps away from the game? Does athlete cognition transfer out to their normal, everyday life?

While Kramer and Voss have shown repeatedly that exercise sharpens the brain, they wanted to find out if consistent training over the years provided an edge in non-sport domains. This type of analysis, known as the cognitive components approach, tests underlying skills such as visual perception, attention, reaction time, memory, and decision-making, but outside of any athletic context.

In a 2010 study,[16] they sifted through dozens of related research papers to find an apple-to-apple comparison of three major themes or paradigms of cognitive performance: attentional cuing, processing speed, and varied attention.

In a team sport environment on the ice, field, or court, most of an athlete's job is to manage the chaos. Overwhelming visual, auditory, and tactile stimuli bombard the brain with information, with only a small amount relevant to that immediate moment in time and space. Does the cornerback covering a speedy wide receiver man to man really care what the left guard is doing? As the ball is crossed from the flank, where should the goalie's eyes be focused?

Paying attention to the most useful cues while ignoring the noise allows an athlete to process information faster and make quick, accurate decisions. The targets, speed, and variety of this attention is critical. Culling an original literature search of 120 studies down to 20, Kramer and Voss then overlaid a common denominator across the 694 total participants. Experts were defined as either professional or college varsity athletes, while novices had little to no sports experience.

Across the twenty studies, brain processing speed emerged as the difference maker between experts and novices. Commonly known as reaction time, being able to react quickly to visual information was a statistically significant advantage of advanced athletes over novices. In other words, the athletes scored higher on reaction time tests (having nothing to do with sport) than the nonathletes. While athletes were slightly better than nonathletes at anticipating where to look, their varied attention test scores were significantly higher than novices' scores.

By arriving at a similar conclusion about processing speed as Mann and his colleagues, Voss, Kramer, and their coresearchers were encouraged that the cognitive components approach could complement the sport-specific expert performance approach: "Based on our results, there is a place for the cognitive component skills approach for extending current knowledge about how sport training affects the brain and acquisition of fundamental cognitive abilities." [17]

Still, the question remains whether athletes are born, trained, or some combination of the two. Some researchers have argued for a hardware-software model, in which we are born with our core cognitive skills (the hardware) and sport-specific training provides the software programs to perform our athletic feats.

"This is the problem of self-selection," Voss, Kramer, and their colleagues wrote. "Which came first, the potential athlete with a particular profile of cognitive abilities, or the potential athlete that acquires a particular cognitive skill set as a result of experience-dependent learning and brain plasticity?" [18]

Since sports are rarely isolated skills but rather an ongoing mash-up of perception, decisions, and movement, a good comparison in everyday life would be a scenario that requires a similar test of total cognition in a tense, risky environment. For anyone who has tried to cross a busy downtown street during rush hour, you know all about the complex visual and auditory stimuli required to make that crucial go/no-go decision—in other words, how not to become a hood ornament. (Cue the Frogger theme music.)

So, instead of a running back dodging linebackers, would that same athlete excel at dodging cars on a busy street more than a nonathlete? Laura Chaddock, a grad student in the Kramer and Voss lab, designed an experiment using a virtual reality world to test this, albeit without the danger of real cars.

First, a group of eighteen Division 1 Illini athletes—two baseball players, one cross-country runner, one gymnast, two soccer players, five swimmers, three tennis players, one track-and-field athlete, and three wrestlers—were matched with eighteen nonathlete college students with no significant differences in age, gender, height, weight, grade point average, or video game experience.

Then they entered "the Cave," [19] an immersive three-sided space that simulated a busy street scene with a treadmill to virtually move forward. Cars traveling randomly at 40 to 55 miles per hour in each direction provided a realistic test of street crossing. Once you make the decision to go, you can't turn back until you cross both lanes or are informed by visual feedback that you've become roadkill.

The athletes were statistically more successful at crossing the virtual street than the nonathletes: 72 percent versus 55 percent. This superior multitasking ability combines quick decisions with confident movements. "Athletes are faster than non-athletes in the coordination of a motor response and the processing of information, which may affect the capacity to process concurrent streams of information," wrote Chaddock et al.[20]

Both groups were also given a simple computer-based reaction time test (pressing a key as soon as an asterisk appeared on the screen). As expected, the athletes were quicker than the nonathletes and that performance correlated with better street crossing.

Since the participants were distracted college students, Chaddock threw a curve into the experiment by having them also cross the street first while listening to music through earphones and then while talking hands-free on a cell phone. Although the music didn't distract from their task too much, holding a conversation while navigating traffic resulted in significantly more virtual collisions for both groups. That level of multitasking—conversation while managing motor skills—was too much even for Division 1 athletes.

These results do make sense when you transfer them to sports. While teammates trade instructions and tactical calls out on the field, their brains are not used to engaging in verbal conversations. (Maybe that's why my sons never appreciated my always helpful commentary during games?) Generic cheering doesn't require players to divide their attention, but specific instructions coming from both coaches and parents disrupts their focus on the task at hand. Whether it's getting hit by virtual cars in the lab or losing the ball to an opponent, split attention causes issues even for accomplished athletes.

Fast-forward to 2013, when Kramer and Voss expanded on these two studies. Their meta-analysis had shown athletes are better at processing speed and some forms of attention. The street-crossing task confirmed that athletes manage a goal-oriented process combining several cognitive skills better than a control group. Still, both researchers wanted to raise the stakes and examine truly world-class athletes to compare their skills with developing athletes in the same sports as well as nonathletes.

Brazilian Dominance

Since Bernardo Rezende, nicknamed "Bernardinho," took over as head coach in 2001, the Brazilian men's volleyball team has won two gold and two silver Olympic medals along with three world championships and one runner-up finish. Coming off their gold medal run in the Rio Olympics, the senior team was ranked number one in the world Fédération Internationale de Volleyball (FIVB) rankings,[21] with the U21 and U19 teams consistently ranked in the top five.

Having previously coached the Brazilian women's national team, Bernardinho's legacy in team selection and training resulted in gold medals at the Beijing and London Olympic Games, even after he left. Despite losing a five-set thriller at the Rio quarterfinals to eventual gold medalists China, the women's senior team, along with the U20 junior team, still ranks in the top five of the world.

It's no different on the beach: Brazilian duos have won three gold and seven silver medals since beach volleyball became an official Olympic sport in 1996, including a gold for the men and silver for the women at the Rio 2016 Games.

So, when Kramer and Voss had the opportunity to study both

men and women from Team Brazil, there was no doubt about their world-class talent. With access to members of both the senior and junior teams, gender and age differences could be measured alongside a continuum of skill from expert to emerging to untrained. A total of 154 participants, including 87 truly world-class men and women players and 67 age-matched control volunteers, were tested across three key cognitive categories: executive control, working memory, and visuospatial attention.

Consistent with their previous studies, Kramer and Voss stayed with a cognitive-components approach using a battery of computer-based tests similar to what we might find in today's brain-training tools, with no sign of a sports context.

Constant shifts between offense and defense in volleyball and other team-based sports demand that a player instantly adjust his mindset, strategies, and movements. Executive control refers to an athlete's ability to switch back and forth between two different sets of goals and instructions. Part of this includes being able to stop an action immediately if new information arrives.

Think of a libero, a volleyball team's defensive specialist in the back row, lined up to dig a spike only to have it deflect off of a teammate at the net. She has to stop her planned movement to one side and instantly dive at a different angle to reach the ball. This inhibitory control mechanism in the brain is often described as reaction time. But there is an extra decision-making step that has to halt the current instruction set and install a new plan for the muscles in a split second, as opposed to a reaction time to a starter's pistol when the "run forward" program is already loaded and waiting.

To test this, the participants were first given a task to switch back and forth between two different instructions. They were shown a single digit between 1 and 9. If the number was shown on a blue background, they pressed one key if it was a high number (5 or greater) and a different key if it was low (less than 5). However, if the screen background was pink, they had to decide if the presented number was odd or even, pressing appropriate keys for each choice. Doing this fast requires activity in the frontal cortex of the brain, often recognized for our executive control decisions.

For the go/no-go decision testing, either a Z or a / appeared on the screen. Everyone was asked to touch the appropriate key on the keyboard as quickly as possible after seeing it, measuring their simple reaction time with both hands. But then a complication was thrown in. In 25 percent of the trials, a tone was randomly played shortly after the symbol appeared. The participants were asked to *not* hit a key if they heard the tone—in other words, exercise inhibitory control. The delay before the tone started at 250 milliseconds but then was increased by 50 milliseconds as each person's speed and accuracy improved. An average "stop reaction time" was calculated for both the athletes and the control nonathletes.

Imagine taking the test: your two index fingers are perched over the Z and the / keys waiting for a symbol to appear. You want to respond faster each time, giving your brain and fingers the green light to go as quickly as the visual information arrives. But then you're asked to process two stimuli, first the confirmation of visual data, then the hesitation waiting for the possible tone. The researchers hypothesized that the elites would be better at both tasks.

The role of working memory in sports is complicated at different levels. At a higher level, tactical knowledge of the opponent's strengths, weaknesses, and tendencies learned from film study and coaching needs to be recalled many times during an actual game. But at a lower level, constantly evolving player movements require second-by-second updates to short-term memory. Tracking teammates, opponents, the ball, and one's own location in space is the skill often referred to as "field vision" or the ability to see opportunities or dangers that others cannot.

In the study, the participants were shown a collection of shapes followed a few seconds later by a single shape. Their task was to remember if the second shape was part of the first group. This was repeated several times, requiring a memory buffer flush with each iteration. As more trials happen, the brain struggles to focus on just this current set, trying to not remember the bits of memory from the group of shapes just shown.

As mentioned earlier, vision makes up about 70 percent of the sensory information that athletes use in competition. So the last test of cognitive skill for the volleyball study was a collection of tasks known as visuospatial attentional processing. First, the useful field of view (UFOV) test measured their ability to pick up object location in their peripheral vision. Next, in the flanker test, the athletes had to pick out the one arrow among several that was pointing in the other direction. Finally, they had to pick out a single change in two otherwise identical scenes.

Sure enough, the expert volleyball players outperformed the nonathletes across several tasks, just as Kramer and Voss expected.

"We found that athletes were generally able to inhibit behavior, to stop quickly when they had to, which is very important in sport and in daily life," Kramer said. "They were also able to activate, to pick up information from a glance and to switch between tasks more quickly than nonathletes."[22]

Task switching, memory storage, and object tracking were clear advantages for the world-class athletes. But even after this fascinating series of studies, Art Kramer could still not solve the "chicken-or-egg" question: Do athletes excel at sports because of an innate cognitive advantage, or do they gain that edge from years of dedicated training?

"Our understanding is imperfect because we don't know whether these abilities in the athletes were 'born' or 'made,'" said Kramer. "Perhaps people gravitate to these sports because they're good at both. Or perhaps it's the training that enhances their cognitive abilities as well as their physical ones. My intuition is that it's a little bit of both."[23]

Clearly there is a perceptual-cognitive difference between the best athletes and the rest of us. Beyond physical advantages, it is this athlete cognition that separates the great from the good. Later we'll dig deeper into this nature-versus-nurture question. Like most debates about the human brain, the answer is probably somewhere in the middle.

But what if we could train young athletes to see better, think better, and ultimately play better? Instead of having a few players who instinctively make better decisions, what if a player development program could teach coaches to teach athletes how to proactively hone their sport-specific perceptual-cognitive skills? If possible, the ratio of great players to just above-average players on a given roster would increase dramatically. So-called B players could grow into A players, at least between the ears.

WHAT IS A PLAYMAKER?

Sidney Crosby, captain and center, Pittsburgh Penguins:

A playmaker is somebody who is able to create things, whether that's for themselves or for somebody else around them. It may be just a subtle play that ends up turning into a play later on. I don't think it necessarily has to be the primary play. A playmaker is able to create things in different ways.

CHAPTER 3

What Gets Measured Gets Noticed

For Justyn Ross, the numbers started to add up. As the top recruit in the 2018 high school class of football-crazed Alabama, he was attracting not only the state's two dominant football programs, the University of Alabama and Auburn University, but over twenty more Division 1 powerhouses, including 2017 NCAA champion Clemson University. As a five-star recruit and a 2018 Under Armour All-American, he ranked as one of the top five wide receivers in his class and in the top twenty of all positions in the country. He was certainly one to watch when he arrived at Buford High School, about an hour northeast of Atlanta, on a warm March Sunday for one of the thirteen regional events of Nike Football's "The Opening," an annual showcase of the top prep players.

With almost 500 local playmakers at each event, getting noticed enough to be one of only 166 players invited to the national final in June at Nike headquarters in Oregon requires both a football résumé of achievement along with stellar performances at the regional event. In addition to position-specific drills and competitions, all recruits have their raw athleticism assessed through the four tests that make up the Nike Football Rating. Scores on a forty-yard dash, twenty-yard shuttle run, a vertical jump test, and a kneeling power ball toss combine to create the single rating metric, also known across sports as SPARQ (Speed, Power, Agility, Reaction, Quickness).

As a six-foot-five-inch, 195-pound junior starring for Central High School in Phenix City, AL, Ross dominated his opposition, catching 38 passes for 663 yards and 8 touchdowns. "He's just a very coachable kid and probably one of the best athletes I've ever been around, period, in my 23, 24 years of coaching," said his head football coach Jamey DuBose.[1]

To be sure, Ross's impressive physical stature at age seventeen is usually enough to put fear in local opposing defensive backs, even in Alabama. But what about when going up against the top defenders from across the South? To be a playmaker on that stage, there has to be more than just speed, power, and agility, since everyone comes to the table with those tools. Like the other players at the Atlanta regional, Ross put up impressive numbers in the four SPARQ tests: a quick 4.87 seconds in the forty-yard dash, 4.40 seconds in the shuttle run, 34 feet in the power ball toss, and 27.3 inches in the vertical jump, for an overall rating of 74.2.

However, of the forty-nine wide receivers at the Atlanta event, Ross's SPARQ rating came in at forty-first place. The five-star recruit could not even place in the top half of his position group in pure athleticism. In the two key measures for a wide receiver, the forty-yard dash and vertical jump, he ranked thirty-seventh and forty-sixth, respectively. Just a bad day of testing? Possibly, until he finds out at the end of the day that he is one of only six players total, out of the entire field of more than four hundred, to be invited to the national event in Beaverton, Oregon.

"It means a lot to me to be invited," said Ross, who has received more than twenty Division I scholarship offers, "because I'll have a great chance to showcase myself against the best of the best across the country."[2]

Ultimately, Ross signed to play for Clemson University, marking the first time the top-rated high school player in Alabama went out of state since Jameis Winston left for Florida State in 2012.

There were other mismatches at the Atlanta event: under-recruited players with high test scores and vice versa. Channing Tindall, a three-star-rated linebacker ranked thirty-seventh-best nationally at his position, was invited to Oregon, thanks to his regional-winning SPARQ score of 125. However, of the top ten SPARQ scores at the event, only Tindall will be headed to the finals.

On the other hand, another finals invitee, Jamaree Salyer, a five-star recruit and the sixth overall ranked 2018 player in the country, only placed fourth in SPARQ among the offensive linemen and seventy-first overall at the Atlanta event. Ja'Marcus "J.J." Peterson, a four-star linebacker also invited to the finals, placed fifth among his position group and twenty-sixth overall. Tindall and Salyer will be teammates at the University of Georgia while Peterson signed with the University of Tennessee.

There's no question that all of these players are elite athletes, but to be a playmaker who attracts the interest of top colleges requires something more. Otherwise the highly coveted recruits would consistently place among the fastest, strongest, and quickest. Physical strength and conditioning is a must for staying on the field, but being the champion of the weight room does not guarantee a spot in the starting lineup. Take away pure athleticism and you're left with cognitive-based, sport-specific skills to differentiate the elite players from the better-than-average crowd.

Still, for some coaches, the allure of the physical specimen with the raw tools is enough to take a chance on, especially at the pro level. Because when all else fails, what can get measured gets ranked, and what gets ranked can justify a draft pick. And that's the allure of the SPARQ rating.

As players progress from high school to college to pro, the talent pipeline filters out all but the best athletes. The marginal differences in physical attributes as well as in-game performance are measured in decimal places rather than whole numbers. Coaching staffs feel confident that they can teach the finer points of the game to these uber-athletes. In football, the drafting philosophy known as "best player available" is a nod to the well-publicized NFL Scouting Combine physical tests, a modified set of SPARQ standards.

According to Zach Whitman, creator of the 3 Sigma Athlete[3] blog, the dream is to find the freak athlete buried somewhere in an underappreciated and lesser-known college conference who can stand up physically to the rigors of the NFL. Whitman has analyzed hundreds of players, comparing a prospect's position-adjusted combine results, what he calls pSPARQ,[4] with their counterparts already active in the NFL. This comparison, known as the z-score, will be 0.0 if the prospect matches the league average for his position. A z-score of 1.0 indicates a prospect who is one standard deviation higher than his position peers. A negative z-score warns coaches and GMs that the player will enter the league as a sub-par athlete, relatively speaking. Whitman's blog name, 3 Sigma Athlete, honors the five prospects who ranked at least three standard deviations (three sigmas) above their NFL peers when they were drafted: Evan Mathis, Byron Jones, Calvin Johnson, Lane Johnson, and J. J. Watt. Being in this exclusive club places you in the 99.87th percentile of NFL players.

As Whitman likes to say, "Not all good athletes are good players. Very few poor athletes are good players. Most great players are great athletes."[5] In a 2015 study,[6] to demonstrate this at a macro level, he plotted the pSPARQ score of every NFL player from 1999 to 2012 against another new age metric, approximate value (AV).[7] Created by Doug Drinen, founder of the Pro Football Reference website,[8] AV[9] is an attempt to measure an NFL player's career impact on the league. Just counting "number of seasons as a starter" or "number of Pro Bowls attended" doesn't capture a player's weekly contribution to his team over the years. Whitman's goal was to confirm the importance of generic athletic skills to an NFL career by comparing raw athleticism, as measured by pSPARQ, with success at the pro level, described by AV3 (the best three seasons of the player's career).

While individual results will always vary from player to player, Whitman found an overall direct relationship of physical skills to production in the NFL when taken as a group. This satisfies two conditions of his maxim, that "very few poor athletes become good players" and that "most great players are great athletes." It does not explain his third axiom: that "not all good athletes are good players." Being physically elite in football may be necessary but not sufficient to being a game-changer.

Even with this relationship established and with the exploding emphasis on strength and conditioning in high school and college football, it would appear logical that average SPARQ combine scores should rise over time as players eventually get bigger, faster, and stronger. Surprisingly, a 2017 analysis[10] found that the individual test results of the so-called offensive skill positions (quarterback, running back, tight end, and wide receiver) were relatively flat from 2000 to 2016. Average height and weight within each position has remained virtually the same. Forty-yard-dash times for quarterbacks and tight ends have stayed consistently at 4.8 seconds, while running backs and wide receivers have hovered around 4.6 seconds, +/–0.1 seconds, over the last seventeen years. Tests of quickness have become very tightly grouped across the four positions, while broad and vertical jumps have been virtually unchanged. Strength, as measured by the bench press, has declined for running backs, wide receivers, and tight ends, with quarterbacks rarely participating anymore.

Yet, the widely held assumption of forward progress in physical development remains. The data disagrees with claims by barstool pundits that athletes are bigger, faster, and stronger than the past generation.

Athleticism and sporting success are linked but not mutually exclusive in either direction. So, while Whitman showed that, overall, being a better athlete corresponds with being a better player, there is still an X factor to being a dynamic playmaker. Because physical training shows improvement in the form of numerical stats that can be tracked and compared, it is an easy target for training sessions. But we're after those intangible improvements in knowledge, awareness, and decision-making that reveal themselves only subtly in competitive team situations. Coaches are convinced that they know a playmaker when they see one, but ideally they would prefer to create a training environment that proactively produces sport-related neural connections, just as speed training adds fast-twitch fibers and resistance training builds muscle.

Success Leaves Clues: Focusing on What Matters in the NBA Draft

With the first overall pick in the 1969 NBA Draft, the Milwaukee Bucks picked Lew Alcindor (thanks to winning a coin flip with the Phoenix Suns). Better known as Kareem Abdul-Jabbar, the three-time NCAA champion went on to become the NBA's all-time leading scorer, a nineteen-time All-Star, and a Hall of Famer, and is still considered one of the greatest ever to play the game. The Bucks were able to win an NBA championship with him before he moved on to the Los Angeles Lakers, where he would win five more rings. Since that franchise-defining pick, the Bucks have had the luxury of three more number one overall picks. Kent Benson, Glenn Robinson, and Andrew Bogut were all meant to be linchpins for hanging more banners next to the lonely one from 1971. But lightning never struck again at the corner of 4th Street and Kilbourn Avenue in Milwaukee.

Hindsight does not require the prescription goggles that Abdul-Jabbar wore throughout his career. NBA general managers and coaches would give away lifetime season tickets to anyone with a crystal ball that predicts the career arc of a college or even high school player. Missing on the top pick can doom a franchise for years, not to mention the GM's career. Since John Erickson, the first Bucks GM, made the obvious choice of Abdul-Jabbar back in '69, the franchise has cycled through eight more GMs. Trying to extrapolate a star college player's talent into a pro career of five, ten, or twenty years is as scientific as picking the draft lottery ping pong balls. Juggling the variables of individual contributions to a team sport goes beyond the basic stats of points, assists, and rebounds. Bottom line, does the team win more games because of this player? Can we allocate a percentage or share of a team's wins to just one teammate? Bill James, the eminent sabermetrician, attempted this for baseball with a statistic he calls Win Shares, or "the number of wins a player contributed to his team." [11] Translating James's original metric to basketball, Justin Kubatko, the creator of Basketball-Reference .com, derived win shares (WS) for basketball using similar logic as AV for football, by combining offensive and defensive statistics,[12] to reflect a player's overall contribution to a team effort.

Calculating a player's career WS establishes their NBA legacy over time, while dividing it by minutes played, WS/48, reveals productivity even for a player plagued by injuries. Not surprisingly, Abdul-Jabbar holds the career record for total WS at 273.4, while Michael Jordan is first in career WS/48. Using WS/48, we can compare current players (with at least 15,000 minutes played or a little more than 312 full games) with retired legends to understand their emerging place in league history even while they are in mid-career. In the all-time top ten, active players Chris Paul, LeBron James, and Kevin Durant can stand with Hall of Famers like Abdul-Jabbar, Jordan, David Robinson, Wilt Chamberlain, and Magic Johnson to determine who is, literally, the most valuable.

Looking at the Bucks' last three top picks, hindsight would tell them to look again. Benson, the big man out of Indiana, ended his twelve-year career with 33.6 WS, at a WS/48 rate of .103. However, it was Marques Johnson, the next Bucks pick after that, at number three, who would go on to be a five-time All-Star and have a much better career WS/48 at .162. Farther down the 1977 list were Jack Sikma, a seven-time All-Star with 112.5 WS, and Bernard King, a Hall of Fame inductee with 75 WS, at number seven and number eight, respectively. In fact, of the nine picks after Benson, all but one had at least the same or more WS.

Another poor season and luck in the draft lottery gave the Bucks another chance in 1994, when they selected Glenn Robinson out of Purdue with the number one overall pick. Despite a nine-year stint with the Bucks and two All-Star seasons, Robinson's career (39.8 WS, .075 WS/48) paled in comparison to the second and third picks that year. Jason Kidd, (138.6 WS, .133 WS/48) would go on to be a ten-time All-Star over nineteen seasons. As the third draft pick that year, Grant Hill (99.9 WS, .128 WS/48), a seven-time All-Star, played eighteen seasons with four different teams.

Surprisingly, the lottery ping pong ball draw favored the Bucks again in 2005. Again, searching for a dominant big man, they made Andrew Bogut, a sophomore out of the University of Utah, the foundation of a rebuilding season. While Bogut's career win shares (49.9 so far) are comparable to the second and third picks that year, Marvin Williams and Deron Williams, it was the fourth pick that, so far, has been the biggest miss. In the same twelve seasons, it is Chris Paul who has amassed 154 WS at an impressive rate of .250 WS/48, which is currently third all-time in NBA history. Already a nine-time All-Star, Paul trails only LeBron James and Dirk Nowitzki in career WS among active players.

In fact, in a 2016 *Sports Illustrated* analysis,[13] the Bucks draft woes made several lists for "most regrettable" picks in NBA history. Benson was the ninth least productive number one pick, in career WS, from 1966 to 2007, while Robinson and Bogut were the eighth and ninth least productive number one picks compared to others available in the same draft from 1966 to 2016. Benson, Robinson, and Bogut may have filled positional needs at the time, but is there a better method that the Bucks coaching staff, or any coach, can use to identify future talent? Is there a signature statistic for "upside" or "untapped potential"?

Florida State University PhD students Jerad Moxley and Tyler Towne tried to nail down this elusive promise of skill growth in athletes jumping up to the next level. Being part of a legendary cognitive psychology department, led by Dr. K. Anders Ericsson and his cornerstone research on expertise, grounded Moxley and Towne in the fundamental differences between skill, talent, and performance. These terms are often muddied in the everyday world of sports coaching and recruiting, with early signs of skill being mistaken for long-term talent. Of course, performance is always relative to the level of current competition. The question on the minds of scouts and recruiters is: Will today's skills that produce star performance grow into tomorrow's talent potential at the next level of sport?

In 2014, Moxley and Towne set out to clarify these definitions so that they could tease apart the variables that NBA GMs should be focused on as they prepare for a draft. In their interpretation, skill is now, talent is future, and "untapped potential" is the difference. To even reach consideration for the NBA, players have already demonstrated quantifiable skill from their past performances. Different teammates, different opponents, and different coaches all contribute to an individual player's résumé, leaving talent scouts to make the apples-versus-oranges comparisons. Solving for the variable of potential is the X factor.

"We will use the term 'skill' to refer to a player's current level of performance," Moxley and Towne explained.[14] "We will simply define talent as different ceilings of performance. Talent can be conceptualized as containing two components, current skill level plus untapped potential."

Has a player already peaked in college (or high school)? Has his growth curve already flattened out? Will the improved training practices, coaches, and facilities accelerate a player's improvement rate after a transition? To give front-office management something to work with, Moxley and Towne contend that, "for scouts, it is important to note that a variable is only interesting if it is systematic and predictable by an observable metric."[15]

Similar to the NFL Combine, the NBA also holds a pre-draft workout event where approximately the top sixty recruits are invited to participate. While there is no use of an overall summary statistic, like SPARQ for football, the players do complete five physical tests: two for agility, two for jumping, and one for sprint speed. Prior to 2013, a bench press tested for strength but was dropped in favor of the shuttle run. In addition, several anthropometric and physiological measurements are taken including height, weight, body fat percentage, hand size, arm wingspan, and standing reach. All data is available to the public at the NBA Draft website.[16]

Moxley and Towne believe that GMs and coaches use these eye-catching combine stats as tiebreakers between two players who are, in their assessment, otherwise equal. However, like an efficient stock market, they contend that a player's physical attributes have already been factored into their past performances, so measuring them again at the combine—and using the data as a separate metric of untapped potential—is redundant.

Gathering data on all combine participants from 2001 to 2006, they built a model consisting of past college performance, quality of college program (as measured by number of players in the NBA), draft combine data, and performance in the first three NBA seasons to determine reliable predictors of success. For both college and NBA performance, win shares were used as the best available metric for individual contribution. The combine data was consolidated to player position (forward, center, or guard), the lane agility test, the no-step vertical leap, arm span, and weight.

Assessing the quantity and growth of NBA win shares in the first three seasons, the researchers confirmed their hypothesis, showing no significant contribution of anthropometric or athleticism variables, independent of college performance, to NBA success. In other words, the combine data added nothing to the analysis.

"The only variables that predicted NBA success were age, player's college win shares and college quality," Moxley and Towne concluded.

But that doesn't stop scouts and GMs from relying on the combine data. In a secondary analysis, Moxley and Towne found that NBA draft order did significantly correlate with combine performance, despite the conclusion that this was not a reliable signal of untapped potential. While success at the previous level can be predictive of success at the next level, there's no need to test players again on the physical building blocks. Traversing backward, then, we need to examine other possible influences on athlete development.

So the search goes on for the origin of the playmaker's advantage, the stuff that consistently grows skill into maximum talent potential. To be sure, strength, speed, agility, and endurance are helpful if not mandatory. Still, in team sports that require integrated technical, tactical, emotional, as well as physical skills, there needs to be a locus of control. As you might expect, we think it is found above the neck.

WHAT IS A PLAYMAKER?

Peter Vint, PhD, former high-performance director of the United States Olympic Committee and former academy director of Everton Football Club:

Vision, decision-making, leadership, the ability to do the right thing at the right time, the ability to understand not only what's happening in the game right now, but what is likely to happen next. Someone that from an academic standpoint may have [those skills], whether it's an implicit or explicit understanding of situational probabilities, and leverage those in really effective ways at really important times.

Perhaps one of the easiest ways to describe [a playmaker] is that certain type of player who makes everybody around them better. I think that's an easy phrase that a lot of coaches like to talk to their athletes about, but I think it's the playmaker who is the one that ultimately ends up being perhaps a bit selfless . . . putting the team in the best position by doing what's necessary at the right times.

CHAPTER 4

The Endurance Thermostat

Diego Simeone was well aware of the battle his football (soccer) team was in for against their crosstown rival, Real Madrid, in the 2016 Champions League Final. Back in 2014, the Atlético Madrid manager was ready to celebrate a 1–0 victory in that year's final, only to be forced into extra time thanks to a headed goal by Real captain Sergio Ramos in the ninety-third and final minute of regulation. Fatigued by the constant Real attacks in the two fifteen-minute overtime periods, the Atlético defenders allowed three more goals to end with what appeared to be a lopsided 4-1 defeat.

Going into the 2016 final, Atlético had beaten Real in nine out of their ten meetings since that disheartening night in Lisbon. Unfortunately, that one loss was again in the Champions League tournament, this time in the 2015 quarterfinals. With two minutes left, Real forward Javier Hernández scored the only goal of the two-game series with an assist from the inimitable Cristiano Ronaldo. Another tournament, another late defensive breakdown.

Playing in their fifty-seventh and final game of a grueling nine-month season, Atlético's French striker, Antoine Griezmann, knew that their fitness had to prevail over their fatigue, especially late in the game right up to the final whistle. "For starters, we're a strong team defensively—that's one of our strong points, and it gives us a platform to work on," said Griezmann in pre-match comments. "We're going to be ready. We'll remain focused every second of every minute, and give our all like always. We'll have to be strong both mentally and physically." [1]

Being strong mentally and physically are two sides of the same coin. Not only does the brain consciously track, analyze, and interact with the dynamic situations on the field, it also subconsciously monitors the overall state of the system to allocate energy resources as needed. For us mere mortals in a typical workday at the office, we maximize our analytical and decision-making abilities while our bodies idle. Out on a run in the evening, we test our cardio and endurance but with the token mental load of putting one foot in front of the other. Playing a sport, especially a team-based, goal-oriented one, taxes the brain at levels not often seen elsewhere.

"If asked to give examples of tasks that require intelligence, the list will usually include math, chess, writing, art, creativity, medicine, science, music, etc.," said Dr. Vincent Walsh, director of the Applied Cognitive Neuroscience research group at University College London, in a recent essay in *Current Biology*.[2] "It is highly unlikely that sport will appear on the list. However, if one considers the challenges that elite sport performance presents to the brain, it is difficult to think of any human activity that places more demands on the brain (with the possible exception of combat soldier)."

Fatigue is often associated with physiological biomarkers that signal when muscles are depleted of energy and can no longer maintain the desired workload. In fact, the brain was traditionally seen as superfluous to the process. Dr. Tim Noakes, professor emeritus of exercise science at University of Cape Town, traced this line of thinking to English Nobel laureate A. V. Hill, who relied on the concept of duality, the notion that the brain and body could operate independently of each other. According to Hill, as quoted by Noakes in a research review,[3] "fatigue was the result of biochemical changes in the exercising limb muscles—'peripheral fatigue'—to which the central nervous system makes no contribution." However, Noakes countered that logic: "The past decade has witnessed the growing realization that this brainless model cannot explain exercise performance."

It is Noakes who is credited with resurrecting the important work of Angelo Mosso, a nineteenth-century Italian physiologist who proposed that fatigue, which "at first sight might appear an imperfection of our body, is on the contrary one of its most marvelous perfections. The fatigue increasing more rapidly than the amount of work done saves us from the injury which lesser sensibility would involve for the organism."[4] Similar to a temperature gauge monitoring the heat of a car engine, Noakes suggested that our brain acts as a "central governor" to constantly observe our physiological state, always on the lookout for overheating muscles. Before we push ourselves too far, our brain sends signals that we're reaching our limit and need to begin a slowdown or even a hard stop. We interpret these messages as pain, exhaustion, or just an overwhelming urge to quit.

"One of the things that Noakes showed from a number of different angles was that we're usually holding back a lot of our physiological capacity because our brain doesn't really care if we win the race," David Epstein, author of *The Sports Gene*, told us in an interview.[5] "It doesn't want us to die. He showed that when you land at altitude, for example, your brain stops recruiting as much of your muscle fibers—immediately. It's not because you're not suffering for oxygen when you're just standing there. It's just whatever your brain and your central nervous system are sensing."

In this theory of an internal thermostat managing our homeostasis, Noakes suggests that the signaling process operates at a subconscious level, which explains why we feel the compulsion to ease up, even when the competitive moment calls for increased output. But instead of a brain-body process that operates below our level of awareness, what if our actual, conscious perception of fatigue is what influences our decisions about level of effort? What if we could learn to override that impulse to slow down?

"Usually, when exercise physiologists talk about the brain, they see it as a center of fatigue and fatigue as a motor function," said Dr. Samuele Marcora, an exercise science researcher at the University of Kent. "They don't talk about psychology or the perception of fatigue."[6]

Marcora's conceptual framework, which he calls the "psychobiological model of exercise tolerance,"[7] combines the emotional with the physiological aspects of a grueling performance. He contends that quitting is still a conscious choice and that, through training, that decision point can be stretched. Like learning how many miles you have left once your car's gas gauge is in the red zone, the secret is to learn how far to push your body even when the needle says you're running on fumes.

"What we call exhaustion is not the inability to continue; it's basically giving up," explains Marcora. "The reality is that the neuromuscular system is actually able to continue. People who wish they can push harder and do more usually can. My idea is that it's basically a safety mechanism like many other sensations. So it certainly gives you a range of flexibility that the traditional model, where you stop regardless of your will, doesn't give you."[8]

It's not just the physical toll of a ninety-minute soccer game that contributes to fatigue. Constant focus shifts, tactical tweaks, and thousands of micro-decisions spike the cognitive load of players. These mental gymnastics pile on top of the incoming signals from the body to create a uniquely demanding effort as described by Walsh. Along with like-minded researchers Aaron Coutts and Mitchell Smith, Marcora turned to soccer players as ideal test athletes to understand the influence and interplay between the muscles and the mind.

"I think people clearly come with different capacity in that respect—not only can it be trained, but it is an essential component of training generally," said Epstein. "There are opportunities to potentially train it explicitly. I've seen the studies where you fool somebody about the temperature in the room and they do a little bit better, or about the distance they have left to go. You can get them to do a little better or worse. That suggests to me if you do that enough times with them, maybe they start to overcome some of those barriers.

"When I was with one of the best Olympic [sprint] teams in Jamaica, Steve Francis, their coach, who I think is a brilliant guy, wouldn't tell them what the workouts were until they got there. Not only that, but they were practicing on about a 310-meter grass track, so they didn't really know what the distances were in some cases exactly, except for by experience. I think those sorts of things help train your brain to say, 'Look we're not gonna die here,' and you liberate more little by little." [9]

The Demands of El Cholo and El Profe

Griezmann and his teammates are no strangers to fatigue. The fitness regimen of Diego Simeone's teams are legendary and a cornerstone of their recent success. Since arriving at Atlético in 2011, "El Cholo"—the nickname was given to Simeone by his Argentine youth coach for his street toughness—has demanded strict physical preparation of his players. His secret weapon is Óscar Ortega, the fifty-nine-year-old, tough-as-nails Uruguayan fitness coach who has been at Simeone's side since his managerial debut in 2006.

In a recent interview with Griezmann on Spanish television, his teammate Koke (Jorge Resurrección Merodio) described one aspect of Ortega's obsessiveness with perfect playing weight: "We are weighed every day. If anyone in the team has put on a kilo or more they have to declare it to the rest of the squad." [10] Playing regularly at Atlético means you survived Ortega's initial boot camp. There is a growing list of players who arrive at Atlético only to crack under the strain of preseason.

In a training methodology that the coach calls mixed integrated training, each player receives a program tailored to his position and to the upcoming schedule. Rather than training physical, technical, and game situations separately, Ortega's plan demands that both brain and body be challenged simultaneously. The four training fundamentals of duration, intensity, complexity, and density are counterbalanced to maximize each session. "In the balance between all these factors lies the secret," Ortega revealed. "I do not have the absolute truth, but it is our method and, for the moment, it works. We create the exercises, but the ball doesn't come to you itself. You have to go and get it. And if it comes to you with an opponent, they don't get by you. Always with elegance." [11]

During early summer, Atlético's richer, rival clubs are touring the world, selling tickets and merchandise. Instead, "El Profe" (the Professor), as Ortega is known, has convinced the team's owners that June and July are when championships are won. Grueling three-a-day sessions set the tone and work ethic required for the rest of the season. "This is hell and he is the culprit," said forward Fernando Torres at the end of the first day last year.[12]

The Atlético coaches understand that the synthesis of brain and body must be trained as a whole. From their pragmatic viewpoint, physical fatigue contributes to mental fatigue, which in turn can affect technical performance. Conversely, an emotional, tactically intensive match that taxes the brain can contribute to a rise in perceived exhaustion. Training at extreme levels of "mixed integration" is what Simeone and Ortega aim for on the practice field. In Marcora's vocabulary, they were preparing the team's "psychobiological exercise tolerance." But would it be enough for the rematch at San Siro Stadium on a muggy May evening in Milan?

"Mental fatigue is a psychobiological state operationally defined as an acute increase in subjective ratings of fatigue and/or an acute decline in cognitive performance, induced by prolonged periods of demanding cognitive activity."[13] This definition from Marcora, Smith, and Coutts contrasts with neuromuscular fatigue, which they define as "an exercise-induced reduction in maximal voluntary force or power." Starting in 2014, the trio started a multiyear research program to isolate and understand the finer details of this reciprocal relationship but particularly for team sports. Rather than individual Olympic sports that require singular feats of running, jumping, or throwing, team sports raise the bar on cognitive complexity. The researchers were hunting for the costs of fatigue, both physical and mental.

A unique aspect of many team sports is intermittent running, that unpredictable mix of speed and direction throughout a game. Evading opponents on offense and chasing them on defense requires continuous adjustments to acceleration and orientation. Unlike running repeated sprints in a straight line or challenging endurance with a ten-mile run, intermittent running meshes physical performance with ongoing decisions of pace and effort. Previous fatigue research used fixed rates of aerobic effort, but Marcora et al. were convinced that if they challenged athletes with a tough brain task first, then measured their performance on irregular chunks of running, the result would be a more realistic test of mental fatigue.

In their first study,[14] a custom-designed sporadic running protocol (a random mix of walking, jogging, running, and sprinting on a nonmotorized treadmill), two groups of athletes were asked to record their best time on a baseline run. Then, a week later, half the group completed an intense ninety-minute computerized brain exercise known as the AX continuous performance test (AX-CPT). In this brain-melting workout, participants watch a string of letters flash on a computer screen. Whenever they see an X preceded by an A, they press the right mouse button as quickly as possible. If that combination is not seen, they press the left button.

The AX-CPT stresses sustained attention, working memory, response inhibition, and reaction time after just a few minutes, not to mention an hour and a half. The lucky control group watched emotionless documentaries. After another round of timed running protocol on the treadmill, the researchers confirmed that cognitive stress takes its toll. Those athletes who had endured the mind-numbing gauntlet reported a higher rate of perceived exertion after the second running session, and their overall time to complete the exercise increased from their baseline. The mentally fresh control group saw no decline in running performance or perceived level of effort.

This estimated workload is key to Marcora's model. "The psychobiological model postulates that endurance performance is a consciously regulated behavior primarily determined by two psychological factors: perception of effort and potential motivation," the authors wrote.[15] Since intrinsic motivation was held constant between the two groups, it is the brain's estimation of workload that impacted the body's performance.

With this first piece of the puzzle in place, Marcora, Smith, and Coutts knew they needed to add other elements to the analysis that would reflect the real-world demands of team sports. In addition to physical performance, players require technical skill execution and tactical decision-making throughout a match. Related studies have shown intuitively a decline in distance covered and technical proficiency toward the end of real games across several sports. But to dig deeper into the details, those skills need to be broken down into bite-sized mini-experiments. To that end, in their next study, Marcora and his colleagues added structured tests of soccer ball passing and shooting in a controlled environment to understand how sport-specific skills are affected by mental fatigue.

Actually, they combined two studies that shared a common cognitive task, the Stroop effect test. Known for its brain-draining qualities, the test, named for the American psychologist who created the English-language version, requires counterintuitive reactions. Lists of color words are printed in different colors: the word "red" may be appear in red ink but more likely appears in blue or green ink. The user's challenge is to read the color of the ink out loud while ignoring the actual word (e.g., "Red" printed in green requires the response "Green"). Similar to the AX-CPT task, the Stroop test stresses selective attention, response inhibition, and executive functioning. Since our word recognition is faster than our color recognition, the brain has to manage the urge to reply with the first answer that comes to mind.

In the first sub-study, twelve soccer players in their mid-twenties were divided into two groups, then asked to complete either thirty minutes of a paper-based Stroop effect test (the experimental group) or thirty minutes of leisurely magazine reading (the control group). Subjective ratings of their mental fatigue and motivation were collected before and after the session. Next, each group completed the Yo-Yo intermittent recovery test, a repeated sprint across a fixed distance requiring athletes to "beat the buzzer" in less time with each iteration. A daunting exercise of "run to exhaustion," the Yo-Yo is well known to soccer players, requiring a determination and decision to keep going. After capturing distance covered, heart rate, and a rate of perceived exertion from each player, the researchers found that the Stroop group ran significantly less distance while reporting higher perceived exertion, even though average heart rate and motivation ratings were similar across the board.

Very similar to their earlier findings with the AX-CPT and the intermittent running protocol, the researchers arrived at the same conclusion: "Mentally fatigued soccer players reach the point of exhaustion during the Yo-Yo IR1 test earlier than in the control condition. This impairment to physical performance seems to be mediated by the negative effect of mental fatigue on perception of effort rather than peripheral changes to the cardiovascular, metabolic, and neuromuscular factors commonly associated with exercise tolerance and muscle fatigue."[16]

It was the second part of this dual study that opened eyes around the sports performance world. Logically, most coaches and players would agree that a tired body contributes to diminished focus, leading to technical mistakes (poor passes, missed shots, bad touches). But how does a tired brain affect the raw motor skills of the sport? For this question, the Stroop test was combined with two tests of soccer skill performance, the Loughborough Soccer Shooting Test (LSST) and the Loughborough Soccer Passing Test (LSPT).[17] Fourteen advanced and experienced players in their late teens were divided into experimental (Stroop test) and control (magazine reading) groups. With a mix of shooting and passing tasks, all under a time constraint, the LSST and LSPT provide a reasonable test of before-and-after skill performance.

As anticipated by the researchers, the "Strooped-out" group made more passing and ball control errors than the mentally fresh control group. Shot speed and accuracy were also better in the control group. An interesting twist was no difference in elapsed time to complete the LSPT and LSST drills. Just as they would be late in a match, the players were motivated to finish the tasks and "play to the final whistle," but their effectiveness declined due to an overworked brain.

Now, the researchers were quick to admit that thirty minutes of Stroop testing would be an odd pregame warm-up. Still, players of all ages have lives outside of sports, and each one arrives at the field with varying levels of stress, preoccupation, and fatigue. The takeaway is that this "mental noise" can directly affect not only physical performance but also technical skills.

Encouraged by their first two studies, Smith and Coutts forged on to discover new angles to the same question. While the structured soccer skill tests were helpful, there's nothing like a real game to understand an athlete's brain. As a soccer training ground staple, small-sided games—usually five players per team, with no goaltenders—offer plenty of ball touches and constant action. Smith and Coutts recruited twenty players from Australia's National Premier Leagues, then divided them into four teams. Using procedures similar to their previous studies, two of the teams were assigned to the thirty-minute Stroop test, computerized this time, while the two control teams just watched a NASA space documentary. Before-and-after subjective ratings of perceived exertion and motivation were gathered followed by a fifteen-minute game, five versus five. Heart rate monitors captured physical exertion while cameras recorded the players' movements to be assessed afterward in terms of performance statistics (passes, shots, ball control, etc.).

Again the mentally fatigued group performed poorly compared to the control group. "Indeed mentally fatigued players had a lower percentage of positive involvements, possessions, accurate passes, and successful tackles, as well as a larger number of ball control errors," the researchers found. "Collectively, these findings indicate that mental fatigue impairs the quality of both offensive and defensive technical performance."[18]

However, in this small-sided environment, physical performance was nearly the same. Just as the time to complete the LSST and LSPT showed no difference between player groups, this new group of cognitively tired players also rose to the occasion, covering the same ground with similar average heart rates. Only cognitively demanding skill execution suffered from a mentally fatigued brain.

Sports statistics or analytics, like those measured in this study, tell us what happened in terms of the end results (passes completed, goals scored, turnovers committed, etc.). To proactively improve sports performance, we need to live inside the playmaker's mind, querying each decision as it emerges. Decision quality in a dynamic team environment is always open to interpretation as to the "correct" choice or the option that generates the highest probability of scoring or preventing a goal. In the capstone study[19] of their series, Smith and Coutts, along with others, did their best to see the game from the player's point of view.

Once more, two groups of experienced players, one completing a computerized Stroop test and the other reading magazines, were then put into a soccer decision-making environment. Rather than real-time play, each group faced a large video screen with recorded game sequences. Across several scenarios, they were asked to take the role of the player with the ball and make the best possible decision of pass, shoot, or dribble under a time constraint. Besides physically taking an action with a real ball at their feet, they also called out their decisions to be sure the observer knew their intent. While they watched the filmed scenes, an eye-tracking system mounted on their heads watched them. As their pupils darted around looking for options, the eye tracker recorded the number of gaze points and the time between their saccades.

"In soccer, successful decision-making also relies on a player's capability to identify, select and then program the correct action in response to opposition or teammate postural cues, recognize meaningful patterns in play and determine situational probabilities,"[20] the study authors noted. Indeed, research has shown that expert soccer playmakers use a more refined visual search pattern than novices to pick out the best next action, often to the point of subconscious reaction time. Smith and Coutts counted on the eye trackers to correlate the players' choices with their actual eye movements. They expected an increased cognitive load from the Stroop test to have impaired both their visual searches and their associated decisions.

Surprisingly, the results only showed half of that picture. Decision speed and quality of the cognitively fatigued group was significantly lower than the control group, but the number of saccades and the length of their fixations were very similar. Smith and Coutts call this "inattentional blindness," where cues that they would normally notice—like an open teammate or an intervening defender—are missed at a higher level of information processing, not because their eyes didn't see them, but because their tired brains didn't choose to focus on them.

Apparently, running performance, technical skills, and even decision-making all suffer from mental fatigue. Coaches stretch physical fatigue's elasticity with a carefully orchestrated endurance training plan focused on cardio capacity and recovery. But what can be done about exhaustion above the neck? When the mind signals an empty tank, can an athlete consciously override the warning, confident that there's enough fuel left to finish the game? Through a regimen he calls "brain endurance training," Marcora believes we can.

Stretching Exercises for the Athletic Brain

Atlético players are all too familiar with El Profe's favorite motivational maxim, "The effort is not negotiable."[21] Ortega prepares the whole player to endure not just ninety minutes of battle but well beyond. By tracking physiological data during tactical training sessions, he can watch for what he calls "leaks" in the workload, when a player may not be performing at the desired intensity.

"When you work six versus six, you can think that the twelve are in their levels, but then you see that one has been below by fatigue, another by a nuisance. [These] are leaks in the workloads, which do not have to be voluntary," said Ortega, translated from his native Spanish. "That your team does two hundred kilometers does not guarantee you win, nor do three hundred correct passes. At a physical level, it is the same as at a tactical or technical level. A coach cannot impose a system on a group that does not have the qualities to do it."

In the 2016 Champions League Final rematch with Real Madrid, the mind-body preparation was at the core of Simeone's strategy. In beating two world-class sides, Barcelona and Bayern Munich, on their way to the Final, he knew the imperative of the underdog was maximizing every ounce of potential from each player. "In wars, it isn't the side with the most soldiers that wins, rather the side that uses its soldiers better," said Simeone after clinching the Bayern match. "In football or life there's no such thing as revenge, just new opportunities."[22]

A first-half goal by Real was answered in the second half by Atlético, sending the game into thirty extra minutes. With no golden goal rule, all 120 minutes of cognitive complexity and muscle meltdown would have to be endured to find a champion. Simeone's prediction that "the game will be very tense" seemed to be an understatement, as the score was still tied after two hours. With a single kick off the crossbar, the injustice of penalty kicks decided the game for Real Madrid, winning their second trophy in three years. But the agony inflicted by El Profe in June paid off the following May. Atlético was able to stay with their Madrid neighbors punch for punch. They did not collapse late but had learned how to live with fatigue, both real and perceived.

"Our intention was clear," said El Cholo in post-match comments. "We had the capacity to attack. We managed to get to 1–1 and then in extra time both teams were very tired. You do your best, you do everything you can. We need to continue working."

Certainly, at this elite level of competition, the physiological gains of these athletes from training sessions are marginal compared to young, developing players. But the untapped potential improvements to perceived exertion and time to exhaustion may unlock a new paradigm in performance expectations. Soccer players often play the full ninety minutes with only a halftime break. So, to manage their energy levels, they may subconsciously conserve their reserves much like an endurance runner managing a marathon route.

By comparison, during the 2007 NBA season, six players averaged over 40 minutes per game (out of a total of 48), with the median of the top one hundred players being approximately 35 minutes per game. Ten years later, despite advances in sleep, nutrition, and training methods, the leader in minutes per game,

LeBron James, averaged just over 38.1. The median of the top one hundred dropped to 32 minutes.[23] In the 2016–17 NHL season, two players averaged more than 27 minutes of ice time per game (out of 60 possible), with a median of 23.5 for the top fifty players. But back in 2006–07, five players exceeded 27 minutes per game when the median was just over 24 minutes.[24] While the differences aren't large in numbers, the trend is surprising. Shouldn't today's ab-ripped, meticulously monitored physical specimens be able to play more minutes per game than their predecessors a decade earlier? If a team needs its best players out there competing, what is holding them back from increasing their playing time instead of seeing it decline over the years?

Again, Marcora points to the brain as the next frontier. "When it comes to performance improvement and the traditional physiological model, there is hardly anything left to be gained," he says. "Innovation will come from a different approach."[25] That different approach relies on toughening up the perception mechanism to build a resistance tolerance. In this brain endurance training (BET), a term coined by Marcora, an athlete learns to tolerate cognitive stress while building physiological endurance. Instead of just running sprints at the end of practice, add a mental workload to the effort. Better yet, let the game be the stressor, with small game variations meant to constantly tax both body and brain. "Applying a cognitive strain can produce an enhanced training effect without adding any additional physiological stress," Marcora observed.[26]

Athletes aren't the only high performers that can benefit from brain endurance training. As Walsh pointed out, soldiers in the chaos of combat make life-and-death decisions by the minute while surviving grueling physical conditions. In a study funded by the U.K. Ministry of Defense, Marcora and Dr. Walter

Staiano, high-performance sport consultant for the Danish Institute of Elite Sport, put thirty-five healthy male soldiers through a twelve-week training program. First, a baseline time to an exhaustion cycling test (peddle at 75 percent of VO2 max until you can't anymore) was recorded from each participant along with a rate of perceived exertion (RPE) ("On a scale of 6–20, how hard was that session?").

Next, everyone returned three times per week for a sixty-minute cycling workout at 65 percent of VO2 max. However, with computer screens attached to their bikes, half the group also included the AX-CPT task simultaneously, while the other half simply pedaled. Marcora and Staiano hypothesized that the brain's plasticity would adapt to the added mental strain over time, helping ease the burden placed on it when bullets are flying out in the field.

After twelve weeks, the BET breakthrough was startling. The control group improved their time to exhaustion by a respectable 42 percent with a gain in VO2 max similar to the BET group. However, the soldiers who balanced physical and cognitive fatigue during training increased their time to exhaustion by a remarkable 126 percent. The constant focus required by the AX-CPT task—not unlike wearing a fifty-pound backpack during a march—became a blended expectation of each workout. When removed for the final time to exhaustion test, the perception of effort dropped and performance took off.

Clearly, a tired brain can slow athletes down even when their muscles can keep going. Yet, the BET model demonstrates that the brain can also be conditioned to withstand stress, including the demands of intense competition. During a game, the burden of perception and decision-making never ends, but BET reinforces support for a training method that includes a mental workload. Decision quality late in the game can decide the outcome, and teams learn quickly if their preparation does not match their opponent's.

After the 2016 Final, Zinedine Zidane, legendary ex-player and current head coach of Real Madrid, learned quickly from his crosstown rivals that the gap between them was closing quickly and that El Profe was right: "The effort is not negotiable." When Zidane took over the team from Rafael Benítez halfway through the 2015–16 season, he inherited world-class talent with above-average fitness. After his first two games in charge, Zidane admitted as much, saying, "You can always improve and physically we have to improve a lot, we will work to be better."[27]

As he entered his late twenties during his playing career at Juventus in the late 1990s, Zidane prioritized his fitness to match his world-class skills. His secret weapon was trainer Antonio Pintus, whom Zidane has described as "an iron sergeant, but serene and open."[28] Training the legendary Bianconeri roster, including superstars like Zidane, Gianluca Vialli, Didier Deschamps, Edgar Davids, and Antonio Conte, Pintus demanded physical preparation with the ball as an integrated training unit, much like Ortega. For Zidane personally, the demanding regimen resulted in being named the FIFA World Player of the Year twice with Juventus (1998, 2000) and then with Real Madrid (2003). When Vialli went on to coach Chelsea in 1998, he hired Pintus, as did Deschamps in Monaco in 2001.

In the spring of 2016, when other managers were chasing top players, Zidane was pursuing Pintus to solve his team's fitness problem. Lured away from Lyon, Pintus arrived at the Estadio Santiago Bernabéu in July to take charge of the current squad of world-class Galácticos. Knowing the work of Ortega and the improvement of Atlético, he wasted no time establishing a new expectation. "If you have two champions at the same technical level, the one that runs faster will be better," Pintus said.[29]

"Pintus is a man from another era; is timid, gentle and attentive in his work," said Maurizio Crosetti, a journalist and childhood friend of Pintus's. "He has gained a lot of credibility in his profession and [this] is shown by the fact that some of his ex-players have wanted to have him at his side."[30]

As the soccer gods would have it, Atlético and Real met again in the 2017 Champions League semifinal. The next test of Simeone versus Zidane, Ortega versus Pintus, and Spanish football versus the world was on display for a two-legged, aggregate score match-up.

At the Santiago Bernabéu stadium, Zidane's emphasis on fatigue preparation paid off. Staying with Atlético in distance covered on the pitch, Real Madrid dominated with 251 more passes at a 91 percent completion rate.[31] And one man, Cristiano Ronaldo, playing in his forty-third game of the season at age thirty-two, displayed his brilliance by scoring all three goals in a 3–0 victory.

Motivated by the goal deficit, Simeone's men challenged the titleholders with two quick goals in the first half of game two. But despite covering more ground during the match, they completed 275 fewer passes than Real. In both games Real controlled 60 percent of the ball possession while committing 21 fewer fouls. Even though Atlético won the game 2–1, it wasn't enough, as Real moved on to their third Final in four years with an aggregate score of 4–2.

Whether it was because of improved physical endurance, managed perception of fatigue, or some combination, the ability to stay fresh and deliver results late in a game was key to Real's performance under Zidane and Pintus. Throughout the 2016–17

La Liga season, Real Madrid scored twenty-seven goals after the seventy-five-minute mark of their games, the most of any team in the five major European leagues.[32] Those late heroics earned them an additional twenty-three points in the standings through wins or ties.

"We get to a point that, after nine months of difficulties, you play it all," said Zidane. "Usually, we arrive at end of season exhausted; to us it happens exactly the opposite. We got really well physically."[33]

As Marcora had shown, it's not how you start but how you finish.

DOC Z'S BRAIN WAVES PART 1: THE OPENING WHISTLE

A Coach and a Scientist: Two Former Students Changing the Conversation

Before he became a two-time Stanley Cup champion head coach for the Pittsburgh Penguins, Mike Sullivan was a student of mine when he attended Boston University, playing for the BU Terriers hockey team. We have remained in contact during his NHL career as a player and coach. What has impressed me most about Mike is his willingness to learn about the mental side of the game, believing that understanding "brain-based" coaching is the next frontier in sport science. For this reason Mike was a natural to write the foreword for this book, and we are very grateful that he took time from his hectic schedule to do it.

Mike's wisdom in working with young athletes comes from many sources, including his time in the youth hockey program in Marshfield, Massachusetts, his high school experiences at Boston College High School, his college career at BU, his pro playing career on four NHL teams over a twelve-year span, and his fifteen years of pro hockey coaching. But, like all of us, Mike learned even more about athlete development as a parent of young hockey players. He and I shared the same difficult challenges of educating parents about the best way to develop young athletes while at the same time developing a love for physical activity, cooperation, competition, and sportsmanship, as well as a lifelong interest in physical activity.

Dr. Avery Faigenbaum, another BU alum and former student whom we feature in this book, is one of the world's foremost experts on strength training in children. With over 220 scientific publications, numerous books, and book chapters on the topic, Avery received a well-deserved lifetime achievement award from the National Strength and Conditioning Association in 2017. His 1992 doctoral dissertation on youth strength training has become the gold standard for pediatric strength training.

Like many doctoral dissertations, there is usually a story to be told about how the topic germinated from an idea to a study, then to numerous peer-reviewed papers on the topic of pediatric strength training. Full of energy and a passion for youth fitness that included strength training, Avery came to study with me in 1989. But the published papers up to that time argued that prepubescents (typically before age twelve) should not engage in strength training for two reasons: first, because they are still developing, strength training is of no value, since testosterone, the hormone needed for muscle development, is not yet readily available in the young athlete's body; and second, because strength training stunts growth of youngsters by putting unnecessary strain on developing bones.

In one of my BU classes, I critically discussed this literature, making the argument that both of these sports medicine claims are probably not accurate, because there is either no science to support the claims or the science is flawed. Two other classic examples in medicine come to mind where the initial thinking and practice was incorrect: recovery treatment for heart attack patients and the effect of performance-enhancing drugs. In the early days of cardiology, physicians prescribed absolute rest following a cardiac event. Then somebody asked the question: What would happen if we exercised the patient with a stepwise protocol? Research showed amazing, unexpected recovery, resulting in exercise becoming a critical part of the treatment for heart attack patients. But a caution came from the cardiac world to use aerobic exercise but not anaerobic (strength training). However, a study I was involved in with graduate student Yael Beniamini disproved this claim as well.[34]

In 1970 the American College of Sports Medicine (ACSM), after reviewing a number of studies on the effects of anabolic-androgenic steroids, published a position paper saying "anabolic steroids had no effect on human performance."[35] Yet, many of us that were around college and pro football, as well as track and field, knew this was not true. At the time, researchers were allowed to use only low "medically prescribed dosages" of the steroid for their studies, which, unsurprisingly, resulted in insignificant strength gains, causing the null effect reported by the ACSM. Meanwhile, in less-than-reputable training facilities around the world, athletes were taking up to twenty times these medically prescribed dosages and showing remarkable changes in strength and body shape.

Similarly, I shared a story with my grad students on the early, misleading opinions on youth strength training. Growing up on a farm in northern Alberta, I observed that my rural friends and I were much stronger physically than the kids who grew up in town. The reason seemed obvious. At a very early age, we had to milk the cows, carry pails of water to the livestock, shovel grain, lift hay bales, and shovel snow. We weren't lifting barbells, but our physical chores were definitely a form of strength training; yet, I saw no evidence of "stunted" growth. If I was giving that lecture today, I would borrow a line from the political comedian Bill Maher, who likes to quip, "I don't know it for a fact, I just know it's true."

Sitting in my class, Avery Faigenbaum accepted my challenge to the graduate students to study the question of how to make kids stronger. He proposed doing a controlled study that would demonstrate to the world that prepubescents on a strength-training program could indeed increase their strength and at the same time increase their self-esteem and confidence, with no negative effects. I warned Avery that two other doctoral students of mine had tried and failed at the same study. Their study subjects, aged eight to eleven, ran away from the exercises, with the only ones getting fit being the doctoral students who chased the kids around the gym. But Avery had a clever plan. We collaborated with Dr. Lyle Micheli, a preeminent sports medicine authority at Boston Children's Hospital, and Dr. Wayne Westcott, an exercise physiologist at the YMCA in Quincy, Massachusetts, where youth-sized strength equipment had been installed for the kids. But the key was Avery himself, who knew how to teach and motivate our young study subjects to comply with the program's goals and get stronger. Confirming that programs like this can work, the study showed that the kids increased their strength by up to 70 percent over an eight-week program. Avery's dissertation ignited new ideas on how to safely engage youngsters in a strength-training program. Following the publication of our accompanying research, the American Pediatric Association adopted new strength-training guidelines for kids that are still effective today.[36]

As we quoted in chapter 1 from our interview with him, Dr. Faigenbaum is absolutely correct in saying today's youth have lapsed into a sedentary lifestyle and as such are underdeveloped in strength and overall fitness, a condition he has labeled "exercise deficit disorder." Many of these kids want to play team sports, but their limited strength and motor skill development prevents them from succeeding while also raising their risk of injury.

Another one of my students, Dr. Dan O'Neill—a noted orthopedic surgeon and physician in New Hampshire who came back to graduate school to get his doctorate in sport psychology—told me recently that he is genuinely concerned about the long-term health of today's youth and adolescents. In his practice, he sees alarming amounts of obesity and the condition of premature dynapenia, or early-onset muscle weakness. Dr. O'Neill says this unhealthy, inactive lifestyle will undoubtedly have severe health consequences as this population ages. Despite the high cost of health care for today's aging baby boomer population, Dr. O'Neill argues that at least they were much more active in their youth, developing a solid base of muscle strength and cardiovascular fitness. He fears today's younger generation simply does not have this baseline of muscular strength and overall fitness to sustain them as they age. Medical conditions such as diabetes, cardiovascular disease, and joint injuries, often due to lack of exercise, will result in massive specialized health care costs at a much earlier age.

Raising physically literate and active kids is the first step toward creating a playmaker. Without a foundation of strength, coordination, and endurance, the finer points of playing sports will be lost. Teaching parents and coaches the fundamentals of child development will help us avoid a generation of underdeveloped athletes.

From the Farm to the Big City: My Search for the Playmaker Advantage

Legend has it that, upon arriving in the region now known as St. Augustine, Florida, in 1513, Ponce de León learned from the natives that sacred anti-aging water was somewhere in the area. Ostensibly, Ponce became obsessed with finding the "fountain of youth" for the rest of his life. He never did find this anti-aging water, nor has anyone else some five hundred years later. Likewise, I was obsessed with finding the answer for what I thought was a simple yet important question: What makes a great hockey player, a great baseball player, a great Olympian?

In other words, what makes a playmaker?

Growing up in Canada, my friends often said I was a "natural athlete," with enough skill and athleticism to be good at most sports. But I realized rather quickly that my "natural" athletic abilities were not NHL- or MLB-level skills. Up in northern Alberta, we didn't have many great coaches, if any, so I always assumed that was my missing ingredient. If only I had had a great coach, I thought, I could have been a playmaker like my heroes Gordie Howe, Mickey Mantle, Willie Mays, and Henry Aaron. On the other hand, was it possible that great athletes simply had "gifts" that were genetically endowed? Did I simply fail to follow the advice of Bertrand Russell, the great British philosopher, to "choose my parents wisely"?[37]

As a ninth-grade student, I was fortunate to hear Murray Smith, the great University of Alberta teacher and coach, conduct a coaching seminar on track and field. After being glued to his every word, I said to myself, *I want to be like that guy*—a teacher and a coach who seemed to know everything. Little did I know that Mr. Smith, who later became Dr. Smith, would be my mentor at the University of Alberta, where I studied education and physical education. Now, Murray was not your average academic. While at Alberta, he was professor not only of physical and general education, teaching undergraduates how to be good teachers, but also of sport psychology before it was an academic discipline anywhere in North America. Incredibly, he also coached the varsity sports of football, hockey, and swimming and diving, and received coaching awards for his accomplishments. Although I learned a great deal about being a teacher-coach from Dr. Smith as well as other legendary coaches, such as Clare Drake (hockey) and Gino Fracas (football), I knew that I was far from understanding exceptionality in sport. Nevertheless, after graduation I started my journey in the central Alberta town of Stettler, coaching every high school sport possible while playing and coaching amateur baseball and hockey.

From a town of only 5,000 people, a surprising number of young Stettler hockey players would go on to play in college, juniors, and even the NHL. One of my students, Perry Pearn, a good player in his own right, even climbed the hockey coaching tree from college to juniors to the NHL. During a recent conversation, Coach Pearn and I agreed that the next generation of coaching would focus on cognitive skills as a key advantage. What we had learned on the frozen ponds around Stettler as a young teacher and an eager student had now evolved to more sophisticated methods to understand a player's thinking.

After a graduate degree at the University of Oklahoma and a PhD at the University of Toledo, I had more questions than answers on the athlete's mental processes. Boston University offered me the opportunity to develop a graduate program that emphasized the psychological aspects of human performance. Now I could finally develop my own laboratory for studying motor skill acquisition and development, putting in motion research opportunities to study exceptional coaches and athletes at the collegiate and professional levels.

Realizing that the European academic community was far ahead of the U.S. in these fields, I embarked on a two-year teaching and research program in Italy and Germany, becoming active in the newly created International Society of Sport Psychology. From this experience I gained a better understanding of mind-body development in young children, so I wrote my first textbook, *Growth and Development: The Child and Physical Activity*, along with my wife, Linda, and graduate student Tom Martinek. We reviewed what was known at the time about physical growth and development, motor skill development and learning, fitness development in children, and perceptual motor development. In keeping with my "mind-body" philosophy, we also integrated the latest research on cognitive development and psychosocial development in young children.

Fortunately, my affiliation with BU provided rare opportunities to peek behind the curtain of elite sporting organizations such as the Calgary Flames and Vancouver Canucks (NHL), the New England Patriots (NFL), the Boston Celtics (NBA), and the Boston Red Sox (MLB). Thirty years ago, their player development cycles, including assessing, profiling, selecting, and training, were just starting to include psychology and science, so I never missed an opportunity to ask players, coaches, and management specific questions. Comparing the fledgling efforts in talent identification to the European model, there was plenty of room for cross-cultural pollination to arrive at a global framework for performance psychology.

These differences were obvious on observing the Spanish national men's soccer team as they prepared for the 2006 World Cup and the 2008 European Championship. Their victory in Austria at the 2008 tournament was the first leg of a remarkable trifecta that included winning the 2010 World Cup and the 2012 European Championship. Watching playmakers like Xavi, Andrés Iniesta, and a young David Silva, I saw firsthand the superior perception and decision-making that have eluded American players. Watching training sessions showed me that Spanish coaches were far beyond the rest of the world in understanding the soccer brain.

Mental Metrics

So why all of this interest in athlete measurement? Quite obviously, it is to be able to predict who will be the playmaker. But as Yogi Berra, the famous New York Yankee catcher and philosopher said one time, "Prediction is difficult, particularly for the future." What a marvelous statement.

Over the five decades that I have worked as an academic and consulting sport psychologist, perhaps the most fascinating, challenging work has dealt with identifying and selecting future playmakers—the prediction factor. Everyone from youth sport organizations to Olympic and professional sport organizations (PSOs) wants to know the standard athlete measures of height and weight as well as physical attributes such as strength and speed. These can all be measured rather easily, but what more can we objectively measure that may contribute to identifying the best athletes? Sporting organizations know psychological and cognitive variables are important, but they're not sure what to measure or how to measure it. For a long time psychological testing has been part of the business world to profile job candidates through personality tests like the Myers-Briggs Type Indicator, the DISC Behavior Inventory, the Big Five personality traits test, and the 16 Personality Factors test. In 1995, Daniel

Goleman popularized the concept of "emotional intelligence," leading to extensive measurement of emotional intelligence in the corporate world and, to a smaller extent, in sport.[38]

While personality testing represents one dimension in the broad field of psychological assessment, another important but poorly understood concept is "athlete cognition," a term that we introduce in this book. Understandably, coaches avoid using the word "intelligence," but that is in fact the correct term. How good is the athlete at making quick, accurate, intelligent decisions during a game under stress?

Perhaps the most controversial intelligence assessment employed in professional sport is the Wonderlic Test, used almost exclusively by the NFL. First published in 1936 by Eldon F. Wonderlic, a graduate student at Northwestern University, the test was intended to screen job applicants as a quick estimate of cognitive ability. It consists of fifty multiple-choice items and needs to be completed in twelve minutes. During World War II the military used it to assist in deciding on good candidates for pilot training. Tom Landry, legendary coach of the Dallas Cowboys, brought the Wonderlic to the NFL Combine in the 1970s. Despite several studies showing low correlation between the test results and success in the NFL, it continues to be used today, despite my best efforts.

In 2001, at a meeting with NFL management on matters relating to psychological testing, I asked pointed questions about its continued use. To paraphrase their response, they said, "We want to measure player intelligence, and although we understand it is a bit off, it is quick and inexpensive." The good news is that a better "cognitive mousetrap" is now available. Dr. Scott Goldman, performance psychologist for the Miami Dolphins and the University of Michigan athletic department, has developed the Athlete Intelligence Quotient, or AIQ.[39] In the early stages of its development, Dr. Goldman and I worked on ways of establishing validity for the AIQ. Developed specifically for athletes, the test battery, given on a tablet computer, measures components of intelligence that are most used in competition, including visual/spatial relations, simple and choice reaction time, processing speed, and memory. Targeted, relevant testing like the AIQ is rapidly gaining acceptance in high-performance sport and will contribute significantly to better understanding the cognitive qualities of a playmaker.

At the same time, the world of high-performance sport did not want to miss this opportunity to also measure personality. When asked by teams in the NHL, NBA, MLB, and NFL, my preference was to use a tool developed by Dr. Robert Nideffer, The Attentional and Interpersonal Style (TAIS) Inventory.[40]

I liked the TAIS for several reasons. First, it had strong theoretical validity that linked attentional characteristics such as awareness, distractibility, and focus with personality characteristics such as self-confidence, competitiveness, extroversion, expression of anger, anxiety, and performance under pressure—all important in the world of sport. Second, the TAIS had an extensive database on leading athletes and "world champions" across many sports, including athletes at the Australian Institute of Sport (AIS), so coaches and researchers can directly compare the results of their athletes with those of champions in their sport to look for similarities. The downside of the TAIS and similar personality assessment tools is that they are self-reported measures. Therefore the question is always asked: Are the athletes being truthful in their responses? Most sport organizations are also interested in the "character" of the athletes they are recruiting or drafting, so I would ask questions in my interviews that attempted to capture their character in a way that was difficult to fake. For example, "Give me an example of a situation where you demonstrated honesty or told the truth instead of telling a lie, when a lie may have served you better."

To provide teams with an overall assessment package, I combined several factors to build a statistical model to predict athlete success. This included athlete performance at a lower level of play (i.e., collegiate or high school), skill ratings by scouts, a battery of physical fitness tests, and measures of character and personality. In recent years I have incorporated a fifth measure, perceptual-cognitive measures, now that we have new devices on the market that are valid and reliable. I would then convert these "raw" scores to what in statistics we call "standard scores" and come up with an athlete index. Teams like this objective approach, but too often they would, unfortunately, revert to "gut" feelings or other "feel" factors in evaluating players. As I look back at my assessments over thirty years, I am convinced a quantitative index proved more accurate than any eyeball assessment. In fact, I have my own *Moneyball* story.

Working with the Boston Celtics from 1998 to 2002, I witnessed how the NBA scouting and drafting process works and how difficult it is to identify the playmaker with absolute certainty. A few weeks prior to the 2001 draft, Chris Wallace, the Celtics general manager, his scouting staff, and coach Jim O'Brien invited prospects to their training center for evaluation. Ed Lacerte, the Celtics head trainer and my former student, supervised and conducted the usual physical evaluations, but Ed also scheduled my one-hour TAIS assessments and player interviews. Two young guard prospects, Tony Parker and Joe Forte, interested the Celtics and were potentially available in the first round.

At our draft planning meeting, I was asked for my psychological analysis of Parker and Forte. In my ten years of assessing and interviewing draft prospects across all pro sports, Tony Parker had the most impressive profile I had ever collected. My interview with him corroborated his self-report and he expressed himself with wonderful elegance. This was impressive, given that Parker was a Belgian-born French speaker and English was not his first language. Then I asked the coaches if he could play. Their answer was vague, confessing it was difficult to compare European players with NCAA players, even though Parker had played on the French national team as an eighteen-year-old. In 2001, the European scouting systems were not well established and video accessibility via the Web was just a dream.

With the tenth pick in the first round, the Celtics selected Joe Johnson, a shooting guard out of Arkansas who became a seven-time All-Star and is still playing today. It was their next two picks that raised eyebrows. With the very next pick, the Celtics chose Kedrick Brown, a small forward from a community college in Florida, who went on to play two seasons in Boston and was out of the NBA by 2007. With yet a third pick in round one, they took Forte, a sophomore from North Carolina. Despite an impressive two years with the Tar Heels, including being named the 2001 ACC Men's Basketball Player of the Year, Forte lasted only one season with the Celtics and one more in the NBA.

Meanwhile, Parker fell all the way to the twenty-eighth pick, landing with the San Antonio Spurs. For the past sixteen years and counting, Parker has led the Spurs to four NBA championships at point guard while appearing in six NBA All-Star Games. Certainly, future playmakers leave clues. We just have to find them.

Dr. Peter Tingling, a professor at Simon Fraser University, whom I consider a leading authority on talent identification, has written extensively on the difficulty of identifying playmakers in the draft across all the major North American sports. He makes the point that the analytics used to date have not been effective mostly because organizations are slow to change. As an avid follower of the NHL player draft, his research has focused on the biases used by hockey front-office staff when selecting their next superstar. "The general point of view seems to be to hope that they are not unlucky in the first round and hope to be lucky in the later rounds," said Tingling. "Our research says nobody is particularly good at making [draft] decisions. The advice that we give is to keep track of which scouts have historically made good recommendations [which surprisingly few organizations do], continue to make individual assessments, and to look deeper in the draft. Our research shows that even teams that pick late can have a great draft."[41]

Avoiding the Wall

Those of us who have worked with coaches in developing young, elite athletes from a psychological perspective have long thought the brain plays a powerful role in how we deal with intense physical and mental fatigue, or what distance runners call "hitting the wall." This belief is in contrast to what the exercise physiologists have been saying about fatigue, which they claim is simply a depletion of oxygen and glycogen to the muscles and the brain has nothing to do with its regulation. As we discussed, Professor Samuele Marcora believes that intense physical and mental effort will induce fatigue, but the athlete's perception is critical in determining whether she will stop or keep going.

In the late 1970s, Polar, a Finnish company, developed a wireless portable heart rate (HR) monitor followed by their Sport Tester PE2000 in 1982. While attending a sport science conference in Heidelberg, Germany, I learned how the monitor was being used to measure heart rates of race car drivers and to monitor and train cross-country skiers in Finland. Of course, I just had to experiment with this impressive bit of technology to pursue my mind-body research interests.

For the first time, the Polar HR monitor allowed researchers to learn about the cardiovascular and fatigue profiles of athletes during training and competition across many sports. Perhaps the most interesting were the world-class runners who came to BU's backyard every April for the Boston Marathon. Since the Polar monitor was a new device, most world-class runners did not train with it and were reluctant to wear the chest strap in the big race. But for those that did, we were able to collect minute-by-minute heart rate data from start to finish and match it with course maps to know when runners were taking on "Heartbreak Hill." To my surprise, elite runners maintained a heart rate in the 170s for the full 26.2 miles of the race.

We were also trying to understand the cognitive strategies that elite marathoners used to fight off the pain of fatigue at the point when the runners "hit the wall." We asked runners questions like "When fatigue begins to set in, do you 'associate' or focus on the sensations your body is experiencing?" and "Do you 'disassociate' or focus on some external event such as imagining you are a steam engine climbing a hill and thus be able to ignore the pain of fatigue?" Dr. William Morgan at the University of Wisconsin had previously published a paper[42] that claimed elite runners primarily used association strategies in competition. But that's not what I saw.

Two of my graduate students had previously won the Boston Marathon, so I interviewed them to discover their mental strategies. Known as the "Run for the Hoses" due to the extreme temperature (100 degrees), the 1976 race was grueling, with many runners dropping out early. But Jack Fultz utilized effective coping strategies to win the race in two hours and twenty minutes, a respectable time, given the conditions. My other student, Greg Meyer, had previously won the Detroit and Chicago marathons and then Boston in 1983.

While on sabbatical leave in Australia in the 1980s, I also met and interviewed Rob de Castella, the great Australian marathoner, who had won races all over the world and at Boston in 1986. De Castella, a three-time Olympian, later became director of the Australian Institute of Sport in Canberra. In addition, I ran with and interviewed another outstanding Australian marathoner, Steve Moneghetti, who won in Berlin (1990) and Tokyo (1994), and competed in four Olympic Games.

My interviews with these world champions combined with the Polar heart rate data convinced me the mind played an important role in "gutting out" grueling athletic endeavors. Unlike the findings of Morgan, these runners told me that, depending upon where they were in the race, they would either focus on body signals or switch to external distractors. This ability to switch focus of attention from "internal" to "external" and back to "internal" focus was the key competitive advantage that separated them from the crowd.

The Importance of Sleep

In 2008, Mike Gillis arrived as general manager of the NHL's Vancouver Canucks as an advocate for contemporary sport science that embraced mind-body training and the use of technology. But convincing the rest of the coaching staff that new ideas would pay off took some time. When Mike asked me to join him in Vancouver to head their sports science effort, I knew the recovery from fatigue was our first challenge. At the time, the only recovery methods used by the strength and conditioning staff were hot/cold contrast tubs and biking for five minutes in the gym after a game. Because of Vancouver's geographic location in the Pacific Northwest, they logged the most air miles of any NHL club, so late-night flights were a necessary evil. During this ten-month span from training camp in September to playoffs in June, players were always practicing, playing, or traveling, a regimen that was physically and mentally stressful.

Consulting with athlete recovery experts around the world, we established recovery protocols for the team. We developed a "mindgym," complete with four biofeedback stations, so that the players could train using heart rate variability (HRV) post-game, and as such recover more quickly. HRV training also helped teach the players how to recover between shifts. Teaching them to breathe at six respirations per minute and synchronizing heart rate with respiration quickly convinced the players—and me—how powerful the brain was in regulating human physiology.

We invested in technology that could better measure fatigue and readiness states in the athletes. We also enhanced the nutrition program so that the players were eating the best possible recovery foods. Since lack of sleep is the biggest barrier to complete recovery following training and competition, I contracted with a Vancouver company to bring their technology and education to the organization. Our experience with the Canucks' sleep, recovery, and performance has now gone global across many sport franchises.

Inertia Still Exists

So what lessons have we learned from the experts on fatigue, recovery, and performance? Many coaches believe more lengthy practices and more games are what make athletes better. But the research shows more is not always better. Athletes at all levels need to train "smart" and use today's knowledge to not overload their physical and cognitive systems. The research on recovery methods for athletes following training and competition is well documented, so pay attention to the mental and physical recovery of your players. Dr. Marcora's research has also showed us that an athlete's thoughts and perceptions, not just their physiological limits, dictate their desire to continue to compete when they hit the wall.

Sharing my expertise with parents in youth sports, many with unrealistic athletic expectations about their sons and daughters, has often been a challenge. As parents of two sons, my wife and I encouraged their participation in traditional sport programs in the Boston area, such as soccer, baseball, hockey, golf, and football.

I quickly learned that most parents were badly misinformed about how young athletes develop. Watching elite athletes and coaches on television or remembering their own sport experiences contributed to treating their kids as "short adults." Despite the latest research, it remains difficult to get current information out to parents and coaches, which is the goal and purpose of this book. There is no magic cookbook recipe for creating a playmaker, but there are many interesting ingredients that contribute to their development.

PART TWO

THE PLAYMAKER'S COGNITION

CHAPTER 5

Search: The Hunt for Opportunities

Expecting a conversation about neuroscience and athletes, Patrick Vieira was a bit surprised by John Krakauer's first question: "What is it about men and their balls?"[1]

Vieira, the legendary midfielder for Arsenal FC and World Cup winner with France, was now the head coach of MLS's New York City FC, whose offices were a short two miles away from the Rubin Museum of Art in lower Manhattan, where the two sat down for a discussion. "That is a really good start," replied Vieira, with his French accent, a chuckle, and a wink to the audience.

As part of the museum's ongoing Brainwave series of talks, Vieira and Krakauer explored the cognitive nature of playing sports. This wasn't the first time that Krakauer, professor of neurology at the Johns Hopkins University School of Medicine, has shared his fascination with the complicated and creative motor skills of athletes, not to mention our obsession with watching them. He prefaced his odd first question to Vieira with "A billion people are estimated to have watched the last World Cup Final. If an alien were to come from outer space, they would say, 'Why are a billion people watching grown men kick a sphere around?'"

As fans, parents, and coaches, despite our intense interest in sports, we often don't appreciate the depth of expertise demonstrated by greats like Messi or James or Crosby or Jeter. Physical talent is put in its own category, tucked away from more traditional forms of mastery, like academics or the arts, even though athletic proficiency has the same reliance on advanced neural connectivity in the brain.

"What does it mean to be physically a genius versus mentally a genius?" Krakauer asked. "We're very schizophrenic in the world when it comes to sport. On the one hand, a billion people watch the World Cup. On the other hand, deep down, we think that it means more to be a 'genius' in mathematics or music than to be able to use the term for an athlete. Now what we've argued and I think what neuroscience is saying is that the distinction is a false one. There is as much cognition in sport as in any other endeavor."

Vieira agreed that the mental aspect of the game needs to be elevated in importance. "We're always talking about the technical and physical talent but in our world, we don't talk enough about the mental talent. For me, this is the number one priority. When we are recruiting players, I put in a bit of time on the mental side of players."

This is why we love watching great athletes just as we enjoy reading a great novel or listening to a concert. We know how to dribble a basketball or write a few paragraphs or play a tune on the piano. We can try to mimic the genius of our heroes at a certain level of expertise. But it's then that we realize how hard it is to do what they do. And the difference between us and them is stored in the brain.

"You watch a single player practicing and go, 'Wow, aren't they good with the ball!' But then when you add on the field you need to have—what we talk about in neuroscience: a cognitive map of the entire pitch—the best players are able to create very complex models of the entire game with all the players in space and then time-advance that now and over time," Krakauer said.

"That's an incredible feat. That is no different from what chess grandmasters do. You can show a grandmaster the configuration of pieces on the board for twenty-five to thirty seconds, take it away, and they can reproduce all the pieces on the board. Players on a pitch, pieces on a board, the same cognitive challenge, the same neuroscientific idea." Viera replied, "I think this is the difference between being a good player and a top player."[2]

Krakauer is driven to study exceptional athletes by more than just an interest in sports. His primary line of research at his Johns Hopkins lab, playfully named BLAM (short for Brain, Learning, Animation, and Movement),[3] is to understand human motor skill development to help those on the other end of the spectrum of movement mastery: brain-injured patients, especially the damage caused by strokes. His eclectic team of neurologists, engineers, developers, and designers create video games combined with robotics to revolutionize both physical and cognitive rehabilitation. By considering the entire spectrum of motor movement abilities, from superathletes to paralyzed patients, he hopes to reveal clues to the elusive brain-body communications loop.

"On one hand, the whole field of neuropsychology is predicated on learning something about the healthy brain by looking at the injured brain," Krakauer said in a recent interview.[4] "The inverse of that may be true as well. We may be able to learn something more about the normal brain by looking at the super brain, too.

"On the other hand, could the study of the normal brain give us insight into super athletes? I think the answer is probably yes. If you want to take any task, whether it is basketball, chess, or violin, and decompose it into its most basic pieces, you can see where to assign credit in terms of motivation, skill, attention, and the like, to better explain why certain people are so good, and what makes them stand apart from others."[5]

As a neuroscientist, Krakauer jumped into the center of what we have named the "athlete cognition" movement with an influential 2009 paper in *Nature Reviews Neuroscience* titled, "Inside the Brain of an Elite Athlete: The Neural Processes That Support High Achievement in Sports,"[6] which has been cited almost three hundred times by other researchers. Along with Dr. Peter Brown, professor of experimental neurology at the University of Oxford, and Kielan Yarrow, cognitive psychologist at City, University of London, Krakauer put a new spin on how we should think about an athlete's thinking with "the aim of bridging the gap between psychological research on expertise and neuroscientific models of the basic mechanisms that support sporting success."[7]

Imagine that: studying the brain itself to understand how the athlete's brain functions. By combining their deep knowledge of neuroscience with the results of dozens of previous studies, Krakauer, Brown, and Yarrow presented a framework to understand athlete cognition at its most fundamental level. "Ultimately, an understanding of the neural mechanisms that distinguish elite sportspeople from others not only provides a rational basis for refining future training strategies, but may also open up the possibility of predictive physiological profiling and, in time, genotyping to foretell the likelihood of success at the highest level,"[8] they concluded.

The ongoing dilemma of studying the brain in any domain is the trade-off of the lab versus the field. To control variables and isolate a finding, a lab experiment breaks down a sport into simpler components. However, the intricacy and interrelationships of multiple moving players in a real game add another dimension of analysis that an isolated task in a lab can't capture.

As a scientist, Krakauer knows this catch-22 all too well. "It's interesting that neuroscience is way behind what's happening in the world of sport and other domains," he lamented to Vieira. "We do very simple experiments, but the problem is those experiments don't have what I was talking about before: the complexity of soccer, the complexity of chess. So we're looking at the brain doing things where the brain is not actually being asked to do what you're describing, so there is a gulf between what we study in the lab and what we know the brain is capable of out in the world. The good thing about sports compared to art and chess is you actually have more variables you can measure because there is all that motor output."[9]

The Athlete Cognition Cycle

In Part 2 of this book, we try to explain these "neural mechanisms," which we define as "Search—Decide—Execute," that are at the root of the athlete cognition cycle that each player creates hundreds of times per game. We believe it is within this repeating process where the playmaker's genius lives. Consistently doing the right thing at the right time in the right way is the essence of the "field vision" or "court sense" or "game intelligence" that distinguishes the playmaker from the masses.

The next three chapters dive deep into each of these major functions. Every action taken by an athlete begins with a *search* of the game environment for cues and opportunities. Starting with anticipation then prediction of what will happen next, the playmaker learns to direct his attention to subtle but strategic focal points. Matching his anticipation with the actual visual stimuli flooding his brain triggers the recognition of patterns that have been seen before and stored in memory. Based on the situation and the opportunities presented and recognized, the playmaker must *decide* on the next action, be it minor (step left versus right) or major (take a shot on goal). Finally, the correct tactical decision is nothing without the ability to properly *execute*, requiring near-perfect, repeated skill performance. But we're getting ahead of ourselves.

At the core of this brain busywork is a goal, be it explicit or implicit, that motivates the athlete to move. Nothing in sport happens without intentional movement. Whether on offense or defense, a player is always trying to accomplish something: complete a pass to a teammate, stop an oncoming attacker, or recover from a fast transition. These goal-directed incentives drive the athlete cognition loop over and over to maximize scoring chances and minimize threats. So, at a high level, an athlete's brain is searching, deciding, and executing to match the immediate needs of the moment but also the ultimate goal of winning the game. Of course, for every well-though-out movement by an athlete, his opponent is going through similar mental computations to do exactly the opposite.

"So, in other words, to become skilled, it's not enough to know how your body's going to respond to commands, but you need to be able to predict what the player or your opponent is going to do ahead of time," Krakauer said in a fascinating discussion on the motor system with Charlie Rose.[10]

As part of Rose's ongoing series on brain science, an entire episode focused solely on how humans plan, generate, and manage their movements throughout the world. Sitting at the same table with Krakauer and Rose were four neuroscience pioneers, Eric Kandel, Robert Brown, Tom Jessell, and Daniel Wolpert.

"Even when we don't engage in movements, our motor systems are simulating the movement. So there's a lot more movement going on in our brain than is visible to the outside world," said Dr. Kandel, Nobel laureate and professor of neuroscience at Columbia University and senior investigator at the Howard Hughes Medical Institute.[11]

"The point is that some people even said that thought is basically movement, planning without the movement," said Krakauer. "And so, from an evolutionary standpoint, you can imagine that if we understood motor planning and simulation without the movement, very likely those planning processes were co-opted for higher-level thought."

In fact, Wolpert, a neuroscientist and professor of engineering at Cambridge University, takes the significance of movement to the next level. "We have a brain for one reason and one reason only, and that's to produce adaptable and complex movement. I think to understand the brain we have to understand movement." [12] He openly admits that he is a "movement chauvinist."

But we cannot study athlete movement without also including perception—the search, as we call it—as we move in response to the environment around us. Kandel agrees with Krakauer's need for a cognitive map to navigate the playing field.

"All sensory perception reaches its completion through the actions of motor systems," Kandel said. "In fact, we can think of the motor systems in some ways as being the mirror image of the sensory system. The sensory systems create a schema, an internal representation in our brain of the outside world. The motor system uses that internal representation in action."

It turns out that the motor skills we use every day are even more impressive than any advanced computations we may learn in school. Consider artificial intelligence systems that play chess against humans. By evaluating millions of possible moves per second, they have used deep game logic to beat grandmasters. Yet, a five-year-old child can outmaneuver the most advanced robot in actually picking up and moving the chess pieces around a board. To understand human movement, we cannot ignore how that motion interacts with the surrounding environment. When we force a basketball down to the floor with an initial dribble, our sensory system has to detect how that action affected the ball's motion. Did it bounce back up to our hand? Did we dribble it off of our foot, sending it in an unexpected direction? Skills that we constantly take for granted demand our attention only when something goes wrong.

We'll look at motor skill acquisition and training in a later chapter. For now, let's start at the beginning of the athlete cognition cycle, searching for the best options.

Search: Taking What the Game Gives You

When you are the greatest player in the history of your sport, your words can sometimes become immortalized, even if they were said with less monumental intentions. The quote above from Wayne Gretzky rivals his other widely cited observation, "You miss 100 percent of the shots you don't take," as the most overused cliché in trying to convert sports tactics into life wisdom. The latter quote was a 1983 reply to Bob McKenzie of the *Hockey News*, who commented, "You have taken a lot of shots this year." [14] While Gretzky did lead the league in total shots during the 1982–83 season, [15] he also scored the most goals and assists with the highest points-per-game average (and seventh-highest in NHL history). In fact, seven of the top ten points-per-game seasons belong to Gretzky.

> "I skate to where the puck is going, not to where it has been." [13]
>
> —WAYNE GRETZKY

From a sports perspective, Gretzky's advice to "skate to where the puck is going" highlights the role of anticipation in the search component of athlete cognition. But it was actually his father, Walter Gretzky, who taught that lesson through a drill on their backyard rink in Brantford, Ontario. As Wayne explained to Rick Reilly in his autobiography, [16] "Some say I have a 'sixth sense' . . . Baloney. I've just learned to guess what's going to happen next. It's anticipation. It's not God-given, it's Wally-given. He used to stand on the blue line and say to me, 'Watch, this is how everybody else does it.' Then he'd shoot a puck along the boards and into the corner and then go chasing after it. Then he'd come back and say, 'Now, this is how the smart player does it.' He'd shoot it into the corner again, only this time he cut across to the other side and picked it up over there." When quizzed "Where do you skate?" by the elder Gretzky, Wayne learned the correct answer was "To where the puck is going, not to where it has been." [17]

Through this simple lesson, the Great One realized smart, pragmatic training will produce results: "Who says anticipation can't be taught?" [18]

Let's start with looking at two similar game scenarios from two different sports, football and soccer. Breaking down each to its most basic objectives, both involve twenty-two players, eleven per team, with the goal of moving a ball down the field into an end zone or a goal. A player with the ball has two options: keep the ball and try to score, or pass the ball to a teammate. Without the ball, a team's players have one job: to prevent either option from happening for the other team.

From this simple setup, one hundred years of tactics, training, and techniques have evolved to trick the other team in their pursuit of ball movement. On the attack, deceptive plays and motion try to fool the defense. Defenders try to anticipate where the ball is going while protecting against mental mistakes offering wide-open opportunities. How a player perceives the movement of the ball, teammates, and opponents directly determines his decisions about his own movements.

Imagine a running back being handed the ball in the backfield. From the play called in the huddle, he knows that the blocking scheme of his linemen should give him an opening between the guard and the tackle on the right side. He starts off toward that hole only to have it closed quickly by an oncoming linebacker. In an instant, less than a tenth of a second, he has to take in the updated visual information, evaluate his options, make a movement decision, and react physically to head in a different direction.

Similarly, think about a soccer midfielder who receives a pass at midfield and begins a counterattack. With the ball at her feet, she quickly observes the location and movement of a dozen or so players—teammates and opponents—in her immediate vicinity. The search for options begins. There's no ultimately perfect choice, as the quality of her immediate decision depends on the success of the actions after that. Did she start a sequence of passes that ended in a goal? Was her pass intercepted, ending in a goal for the other team? Had she chosen a different action, would that have had a higher probability of success? To start to answer these questions, we can look at relevant research that compares elite athletes to identify where exactly they have an edge over less experienced athletes.

Just as the physical assets of size, strength, and speed provide a competitive advantage for an athlete, it would be easy to assume that better eyesight would boost an athlete's perception. Of course, less than 20/20 visual acuity is a disadvantage anywhere, but beyond reading small letters on an eye chart, there are several other vision metrics that, logically, should make a difference. In the scenarios above, the running back in motion toward the line needs to focus on other players, who also are moving, a vision skill known as dynamic visual acuity. In the same way, the midfielder needs to track the ball at her feet, teammates available for a pass, and the defenders who are covering them. They both need to rely on peripheral vision to alert them to movement on either side of their immediate focus. Sports that require dribbling or stick handling add the element of near-far quickness—in other words, being able to change focus back and forth between the ball or puck and the surrounding environment.

But there is no agreement yet among researchers whether elite athletes or playmakers have better basic visual function in a sports or non-sports setting. In a review of the available literature, researchers Paul Ward and Mark Williams could not find definitive proof of this "hardware" advantage. "The notion that skilled performers are endowed with enhanced visual systems has intuitive appeal. For years, anecdotes of the best players possessing great vision have pervaded the locker room, terraces, and popular press. The empirical evidence, however, is at best inconclusive." [19]

For example, a 2017 study out of Liverpool John Moores University tested the visual function of 49 English Premier League players (high performers) and 31 college-level players (intermediate performers) against a normative database of 230 healthy but nonathletic adults. Across the test battery of five visual functions (visual acuity, contrast sensitivity, near-far quickness, target capture, and perception scan) both sets of soccer players performed significantly better in three of the five domains than the nonathletes. However, there was no difference at all between the elite EPL players and the college players. So the athletes did have an advantage over the nonathletes in a few of the vision functions but not enough to distinguish between elite and average athletes.

Measuring and training raw vision attributes in isolation from a sports context may be the problem, since, according to Ward and Williams, "the visual system does not function in isolation from the perceptual-cognitive system; these two components work together in an integrated manner to facilitate effective perception." [20] To put it another way, if we're going to attempt to train an athlete's vision, let's try to do it within a sports context to combine incoming sensory data with the rest of the athlete cognition cycle.

If perception and action (i.e., search and decide) are linked, then what is it that playmakers do differently? Two areas, cue utilization and pattern recognition, provide a peek into the playmaker's advantage.

Cue Utilization: Reading the Opponent

After playing more than nine hundred games as a defender for AC Milan football club, you would think that Paolo Maldini certainly must rank among the all-time leaders in number of career tackles, simply because that is what a defender is supposed to do. Not true, according to the man known as "Il Capitano" ("the Captain"): "If I have to make a tackle then I have already made a mistake."[21] By anticipating an attacker's moves and passing lanes, he was consistently able to be there a step ahead, avoiding the need for a rash, last-second lunge. While today's top defenders are celebrated for an average of four to five tackles per game, Maldini only needed 0.5 tackles per game across his twenty-five-year career.

Xabi Alonso, a longtime admirer of Maldini and an equally gifted defensive midfielder for Liverpool, Real Madrid, and Bayern Munich, stresses anticipation, not tackling, as the key training goal. "I don't think tackling is a quality. It is something you have to resort to, not a characteristic of your game," Alonso said. "I can't get into my head that football development would educate tackling as a quality, something to learn, to teach, a characteristic of your play. How can that be a way of seeing the game? I just don't understand football in those terms."[22]

"Seeing the game" as a key teaching objective sounds logical but is difficult to do without some understanding of how our visual perception operates. When we make an athletic move—let's say dribbling a basketball—our brain constantly makes adjustments based on two sets of information. First, our senses, particularly vision, touch, and hearing, provide multiple data points about the position of the ball in relation to our hands. At the same time our brain is monitoring the dribbling task and making numerous predictions per second about where the ball should be. After pushing the ball down with your hand, the brain also receives the touch feedback from the fingertips. The neural simulator in our brain, using thousands of prior dribbles as data points, estimates that we should feel the ball again on our fingertips in less than a second. Most of the time the ball bounces back up, we touch it again, and our dribbling motor program continues in the background while we focus on more important decisions on the court. But as soon as the prediction and the sensory data don't match up, we are alerted to a problem: the ball took a weird bounce requiring immediate visual attention to recover it.

Daniel Wolpert refers to this variation as noise, described as the movement variability in a world of uncertainty. "Imagine you're learning to play tennis and you want to decide where the ball is going to bounce as it comes over the net towards you," Wolpert explained in his TED Talk.[23] "There are two sources of information . . . There's sensory evidence—you can use visual information and auditory information, and that might tell you it's going to land in that [certain] spot. But you know that your senses are not perfect, and therefore there's some variability of where it's going to land . . .

"[B]ut there's another source of information not available on the current shot, but only available by repeated experience in the game of tennis, and that's that the ball doesn't bounce with equal probability over the court during the match. If you're playing against a very good opponent, they may distribute it in [this] area . . . making it hard for you to return. Now both these sources of information carry important information. . . . You might have a little predictor, a neural simulator, of the physics of your body and your senses. So as you send a movement command down, you tap a copy of that off and run it into your neural simulator to anticipate the sensory consequences of your actions."

Wolpert terms this "the optimal way of combining information." [24]

This movement analysis system is so useful that we even call on it, subconsciously, to predict the movements of others. Since we have mastered the task of dribbling a basketball, we understand the physics of the motion, even when watching someone else do it. While observing a player with the ball coming at us, our brain monitors the ball using the same combination of visual stimuli and internal prediction code as if we were dribbling. Experienced players use this finely tuned monitoring program to anticipate and guard oncoming attackers.

In a fascinating example of this, Italian researchers found that expert basketball players could predict the success of another player's jump shot before the ball even left the hand of the shooter. [25] They asked three groups of volunteers—professional basketball players, coaches, and those who never watch basketball—to view partial video clips of jump shots, then guess if the shot went in or missed; both were equally represented in the sample of shots. The video was stopped at several different points, including before the ball left the shooter's hand to several points in the arc of the shot toward the basket. By comparing expert players to coaches, the researchers tried to tease apart the neural advantages of playing the sport versus just watching the sport.

Sure enough, the players were better and faster at predicting the outcome of a shot than either the coaches or the neutral observers, even before the ball had left the shooter's fingers. "This indicates that elite athletes, but not expert watchers or novices, were able to extract relevant information on the fate of the shots at the basket by using kinematic cues from the player's body movements," the researchers concluded.

Two other facets of the study confirmed that the players' brains were specifically tuned to basketball. The groups also watched video clips of soccer penalty shots, but the expert basketball players were no better than the other two groups in predicting the success of that different type of movement. Their neural simulation algorithms were coded just for basketball. And when the researchers measured the brain activity of the groups during the videos, they found that the players and coaches showed excitability in brain regions associated with motor movement, while the novice group remained neutral.

"It looks as though before the ball ever leaves the hand, there is differing degrees of activations in the expert observer's motor cortex that go to the very same muscles they themselves would use to perform this task," commented Krakauer on the study. "And that seems to be a readout or simulation of what's happening when they're watching the player. That's why they can predict if the ball will go in or not, because in a sense they've simulated doing it themselves."[16]

Seeing these kinematic cues in an opponent helps anticipate their next action, which may be how playmakers like Maldini seemed to always be a step ahead in man-to-man situations. However, in a team sport, reading individual actions is not enough. The dynamic movement patterns of all the players provide even more opportunities.

Pattern Recognition: Seeing the Forest for the Trees

When Torbjörn Vestberg prepared to test Xavier Hernández Creus, better known to the soccer world as Xavi, he knew the results would be skewed to the upper end of the normative scale. As part of a larger 2012 experiment, Vestberg, a psychologist and researcher at Sweden's Karolinska Institutet, had already tested the executive function of more than fifty players from the top three professional divisions of Swedish soccer. As a measure of cognitive control, executive function combines working memory, attention, inhibitory control, and pattern recognition to understand how we confront new situations to plan and make decisions. Using the D-KEFS test battery of executive functions,[27] he found that higher-division players scored better than second-division players, while both player groups outperformed a control group of nonathletes. In addition, the players' on-field performance for the next two seasons showed a clear correlation between higher test scores and total number of goals and assists. While the result seems logical now, the study was one of the first to link generalized cognitive abilities with specific sport performance.

"We can imagine a situation in which cognitive tests of this type become a tool to develop new, successful soccer players," commented Vestberg. "We need to study whether it is also possible to improve the executive functions through training, such that the improvement is expressed on the field."[28]

In 2014, as part of a documentary for NHK,[29] the national Japanese TV network, Vestberg was given the opportunity to conduct similar tests with two of the game's greatest playmakers, Xavi and Andrés Iniesta, who formed a dominant midfield partnership for almost eighteen seasons, winning thirteen trophies for FC Barcelona and a World Cup for the Spanish national team. In fact, Xavi won the "World's Best Playmaker" award from IFFHS four consecutive times from 2008 to 2011, followed by Iniesta in 2012 and 2013.[30]

Design Fluency, one of the D-KEFS sub-tests given to both players, specifically assesses planning, working memory, and pattern planning by asking the user to create novel connections among a grid of dots time after time. The first four or five iterations are simple enough for most test takers, but to generate numerous unique combinations and patterns in a one-minute time constraint becomes challenging. However, Iniesta and Xavi scored in the top 0.1 percent of all test takers, according to Professor Predrag Petrovic, senior researcher at Karolinska Institutet's Department of Clinical Neuroscience and a coauthor on the 2012 study and a colleague of Vestberg's.[31] In fact, when Len consulted with the Spanish national team in 2006, he saw firsthand how their superior perceptual-cognitive skills transferred every day to the training pitch.

Finding new ways to connect the dots defines the playmaker's job. Seeing patterns and solutions where others don't is part of the cognitive mystery that is hard for even them to describe. "Think quickly, look for spaces," said Xavi, trying to explain his constant searching on the field. "That's what I do: look for spaces. All day. I'm always looking. All day, all day. Here? No. There? No. People who haven't played don't always realize how hard that is. Space, space, space. It's like being on the PlayStation. I think . . . the defender's here, play it there. I see the space and pass. That's what I do."[32]

Andrea Pirlo, the Italian midfield maestro known to fans as "L'Architetto" ("the Architect"), described this search for patterns in terms of vision: "I've understood that there is a secret: I perceive the game in a different way. It's a question of viewpoints, of having a wide field of vision. Being able to see the bigger picture. Your classic midfielder looks downfield and sees the forwards. I'll focus instead on the space between me and them where I can work the ball through. It's more a question of geometry than tactics."[33]

Even for the goal scorers, the players on the receiving end of an Iniesta or Pirlo pass, being able to see the play develop in the future creates opportunities.

"It's like when you play snooker, you're always thinking three or four shots down the line," explains Wayne Rooney, Manchester United's all-time leading goal scorer. "With football, it's like that. You've got to think three or four passes where the ball is going to come to down the line. And the very best footballers, they're able to see that before—much quicker than a lot of other footballers . . . [Y]ou need to know where everyone is on the pitch. You need to see everything."

Rooney pointed out that "what people don't realize is that it's obviously a physical game, but after the game, mentally, you're tired as well. Your mind has been through so much. There's so many decisions you have to make through your head. And then you're trying to calculate other people's decisions as well. It's probably more mentally tiring than physically, to be honest."[34]

Thomas Müller, star attacking midfielder for Bayern Munich and World Cup winner with the German national team, agrees: "I'm an interpreter of space. Every good, successful player, especially an attacking player, has a well-developed sense of space and time. Every great striker knows it's all about the timing between the person who plays the pass and the person making a run into the right zone."[35]

While their initial study focused on experienced adult players, Vestberg and Petrovic wondered if executive function testing could help find the next playmaker in the haystack. "This is interesting since soccer clubs focus heavily on the size and strength of young players," said Petrovic. "Young players who have still to reach full physical development rarely get a chance to be picked as potential elite players, which means that teams risk missing out on a new Iniesta or Xavi."

In an updated 2017 study,[36] the researchers found similar results when testing thirty young, talented playmakers aged between twelve and nineteen. Not only did they outperform a normative group of age-matched teens on the executive function tests, but they also showed correlation with strong goal-scoring performance over the next two seasons. In addition to the D-KEFS tests, they showed superior performance on a working memory test that did not surprise the researchers from Cogstate.[37] "This was expected since cognitive function is less developed in young people than it is in adults, which is probably reflected in how young people play, with fewer passes that lead to goals," Petrovic said.[38]

Their next step is to see if certain playing positions call for specific cognitive profiles. "We think that the players' positions on the pitch are linked to different cognitive profiles," Petrovic explained. "I can imagine that trainers will start to use cognitive tests more and more, both to find talented newcomers and to judge the position they should play in."[39] In fact, the Cogstate test is one of four tests included in a concussion baseline suite that thousands of young athletes have already taken. Petrovic thinks this may become the next generation of talent identification testing. "These could be used in many ways, such as selecting gifted soccer players at an early age, or testing and selecting from the large, untapped pool of soccer ability in a global soccer world. We expect that soccer players would want to take these tests to learn about their strengths, and to identify potential weaknesses that can be improved with training. And managers could use these methods to find the perfect set of profiles for a winning team, and identify the missing players in this jigsaw."[40]

As the superstar playmakers indicated, they find openings by studying space and time in relation to the players on the field. For the running back heading to the hole called in the huddle, the unexpected movement of players, both teammates and opponents, changes the space and time parameters they have to work with in a split second. Reaction time to these changes is the difference maker. While players can't quite explain exactly how they make these adjustments on the fly, researchers have been trying to isolate and identify the important cues that trigger redirected actions. Across different sports, this has been tested with two main memory features, recognition and recall. A recognition task asks the athlete, "Have you seen this pattern before?" Multiple images or video sequences of structured and unstructured game action are shown, with the athlete picking out which pattern of play has already been displayed. Conversely, a recall task asks the athlete to reconstruct the scene after seeing an image or video of a game situation. So, for example, after seeing five seconds of game action, they are given a blank field or court template and asked to place X's and O's to reenact the scene from memory with the relative positions of all the players.

Early studies of recognition and recall started with chess, in which grandmasters display their photographic and encyclopedic memory of game situations. They are able to both recognize chess boards they've seen before as well as recall and reconstruct a board after seeing it for only a few seconds. In the same way, expert athletes consistently outperform novices in recognition and recall. But every soccer, basketball, hockey, and lacrosse game is unique, with different players, uniforms, playing environments, and game action. What exactly is the brain remembering about these patterns of movement that can be accessed quickly and subconsciously later?

In a 2006 study,[41] three unique experimental conditions teased out some important differences. Two groups of soccer players, experts and novices, were shown ten-second action sequences from a video camera that was high above one goal, giving an end-to-end point of view of the entire field. The initial experiment confirmed that the experienced group could recognize previously viewed clips better than the novices. But then it got interesting. The researchers converted the game film to point-light displays, so instead of seeing actual players, only different-colored light dots representing each player were shown on the field. This stripped away all of the contextual clues of uniforms, colors, body size, and other details that a visual memory might capture. Again, the expert players outperformed the novices, telling the researchers that the recognition keys must be in the relative positioning and movement of the players rather than any superficial cues.

In the final experiment, using the original game film, a few key individuals were omitted from the scene entirely. This is where the expert-novice difference disappeared. No longer could the experienced players beat the newbies in recognizing previously seen patterns. Like removing a few pawns and bishops from the chessboard, the connected network of player positions is no longer intact, removing the underlying tactical logic of the play.

"It would appear that the positions and movements of these players, or the relative motions between these players and their team-mates, provide participants with the important information needed to make accurate familiarity-based judgments," the researchers concluded.[42]

In fact, it is this understanding of time, space, and movement that gives playmakers an advantage not only in their own sport but also in similarly structured sports. In a study involving experienced soccer, field hockey, and volleyball players, each sport group was asked to watch filmed play sequences of the other two sports (e.g., soccer players watched field hockey and volleyball game clips). Because of their tactical similarity, the soccer and hockey players scored well on recognizing patterns of play for the opposite sport, while the volleyball players struggled when watching soccer or hockey clips. The argument for kids playing multiple, related sports gets a boost from this study, which "suggests that such sporting diversity is only likely to benefit the acquisition of expert 'game reading' skills in a specific sport, if the sports in which participants engage are 'structurally' similar."[43]

Apparently, the athletic genius of Gretzky, Maldini, Xavi, or Iniesta starts with their interpretation of the external world, converting sensory input into opportunities. What they do with those nuggets of knowledge and the quality of their decisions drives their performance.

WHAT IS A PLAYMAKER?

Valter Di Salvo, director of football performance and science at Aspire Academy and former fitness and performance coach at Real Madrid FC and Manchester United FC:

Practically the playmakers are the players that make other players better, because without them, it's the missing the link between the positions. It is the player that controls the traffic in moving through the field. As a traffic light, you should control the situation, by making a connection between areas, between lines. Normally the playmaker is considered to be the person that controls the attacking phase. From my point of view, the playmaker is, of course, the player that puts on the lights for the attacking phase, but the modern one is also the person that should connect people in the defensive phase. There are lots of playmakers that have a capacity for connecting offensive movement, but not the capacity in connecting defensive movement.

CHAPTER 6

Decide: Choose Wisely

Dwane Casey knew his team had the knowledge to beat the Milwaukee Bucks, it was just a matter of making the right decisions at the right time during a game. "We have a 0.5 rule and we haven't been sticking to that very much until tonight," said the Toronto Raptors head coach after their crucial game-five win in the first round of the 2017 NBA playoffs. Every 0.5 second that elapses before a player makes his next decision gives their opponent a chance to react faster. "I thought the guys made excellent decisions out of the double team, out of the trap, and everybody that caught it was ready to play, ready to either drive it, pass it, or shoot it."[1]

That half-second rule may be the reason behind the Raptors organization building one of the most sophisticated training systems in sports. In 2011, when the NBA made the SportVU camera system available to teams, Toronto was one of the first to sign up for the $100,000-per-season data monster. Providing real-time (twenty-five times per second) X, Y position coordinates of every player on the court, as well as three-dimensional X, Y, Z coordinates of the ball, the SportVU system converts the motion of the game into useful data, enabling the tracking of thousands of micro decisions by individual players. Traditional basketball stats, which simply define who scored a point, made a rebound, or provided an assist, lack information on the constant weave of movement throughout a developing play.

Of course, the time-tested teaching tool of game film allows coaches and players to review their decisions, both good and bad. But converting this video-based action into digital 0's and 1's opens up game analysis to artificial intelligence, machine learning, and big data manipulation. This is where the Raptors took it to the next level. As Zach Lowe of *Sports Illustrated* explained, "The Raptors' analytics team wrote insanely complex code that turned all those X, Y coordinates from every second of every recorded game into playable video files. The code can recognize everything—when a pick-and-roll occurred, where it occurred, whether the pick actually hit a defender, and the position of all 10 players on the floor as the play unfolded. The team also factored in the individual skill set of every NBA player."[2]

Bring in the Ghosts

The result is a computer screen that looks like a basketball coach's clipboard with a floor diagram and ten little circles, each with a player's team color and uniform number and a dot for the ball. Clicking "play" on a game snippet puts the player circles and ball into action, just as it occurred in the real game. "So what," you may say, "we could just watch the game film to see this." But it's here that the magic happens. In addition to the ten actual player circles, there are five more circles on the screen, denoting the "ghost" players. Toronto's analytics staff factored in what the five Raptors players *should* have been doing on that play based on the coaching staff's ideal tactical scheme and the expected possession value (EPV) of each moment. Created by Kirk Goldsberry, former Harvard professor and now VP of strategic research for the San Antonio Spurs, specifically for the world of

SportVU data, the EPV statistic defines the best possible outcome of a possession given the players on the floor and their exact position at a moment in time.

"Every 'state' of a basketball possession has a value," Goldsberry explained in his 2014 article describing the new metric. "This value is based on the probability of a made basket occurring, and is equal to the total number of expected points that will result from that possession. While the average NBA possession is worth close to one point, that exact value of expected points fluctuates moment to moment, and these fluctuations depend on what's happening on the floor."[3]

Just like a coach hitting the pause button on the game film and explaining what should have happened instead of what did happen, the EPV is able to compute the ideal possible outcome and then compare it to the actual result. Indeed, it allows the grading of player decisions on every single possession rather than a summary of end-product stats.

"We can use EPV to collapse thousands of actions into a single value and estimate a player's true value by asking how many points he adds compared with a hypothetical replacement player, artificially inserted into the exact same basketball situations," Goldsberry noted.[4]

Based on second-to-second EPV, that ghost player circle on the Raptors' graphic visualization represents ideal decision-making and movement.[5] In fact, the analytics team built simulations that show what a set of "average" NBA players would do in that situation as well as, more importantly, what the best NBA teams would do. By superimposing the ghost players on the same screen as the real players, the effect is eye-opening as the ghosts demonstrate the optimal movement in that scenario. It's as if the coach called a time-out, diagrammed the perfect X's-and-O's scheme, and then hit the "play" button to bring it to life. This allows both coaches and players to review past games and to preview upcoming opponents based on their historical patterns. Coaches can see flaws in their tactics and opportunities to exploit other teams' weaknesses, all supported by EPV stats and probabilities.

Of course, at the end of the day, this is still just analytics, albeit at a more advanced level. In the NBA as well as all high-level sports, some basic truths still hold, like having a few players with world-class size, talent, and drive. But for the first time decisions can be quantified and measured to augment teaching on the court.

"It's a good backup for what your eyes see," said Casey. "It may also shed light on something else."[6]

"You need that coaching perspective," said Alex Rucker, who managed the development of the Raptors' system and is now VP of analytics for the Philadelphia 76ers. "But we are still looking for where the rules are wrong—areas where there are systemic things that are wrong with what we do on the court. But any system needs to comply with what the coaches want, and what the players can do."[7]

The one drawback that the Raptors found was the daunting, tedious manual task of entering data for every player to create these engaging visuals. Enter some even more impressive brainpower to automate this process. Researchers from California Institute of Technology (Caltech), STATS (the owner of SportVU), and Disney Research used machine learning—more specifically imitation learning—to teach a computer to behave like a human player. They learned from the Raptors' experience and turned their attention to soccer, training a neural network, a software system that learns logical connections between volumes of data using 17,400 soccer play sequences across 100 games.

"At a high level, artificial intelligence [AI] is simply about designing computer programs that can behave in increasingly complex ways," said Yisong Yue, an assistant professor at Caltech. "In this case, we want the trained AI agent to mimic the decision-making of professional soccer players as represented by trajectories. Coaches do this all the time when they draw up plays on a chalkboard, and ask their players to execute certain trajectories in different situations."

Presenting at the 2017 MIT Sloan Sports Analytics Conference,[8] the mecca of all things analytics, the research team described how they created a soccer ghost team based on data from actual sequences in an English Premier League game between Fulham and Swansea. The optimized, virtual, defensive ghost players were able to lower the expected goals (xG), the odds that a goal would be scored in that exact situation, from 72 percent using league-average defenders to 42 percent using learned behaviors from one of the best defensive teams in the EPL. In other words, mimicking the decisions and movements of the ideal human defense could predict a better outcome and should probably be taught by the coaching staff in training. Over time, fundamental questions that have stumped coaches for decades could be anticipated.

"Given an attacking play by a team, how did that team defend, or how should they have defended?" said Patrick Lucey, director of data science at STATS. "How should they have moved to minimize the likelihood that that team scores?"[9]

According to many pundits, soccer is a relatively simple game. Are there really that many different decision combinations available, other than dribble, pass, or shoot? "In soccer, there are 3.5 billion permutations in how those [ten field] players can be switched around," said Lucey. "When you include the opposition, there are more permutations than there are atoms in the universe." That sounds like a lot of choices. Choosing the right option at the right time requires some heavy-duty artificial intelligence computation that is based on the best human decisions by world-class players. So how do developing athletes, playmakers in training, learn to choose correctly? What are the strategies used by the brain to sort through the dizzying array of possibilities at any given second? In basketball, soccer, hockey, or any fast-moving team sport, how can a coach teach individual decision-making to achieve a coordinated, orchestrated flow of players?

Decision-Making Is Messy

A recent inventory of published judgment and decision-making theories catalogued up to three hundred variants of how humans make choices.[11] Of this overwhelming list, only twelve theories have been applied and researched specifically in sports settings. Clearly, we cannot decide how we decide or even how we should study our decision-making process. For decades, researchers used a top-down, experimental approach of hypothesizing a theory, then designing experiments in controlled lab-based settings to test it. Without the stress, confusion, and competing priorities of everyday life, test volunteers, kept within the lines of constrained variables, may show a rules-based logic to their choices. However, throw them into the real world and decisions get messy. It's no different for athletes who study film on their laptops, listen to their coaches in quiet meeting rooms, and memorize their two-dimensional playbooks. In those safe places, they analyze and select the best course of action. But on game days, they enter stadiums of screaming fans and high expectations where the windows of opportunity close in fractions of seconds.

> "An expert is someone who has succeeded in making decisions and judgements simpler through knowing what to pay attention to and what to ignore."[10]
>
> —EDWARD DE BONO

Decision theories that emphasize calm and reasoned analysis of options simply don't work in this environment. Athletes in competition certainly do not reflect the "economic man" concept of rational and predictable decision-making.[12]

Gary Klein knew that, as humans, we need to be studied in our natural habitat. As a research psychologist, he preferred to observe decisions being made in the moment during high-stress, time-constrained situations, noting the methods adopted and the mistakes made. "Instead of beginning with formal models of decision making, we began by conducting field research to try to discover the strategies people used," Klein explained. "Instead of looking for ways that people were suboptimal, we wanted to find out how people were able to make tough decisions under difficult conditions such as limited time, uncertainty, high stakes, vague goals, and unstable conditions."[13]

One of the first populations he studied was firefighters, especially commanders, who were required to make fast, correct, life-saving decisions. Klein first hypothesized that these commanders would choose from an array of options (keep current position, proceed to next room, evacuate immediately, etc.). Instead, he discovered, through task analysis interviews with the commanders soon after an event, that they used a serial evaluation process. "In fact, the commanders usually generated only a single option, and that was all they needed," Klein found. "They could draw on the repertoire of patterns that they had compiled during more than a decade of both real and virtual experience to identify a plausible option, which they considered first. They evaluated this option by mentally simulating it to see if it would work in the situation they were facing . . . If the course of action they were considering seemed appropriate, they would implement it. If it had shortcomings, they would modify it. If they could not easily modify it, they would turn to the next most plausible option and run through the same procedure until an acceptable course of action was found." [14]

Much like a quarterback working through his progression of receiver options, the fire commanders would sense and internally compute the feasibility of the first option that came to mind, then proceed down the list of next-best alternatives. Known as "satisficing," a mash-up of "satisfy" and "suffice," this strategy goes with the first option that passes an acceptable threshold for the situation. Originally conceived by psychologist and computer scientist Herbert Simon, this method helps prevent analysis paralysis in a fast-moving situation. "Decision makers can satisfice either by finding optimum solutions for a simplified world, or by finding satisfactory solutions for a more realistic world," said Simon in his 1978 Nobel Prize acceptance speech. "Neither approach, in general, dominates the other, and both have continued to co-exist in the world of management science." [15]

In addition to firefighters, Klein and his team have studied military commanders, anesthesiologists, pilots, nurses, and even nuclear power plant operators—decision makers in critical situations with limited time. The spontaneous list of options that they consider is generated by recognizing patterns in the environment that trigger recollections of past encounters, much like we discussed in the previous chapter. Naming this process the recognition-primed decision (RPD) model, Klein explains how people make the best decisions without taking the time to compare every option. "When people need to make a decision they can quickly match the situation to the patterns they have learned," he wrote. "If they find a clear match they can carry out the most typical course of action. In that way, people can successfully make extremely rapid decisions." [16]

RPD, part of a broader naturalistic decision-making (NDM)

framework, combines intuitive, quick retrieval of similar patterns with the slightly slower simulation and analysis of the best option generated. A running back does not have time to weigh the pros and cons of the multiple directions he could cut when the initial play breaks down. Based on the visual stimuli his brain receives, the experienced back instantly recognizes the pattern of movement in front of him and then simulates the success rate of the first option considered. If acceptable, he commits to the decision and attacks. Ideally, the whole process happens instantly and automatically with no conscious thought needed. Another Nobel Prize winner revealed how this happens.

Thinking About Thinking

Just like Klein's bottom-up approach to studying decision-making, Daniel Kahneman observed humans as we are, not how we wish to be. We are not logical robots but living, emotional beings that are easily influenced by other people and circumstances. Along with his longtime collaborator Amos Tversky, Kahneman held a mirror up to the world's face to show us how we think, in an imperfect and biased way. The two Israeli psychologists created several groundbreaking theoretical concepts in judgment and decision-making as well as creating the field of behavioral economics. Most of the nonacademic world discovered Kahneman from his 2011 book, *Thinking, Fast and Slow*,[18] in which he summarized his forty years of research. In fact, Michael Lewis, author of *Moneyball: The Art of Winning an Unfair Game*,[19] credits Kahneman and Tversky, belatedly, as the big thinkers who ex-

> "We are prone to blame decision makers for good decisions that worked out badly and to give them too little credit for successful moves that appear obvious only after the fact."[17]
>
> **—DANIEL KAHNEMAN**

plained the decision-making behaviors of the biased baseball scouts and coaches whom Lewis described. It took two book reviewers, one of them an economics professor and former student of Kahneman's, to reveal to Lewis that the traditional player evaluation errors that were corrected by Lewis's protagonist, Billy Beane, had already been described by Kahneman and Tversky years before.

"And so, once the dust had settled on the responses to my book, one of them remained more alive and relevant than the others: a review by a pair of academics, then both at the University of Chicago—an economist named Richard Thaler and a law professor named Cass Sunstein.[20] Thaler and Sunstein's piece, which appeared on August 31, 2003, in the *New Republic*, managed to be at once both generous and damning. The reviewers agreed that it was interesting that any market for professional athletes might be so screwed-up that a poor team like the Oakland A's could beat most rich teams simply by exploiting the inefficiencies. But—they went on to say—the author of *Moneyball* did not seem to realize the deeper reason for the inefficiencies in the market for baseball players: They sprang directly from the inner workings of the human mind. The ways in which some baseball expert might misjudge baseball players—the ways in which any expert's judgments might be warped by the expert's own mind—had been described, years ago, by a pair of Israeli psychologists, Daniel Kahneman and Amos Tversky. My book wasn't original. It was simply an illustration of ideas that had been floating around for decades and had yet to be fully appreciated by, among others, me."[21]

Slightly embarrassed that he had missed it the first time and intrigued with the lifetime of work that led to a Nobel Prize in economics for Kahneman, Lewis cajoled his Berkeley neighbor to let him tell the story of Kahneman and Tversky's discoveries, which he titled, *The Undoing Project: A Friendship That Changed Our Minds.*[22]

Of interest to playmakers, Kahneman introduced two characters living inside the brain, System 1 and System 2. We have seen both of these notions, with different names, in earlier chapters. System 1 is your automatic, knee-jerk responses to situations. What is 2 + 2? *Boom,* the answer immediately came to mind without thinking. You drive down a lonely, empty road lost in your thoughts. Don't worry, System 1 is there to switch on autopilot. A fastball is headed directly for your face, but System 1 is there to make sure you duck. In a gym full of loud fans, you hear a particular voice yelling from the sideline and instantly know, without looking, that it's your coach. In Klein's world, it provides the instant pattern recognition on the field. System 1 operates on its own based on a lifetime of learning that has been passed on to it from its partner in crime, System 2.

When we need to stop and think, System 2 is our slow, conscious, effortful tool. Sure, 2 + 2 was easy, but what about 17 × 234? You know you can solve it in your head but it requires focus, concentration, and effort. Learning a new offensive play with its unique visual cues and alternative options relies on System 2 thinking. While System 1 is very confident in its beliefs, or heuristics, System 2 sometimes has to step in and verify an educated guess. When a quarterback hesitates for just a second before passing to a receiver, his System 1 has asked for a double check with System 2. While the confirmation may prevent an interception by an unseen defender, the delay may also close the tiny window that was available. The goal of skill acquisition, which we will look at closely in the next chapter, is to hardwire System 1 with the recipe so that it can be performed subconsciously. When an athlete begins to focus on the individual components of a learned skill, System 1 has broken down and

System 2 has been asked to check the process, resulting in a loss of automaticity and form.

The reflexive decisions doled out by System 1 can also be described as that vague notion of intuition. Just as Klein studied the intuitive feel of fire chiefs as to when a burning floor was about to collapse, a hockey defenseman's instinct when to commit to an attacker is a combination of System 1 pattern recognition, timing, and best-available-option selection. While their theories fit together at several integration points, Kahneman and Klein did not always agree with each other. While Klein marveled at the magic of expert decision makers, searching for the secret of how they performed at such a high level, Kahneman sought out the causes of faulty thinking, which he labeled heuristics and biases, whereby our confident but sometimes flawed System 1 makes poor decisions. In an unusually cordial collaboration that lasted almost nine years, they worked together to reconcile their different viewpoints. Instead, they found that they actually agreed on quite a lot, as captured in their capstone paper title, "Conditions for Intuitive Expertise: A Failure to Disagree."[23] The answer to their primary question—under what conditions are the intuitions of professionals worthy of trust?—was the need for a "high-validity" environment along with plenty of practice time to learn from that world.

"We describe task environments as 'high-validity' if there are stable relationships between objectively identifiable cues and subsequent events or between cues and the outcomes of possible actions," they concluded. ". . . If an environment provides valid cues and good feedback, skill and expert intuition will eventually develop in individuals of sufficient talent."[24]

Sports offer ideal high-validity learning spaces. Rules of the game, immediate consequences, and measurable outputs give athletes plenty of opportunity for System 2 to develop the predictable rules of thumb and cause/effect relationships that will eventually transfer to System 1. The challenge is not with training a young playmaker who has a relatively empty expertise container to fill but with breaking old beliefs of more experienced players. Just as it was difficult for the Oakland A's baseball scouts to change the way they evaluate players, it was also hard for experienced players to change based on the suggestions of an AI system. System 1 can be stubborn, not open to reprogramming attempts. When Raptors coaches introduced more aggressive defensive coverage based on the ghost system, they ran into resistance—even though the ghost movements were based on superior human teams. "Guys don't want to be embarrassed, or see themselves on TV giving up a dunk or an open 3," said Micah Nori, Raptors assistant coach. "Even though basketball is essentially five guys guarding the ball, it's hard to get players away from the concept of, 'This is my guy.'" Even Coach Casey started to sound a bit like an A's scout when asked about the system's suggestions: "You can't make all your decisions based on it, and it can't measure heart, and chemistry, and personality."[25] Now, that would be something. Perhaps we'll call it System 3.

Take the First Option

While Klein and Kahneman built a foundation for thinking about decision-making in chaotic, time-sensitive environments, it would be helpful to have some validation that athletes act this way in their stress-filled world. While basketball and football have a more structured play-calling system, sports like soccer, hockey, lacrosse, and rugby rely on a style of play that combines creativity with some tactical guardrails. When a playmaker scans the field, she knows there are constraints to her options that are immediately off the list: *Don't do this or you'll get yelled at.* But then, using the overarching tactical game plan, she monitors opportunities that match the strategy that the coaching staff embedded into her memory in the pregame preparation. A so-called functional strategy gives her guidelines of when to carry out a certain task, like dribble, pass, or shoot, while a spatial strategy provides a preferred directional focus, like *Attack the left side of the defense*. But how do these different strategies affect the number and quality of decision options that playmakers create on the fly?

Enter Markus Raab and Joseph Johnson, two decision researchers who have used sports as their laboratory. For the last fifteen years, they have tried to figure out how people choose what to choose from. That is, how do people generate possible solutions to a task when they are not restricted to selecting from among a set of alternatives given to them?[26] Sounds like a situation all too familiar for a playmaker. Following in Klein's footsteps, Raab and Johnson agreed with the RPD model but wanted to find out if athletes typically take the first option that satisfies an immediate goal. Also, they added a branch on the tree by defining the underlying search strategy that the playmaker has looming over her play, including the "what" and the "how."

"Across sports, one of the most common decisions is what a player decides to do with the ball and how he does it," they explained. "For example, in soccer, basketball, and handball, the options may be to move somewhere with the ball, pass it to a teammate, or shoot it at the goal; in tennis and golf, the options concern where to place the ball, and how (e.g., with or without backspin). When a sports player has to decide quickly what to do in a given situation, such as how to allocate the ball, the possible options can be classified based on their spatial result (to the left wing player, to the right sideline, etc.) or on their functional result (pass, shoot, lob, spike, etc.)."[27]

They predicted that the number of options generated would

depend on which strategy, functional or spatial, is used. Also, they believed that as the option list grows, the quality of choices goes down, as does the consistency between the first option considered and the final one selected. To confirm their ideas, Raab and Johnson turned to team handball, an Olympic sport and the second most popular team game in the world behind soccer. With six players and a goalie on each side, the gameplay mixes elements from basketball, hockey, water polo, and soccer. While the object of the game—throwing a ball a little smaller than a basketball into a net about twice the size of a hockey goal—is straightforward, the speed of the game and the decision complexity matches those two sports.

Gathering eighty-five local professional players, Raab and Johnson asked them each to watch a series of video game clips presented on a large screen in front of them. Each of the thirty-one clips was ten seconds long and ended with one team in possession of the ball and on the attack. As quickly as possible, each player was asked to say out loud (into a microphone and recorder) the first decision that intuitively popped in his brain, followed by a list of as many other alternatives as he could think of. Finally, of all his ideas, he chose the best option. In this way, his first, intuitive choice could be compared to his final, optimal choice to see if he really should just go with the first decision that occurred to him.

Surprisingly, the players came up with a total of 107 different options across the video clips, some using a spatial strategy (move left) and some using a functional strategy (pass to number 9). All of the choices generated by the players were rated by expert coaches to determine decision quality in the specific situations. After the video sessions, all of the players participated in scrimmage games in which they were rated by the same coaches to provide an assessment of the skill level of each player.

After the data was analyzed, the researchers found that players who used a functional strategy generated more options than those using a spatial strategy. However, the quality of their best, final options was lower, as rated by the coaches. In fact, those players who had shorter lists of options had higher-quality first and final choices, confirming what Raab and Johnson call the "take the first" (TTF) method of decision-making. "In fact, had participants not generated *any* options but instead relied solely on their first choice . . . they would have, on average, chosen options with higher quality . . . ," they concluded.[28]

As athletes gain experience, their intuitive (System 1) first choice is usually their best bet, which matches with a coach's instructions to trust your gut and don't overthink it. "In familiar yet ill-defined tasks, choose one of the initial options generated once a goal (and strategy) has been defined, rather than exhaustively generating all possible options and subsequently processing them deliberatively," Raab and Johnson advise.[29] Over time, the athlete will be able to pick the best entry point in her memory to start searching for the first option, a process they call "fast and frugal heuristics."

But Raab and Johnson didn't stop there. Following up on their 2003 study, they still wanted to know how an athlete's decision-making skill evolves over time. Using the same experimental setup of viewing shortened video plays, they recruited sixty-nine players at three skill levels—expert, near-expert, and nonexpert—based on their years of experience and team membership. They tested the groups every six months for two years. "It is one thing to say that experts and nonexperts differ, but it is far more productive to understand why and how they differ," they said. "In particular, we focus on three distinct processes that serve to guide the ultimate selection of a course of action—

information search, option generation, and deliberation producing choice."[30]

In addition to a longitudinal timeframe, the researchers used a revealing tool to track the players' vision as they searched the field for options: eye-tracking glasses.[31] Coaches ask players all the time, "Where were you looking on that play? What were you focusing on?" Of course, in hindsight, a player will try to give the correct answer to cover up any mistakes made. However, eye-tracking glasses can show exactly where the eyes were fixated in the target environment and for how long. These glasses have two cameras, one that faces out, capturing what the player sees, and one that is pointed at the player's pupils to capture his continuous focus shifts, or saccades.

At any one time, the human retina, specifically the fovea, can only capture about 1 to 2 degrees of vision, with the rest of the scene being filled in by peripheral vision and the brain. By constantly shifting this high-definition focus to different points, the eyes create a mosaic of the environment. In real time, eye-tracking software can combine the two video streams to be displayed on a computer screen. A crosshair is placed on the view of the playing field that represents exactly where the player is looking. When the gaze shifts from a teammate to the ball to a defender, the crosshair jumps around the screen, reflecting the current gaze. This entire sequence can be recorded and replayed to the player to teach him his search pattern habits.

Wearing the eye-tracker glasses, the handball players called out their first options, listed all possible options, and then selected their final, best options. As expected, the players' gaze behavior matched their search strategy. Those who looked for a functional solution (dribble, pass, or shoot) scanned the entire environment first, while those who were focused on a certain region (left, center, right) verbalized spatial strategy options. More importantly, their initial gaze matched their first and best options. Expert players generated shorter lists of options of higher quality with fewer gaze fixations using, primarily, a spatial search strategy. Over the course of the two-year study, players showed consistency in using the TTF approach and improved the timing and accuracy of their options.

So, what Raab and Johnson's research shows is that when an expert playmaker brings the ball into the attacking zone, he tends to look first for spaces to exploit rather than functional acts (dribble, pass, shoot). From experience, his gaze recognizes an opening producing a first-choice option. Like Klein's fire commanders, he internally simulates a move into that space to test the probability of success. If it passes an acceptable threshold, he immediately picks that choice as his decision rather than continuing the search.

While expert playmakers get better at these quick, intuitive decisions, talented kids apparently use the same TTF strategy. In a 2017 study, Raab and colleagues asked ninety-seven young soccer players, ages six to thirteen, to call out decision options after viewing clips of soccer sequences. Sure enough, the kids produced two to three options per play and chose their first options as their best options 74 percent of the time. When pressed for time, the option lists got shorter but their quality increased.

Stopping the Mental Mistakes

Over time, young players build their heuristics library to be able to call on it in future games. "It really depends on the player," said Brad Stevens, head coach of the Boston Celtics, in an interview. "With Al Horford, you don't have to spend much time on anything because he's lived it all. He's experienced it for ten years. When a young 19-year-old like Jason Tatum joins your team, you have to cover everything and show him where the right basketball plays are to be made, even though he's had elite coaching. Even though he had great coaching in high school and had one of the game's greatest coaches ever in [Duke's] Mike Krzyzewski, he's only 19. So he's got a long way to grow." [32]

Stevens, who has made the transition from coaching college kids to coaching experienced professionals, believes decision-making skill starts in practice.

"First of all, I think everybody can get better in that regard no matter where their starting point is. To me it is compartmentalizing each possession and understanding what your job is on that possession, and that's why you practice. That's why you watch film. That's why you rehash the game before that you played, and that's why you preview the game ahead that you're playing against your opponent. So, I think it's about being able to stay in the moment and do the job that you worked hard and trained yourself to do."

Breakdowns in decisions—what many call mental mistakes—are a combination of lack of preparation and not being able to recognize and recall patterns and coaching points.

"A mental mistake can be a number of things," said Stevens. "It can be something that happens on the fly where you decide to guard a screen a certain way but it doesn't take into account understanding who you're guarding. For instance, if you go under a screen on Kyle Korver, it's just a huge mental mistake in a game. If you guard a post player that always goes to his left shoulder and you give him his left shoulder, that's a huge mental mistake in a game. If you don't run a play right that you've worked on over and over or don't come from the timeout to the floor and execute a play, [it] is a huge mental mistake in the game.

"Some of those are preparation errors, so it may be more how you focused in your preparation than it was in how you're focusing in the game. Some of them may be just lack of ability for whatever reason to carry out the task."

Mark Newman, former senior vice president of baseball operations, who supervised player development and scouting for the New York Yankees, agrees that improving decision-making needs to happen in practice as well as in games by empowering the players to call their own shots, even at a young age.

"You can't expect them to grow in their decision-making ability by looking over at the coach all the time," he told us. "You see in youth sports today young players looking toward a coach or even a parent for in-game direction. Even a ten-, eleven-, twelve-year-old, those kids are capable of making decisions. Initially they'll make a lot of wrong ones, but then they'll make better ones. I've seen amazing results with young kids where they were given reasonable freedom to make decisions and mistakes, and they have to go together." [33]

It's a matter of setting up multiple game scenarios in practice with different variables to expose players to a wide variety of patterns and the options available. In his eighteen years as a college coach and twenty-five years with the Yankees, Newman has experimented constantly with the best teaching methods.

"We will present our players with all possible game situations in the practice setting. Some of the rare situations, like runners on first and third and we are up two runs and there is a sure double down the right field line in the bottom of the seventh inning: How do we respond defensively? These rare situations will be covered, but probably not very often as we spend most of our practice time on plays and situations that occur more often or have more regular impact on game outcomes. There are certain players, like Derek Jeter, who we saw make great intuitive plays over his long career, that possess the ability to respond correctly to these difficult situations. There are many other players who have the opportunity to make those plays but don't.

"Our training process is founded on correct repetition after correct repetition. We will instruct, assess, and instruct again. We are constantly asking players for feedback about what they are experiencing during these repetitions. We want them to make decisions and we have to show patience while they are engaged in the process of learning how to respond to competitive situations. This is an active patience. When mental mistakes are made we are going to coach players, but it will be done in a tone and manner that strongly implies that we trust the player to make decisions. They have to keep playing freely and fearlessly."

Since those late-game actions are usually influenced by fatigue, a player's brain has to rely on decisions made below his level of consciousness. "In rugby, there's a time for watching and reacting and there's a time for thinking," said Dave Hadfield, an educator and coach who has worked at the elite level of New Zealand rugby for twenty years. "And if you're thinking when you should be watching and reacting, you're in trouble." [34] While Hadfield has helped players build their mental skills for years, he believes his biggest impact is teaching coaches pedagogy principles to use with their athletes. Take a scenario that happens hundreds of times in a game of rugby, basketball, soccer—really any team invasion sport. Hadfield stresses that the quick, automatic decisions are made in the subconscious mind, so when things go wrong, it takes some digging to fix it.

"If we believe that decisions in sports are made at the subconscious level, then when something goes wrong, we need to shine a light on that hidden space to correct it," he told us. "As an example, consider a player with the ball who senses a defender next to him. Instead of passing the ball to a teammate to his left, he decides to try to evade the defender but gets tackled.

"When reviewing the game film the next day with his coach, he admits that the 'correct' decision was to pass the ball and realizes his mistake. Now we need to understand why he did what he did in the moment so it doesn't happen next time.

"Did he do it because he doesn't understand his functional role on the team? Does he not understand the game tactics? Was he distracted in that moment, thinking about what he was going to do next? We have to diagnose where the error was in that decision and where did it come from. We have to talk about it and perhaps design some training drills to correct it until it's locked and loaded back in the dark of the subconscious."

That's why Newman still encourages coaches to find new ways to get through to their players, especially in cognitive development. While Aaron Judge might seem to be an obvious prospect for MLB success, how many were left behind?

"The question I continue to have is about the ones that did not make it," Newman added. "Had we trained them differently, could they have acquired those playmaking skills? When I look back at my coaching career, I am at times somewhat embarrassed by some things I didn't do or did do and shouldn't have done. My challenge to coaches is to ask: If you look ten years into the future, what are you doing now or not doing now that you're going to look back on and regret?"

WHAT IS A PLAYMAKER?

Mark Newman, former senior vice president of baseball operations for the New York Yankees:

What the term means to me is someone who takes talent and skill, and is able to use them in game situations. During my many years with the Yankees we signed and developed many outstanding players. We also signed several players who we thought were going to be outstanding and for some reason fell short of the potential we saw in them. This experience makes a person acutely aware of the gap between talent and performance. The bridge over that gap is all the cognitive skills that allow a player to go from being a prospect to a performer. That's what distinguishes the playmaker from the one who aspires to be a playmaker.

Certainly, in everything there are degrees, but [a playmaker is] one that can translate talent into execution, make plays, as the term suggests, and that requires a level of skill development. Beyond that is this cognitive development: the ability to mentally and emotionally be tuned in to the environment and respond appropriately to it.

CHAPTER 7

Execute: Make It Happen

Think back to the fall of 2016. You might remember one team that defied the odds and exorcised the demons of futility in a postseason for the ages. Founded in 1877, they had won just one championship in the last 110 years with only one other runner-up finish. In the meantime, mediocre seasons led to twelve different managers in the last forty years. Yet, a new leader in 2015 sparked hope among players and fans with an unusual chatter of optimism. And then it happened: a magical run through the playoffs that had most of the country rooting for the underdogs, culminating in the final game of the season to mercifully end the long, fabled drought. Maybe the Chicago Cubs drew some inspiration from those unlikely champions.

Playing in their first Australian Football League (AFL) grand final match since 1961, the Western Bulldogs beat the favored Sydney Swans to raise their first flag in sixty-two years, becoming the first premier, a title given to the champs, in the 110-year history of the league to start the postseason as a seventh seed (out of eight teams). The crowd that packed the 100,000-seat Melbourne Cricket Grounds stadium and the millions who watched on TV witnessed a true David conquering a Goliath—the Swans appearing in their third Grand Final in the last five years, having won in 2012 and finishing tied for first place during the regular season.

"We won a lot of close games [this year], and we were able to stay calm under enormous pressure, but still find a way to play with some freedom," said Luke Beveridge, head coach of the Bulldogs.[1] His counterpart, John Longmire, admitted his Swans players just didn't perform to expectations: "You need everyone with their noses to the grindstone and we didn't have that even contribution we definitely needed."[2]

For anyone who has not watched an Australian rules football match (affectionately known as "footy"), staying calm under pressure while your nose feels like it is chained to a grindstone is one of the ultimate tests of sports. With the speed of an NBA fast break, the kicking skill of an EPL striker crossed with an NFL punter, the catching skill of an All-Pro wide receiver, and the physical violence of an NHL mid-ice collision, Aussie football stretches the limits of sensory perception, decision-making, and skill execution.

The last few minutes of the Bulldogs' decisive victory showcased the sport's chaotic, adrenaline-fueled rush of skilled movement. With a tenuous nine-point lead with under six minutes to play, the Swans sent a high, lofted kick, similar to a targeted punt, to their star forward, Lance Franklin. But veteran Bulldogs defender Dale Morris was there to tip the ball away, which, in footy, results in a mad scramble for the live ball, much like a fumble in the NFL. After a few short handball passes (think underhand volleyball serve) between Swans players, Franklin got the ball back and headed for open field. Relentlessly, Morris stayed in pursuit, tackling Franklin from behind despite giving up four inches and thirty-three pounds to the six-time all-Australian, knocking the ball free. Tom Boyd, the Bulldogs' six-foot-seven-inch power forward, scooped up the ball, took two steps, and ripped a sixty-five-yard kick that bounced once in front of the center goalposts and then across the line for six points and a crucial fifteen-point lead with five minutes left.

In those thirty seconds, the primary skills of Aussie rules football were displayed: passing with the foot, catching a pass (known as a mark), pickup of a loose ball, passing with the hands, pursuit followed by a tackle, and a scoring kick. Breaking those skills down even more, there were four fundamental elements: targeting a ball to a teammate or goal with a foot or hand; catching a ball; pursuing a player with the ball; and evading defenders when in possession of the ball. Now think about similar team-based invasion sports like soccer, basketball, hockey, lacrosse, and American football. Again, only four core skills are necessary: throwing, catching, pursuing, and evading. Each of these has an intentional purpose to them: to get possession of the ball, advance the ball toward your opponent's goal, and score. When not in possession, reverse the process to get control of the ball. Of course, many micro skills live inside each macro skill: there are at least six different types of footy kicks. But to manage the complexity, the human brain clumps comparable skills into categories to provide a hierarchy for learning them. In basketball and soccer, it's dribble, pass, or shoot. In hockey, it's stick handle, pass, or shoot. In American football, it's carry, throw, or catch the ball. With the ball, you evade the defenders. Without the ball, you pursue the attackers.

As we've learned from previous chapters, perception and interpretation of the playing environment, followed by a decision to choose the best option—often the first one considered—leads an athlete to the point of no return, executing the skills that the moment demands. Dale Morris did not methodically break down the process as we do in this book but rather instinctively repeated the athlete cognition cycle multiple times in those thirty seconds.

Tom Boyd had no time to slow down for a lengthy analysis of options. In three seconds he executed a pickup of the ball, positioned himself for a kick, glanced at the goalposts, and performed a complex set of motor skill instructions to send the ball between the goalposts, over sixty yards away. Skill execution is the ultimate payoff across sports.

A veteran of two hundred AFL games as a player, John Longmire is a coach who has walked the walk. Add in an assistant coach apprenticeship under Swans legend Paul Roos, and Longmire was well prepared to take over as head coach when Roos retired at the end of the 2010 season. In seven seasons with Longmire in charge, the Swans have won over two-thirds of their games, which places him third all-time in winning percentage among AFL coaches with more than one hundred games coached.[3]

"He has got an amazing track record. He cut his teeth over a significant period of time working with Roosy and then he brought in his own style and his own brand after that," said Beveridge of his rival. "I think in many ways the Swans were transformed when he took over. The consistency of his success and finals footy is a great credit to him and his people. We aim to be like that. We aim to be envied like the Hawks and Swans."[4]

Despite twenty years at the top level and a lifetime of footy, there is still at least one mystery that Longmire is trying to solve. When we asked him which playing skill was the most in demand but the least in supply, he emphasized that instant, intuitive decision-making followed by flawless skill execution under pressure was the holy grail.

"Athletes come to us having mastered most of the technical demands of the game, such as kicking, advancing the ball, catching, and tackling, but without question the biggest challenge our coaches face is teaching our players how to make quick and accurate decisions on the field," said Longmire. "As coaches, we have learned how to make our players stronger, faster, and more fit through our sport science programs. We review a lot of video with the team and structure training sessions to simulate games as much as we can.

"But we have not come up with a good strategy for teaching perhaps the most important skill in our sport: decision-making. All football players are capable of making decisions on the field, but when the game is perceived as important, this psychological pressure changes how a player makes decisions. Likewise, when your opponent applies a lot of pressure by taking away space and time, decision-making is affected. So our challenge now is to creatively teach decision-making." [5]

"I Do Not Like Green Eggs and Ham"

During a technical presentation to an audience of elite coaches, Damian Farrow showed a photo of Theodor Geisel, asking the audience, "While he's not a sport scientist, do you know who he is?" A few in the audience, most likely parents, nodded. "That's Dr. Seuss," exclaimed Farrow. "He is the master of manipulating cognitive load to get it to an optimal challenge point." Farrow, a professor of skill acquisition in the Institute of Sport, Exercise and Active Living (ISEAL) at Victoria University in Melbourne and an expert coach with the Australian Institute of Sport, had been laying out the case for training sport skills much like physical conditioning, using periodization techniques that break up practice time into alternating chunks of knowledge. "All of these books [by Dr. Seuss] with their rhyming phrases repeat time and time again, then they switch, then they repeat, then they switch. This is essentially what we've been talking about with this in-task switching and he is the master of it. Most of us with kids have taught them to read using this type of material. The same principles readily transfer over to skill learning as well from the physical perspective." [6]

Indeed, Dr. Seuss's *Green Eggs and Ham*, one of the all-time bestselling children's books, uses just fifty words, but in different combinations and rhythms. [7] Related to skill training, Farrow advocates for random repetition of tasks in a coach's practice design rather than block training that sequentially orders drills according to skill. Like a Dr. Seuss story, randomizing training by circling back to a skill in a new and different way teaches adaptation in different contexts.

Farrow, who has extensive experience working with many different teams in invasion-based sports, recognizes the disconnect between scheduled, structured practice environments and muddled, disorganized game situations. "Skill is, really, technique under pressure," he said in a recent presentation. "When we're looking at methods to train skill, are we preparing our athletes to hold their technique under pressure? If we're not, we're really not meeting the needs of our athletes." [8] Most coaches, according to Farrow, don't separate two very different types of practice, learning a skill versus performing a skill. When teaching a new movement for the first time or at an elementary level, pressure and fatigue can be set aside until the skill has advanced to being repeated consistently. But when preparing for competition, a practice environment that simulates actual game stress will build the adaptations needed and that coaches like the Swans' Longmire demand.

Part of the problem is that managing the skill development process for athletes has been a bit murky, with no unifying methodology for long-term player development (LTPD). "When you look at the skill acquisition literature, there is no real framework for how we develop skill. We have a lot of theories and principles that we tend to follow and apply but a high-performance framework is absent." [9]

However, physical conditioning, the other side of the LTPD coin, has a well-established foundation to plan, measure, and manage the process of getting stronger, faster, and fitter. "The strength and conditioning community is very good at being systematic in the prescription monitoring of the interventions they do." [10] In particular, the concept of periodization to plan and schedule workouts defines a twelve-month calendar designed to have an athlete peak physically at the ideal point in time in their competitive season. Using three phases of development—preparatory, competitive, and transition—periodization customizes the year to fit the specific demands of the sport with the individualized progress of each athlete. [11] Since sport coaches are already familiar with this concept from their strength and conditioning specialists, Farrow envisioned using this planning technique to communicate skill development.

Samuel J. Robertson agrees with Farrow. In fact, they wrote a paper together describing this skill acquisition periodization framework. [12] But Robertson has no intention of letting it die a dusty death in an academic journal. In addition to being a researcher and peer of Farrow's at Victoria University, he is a sport scientist with the Bulldogs, heading up their research and innovation. With a doctoral degree in skill acquisition, Robertson has dived headfirst into data analytics and machine learning to bring more rigorous discipline to LTPD.

"From a recruiting perspective, it's far more about the skill side of things than the physical. Australian football went through a phase where everyone was looking for the best athlete they could get their hands on, but it's still a skill-based sport," said Robertson. "That's first and foremost what we're looking for—players that can kick and handball, because that's more fundamental to the game. It's probably easier to teach someone to run better later down the track rather than teaching them to kick.

"It helps because we've got a really strong idea at the club for the types of players we want to have here," Robertson continued. "It sounds obvious but a lot of clubs don't have that. We can evaluate our system against those values we've got here.

"It's just also basic intelligence, we can pick out the education we're going to provide them and make sure they're going to understand it quickly. If they do that they'll be more likely to play for us earlier," he concluded.[13]

Bringing together the objective metrics of data analysis with the planned methodology of periodization, Farrow and Robertson turned to a well-known acronym used in physical conditioning: SPORT—Specificity, Progression, Overload, Reversibility, and Tedium. Organizing skill development using these principles would provide the discipline and metrics needed to evaluate progress throughout the season.

"Monitoring of skill training to date has largely centered on the outcome of a skilled performance (i.e., whether a kick resulted in a score) rather than the underpinning process measures of skilled performance (i.e., attentional capacity, kinematics, etc.)," they wrote.[14]

Specificity: Keeping It Real

If there's one question that annoys teachers, it's "Will this be on the test?" The implication is if the student is never going to need to use something later, then there is no point in learning it. Hence the principle of specificity, the degree to which the training task matches a skill that will be used in competition. Dribbling around cones may be easy to set up, but defenders in a game typically don't stand still in an evenly spaced straight line.

Based on the concept of "representative learning," Farrow and Robertson describe specificity as "the constraints of training and practice need[ed] to adequately replicate the performance environment so that they allow learners to detect affordances for action and couple actions to key information sources within those specific settings." In other words, use constraints to squeeze the skill learning into a tighter time or space, but don't change it fundamentally from what they do in a game. Instead of dribbling around cones, create different games of dribbling but against their teammates. Varying the amount of time to get from point A to point B, the number of defenders they have to face, and the size of the playing space challenges them at different levels but also keeps it real in terms of gamelike scenarios.

Progression: Finding the Challenge Point

By constraining a skill drill, a coach can manage the rate at which the athlete learns. By getting ever closer to a full-speed task environment, an athlete progresses in her capacity to use the skill. This is the job of Ericsson's deliberate practice of continually ramping up the difficulty of training to eventually meet elite levels of performance. This improvement over time allows a coach to compare actual growth with scheduled growth in skill development to meet the competition calendar ("We have three weeks until our first game and our free throw shooting percentage is not on pace to meet our goal"). That optimal end goal is the target that keeps getting bumped up over time, or what Farrow calls the "optimal challenge point." While most athletes achieve a certain plateau in their skill development, Farrow has observed that "the very best athletes don't get comfortable, they keep challenging the status quo of what[ever] level of performance they're at and they find a way to progress further."[15]

Take passing the ball as an example. As coaches plan ways

to constrain the passing drills, they should constantly assess the current level of skill of their players to find today's challenge point. By tracking the complexity versus the frequency (repetitions) in practice, a "skill load" can be computed (complexity × frequency). This load metric can be compared to actual pass completion rates in scrimmages or games to measure the progression over time. Being able to directly link practice to performance validates whether training drills are working. The time-consuming but ultimately rewarding part is to treat each player as a separate learner and create a customized lesson plan that constantly challenges his specific journey. That can only be accomplished through data collection, especially for a larger roster.

Overload: Learn from Mistakes but Motivate by Success

From a strength-training perspective, a muscle needs to be burdened beyond its current capacity to grow. Loading and overloading challenges the muscle to rebuild and add to current fibers to handle more work. In skill acquisition, the load is cognitive rather than physical but just as important to manipulate in training and manage during games. When we asked Farrow for his definition of a playmaker, he replied, "We have a term in Australia, 'a good driver in heavy traffic.'"[16] When surrounded by cars going 70 miles per hour, our senses and concentration can be overloaded by monitoring and anticipating the actions of other drivers who are just yards away. In the same way, a midfielder or point guard needs to learn fundamental sport skills in an environment of chaos and confusion. Overloading attention and demanding multitasking in training provides better transfer to the game atmosphere.

"From a learning point of view, you learn from mistakes but are motivated by success," said Farrow. "We can take a very scientific approach to capturing the amount of mental error but we also need to be mindful that we're also manipulating athletes' emotions and motivation." [17] During a game, an athlete's working memory must not only manage constant motor movement but then layer in tactical decision-making. Stretching the brain's capacity to process both requires cognitive overloading during practice. By manipulating the task constraints to push past the optimal challenge points at each practice, mental load can be increased to near-gamelike levels. Asking athletes for their rate of perceived exertion after every practice often captures their physical exhaustion, but also asking for ratings of "mental demand," "effort," and "frustration" will reveal their level of mental fatigue. Comparing mental fatigue in practice to similar ratings after a game can tell a coach how well training matches competition.

Reversibility: Use It or Lose It

Just as our fitness levels begin to deteriorate when we stop exercising, specific sport skills can slip away over time, albeit more slowly. Just as we never forget how to ride a bike, other motor skills are never completely forgotten. Yet, keeping a sport skill at its peak requires regular practice. Part of the periodization scheduling process is to juggle all of the training balls at once, advancing each component forward throughout the year. A real test of specificity, progression, and overload is the extent that the skill is embedded in memory, as measured by its ability to withstand reversibility. To the coach's eye, a slight reduction in skill level may not be noticed in a busy practice session, which is why structured drills that offer trackable data are needed.

Tedium: Time to Milk the Cows

When daily training becomes tedious and boring, Farrow muses about how athletes behave like cows: "They come in every day, get milked and out they go." There's very little engagement from the athlete in the process. The goal is to get "repetition without repetition," meaning build the skill by repeating it in different contexts and situations. Since no two athletic movements are ever exactly the same, training them should not be identical, and monotonous drills that provide no variety from day-in, day-out should be avoided. If playing outside, practice kicks in the rain, on multiple surfaces, at different times of the day, and at varying levels of fatigue. Have athletes design their own drills to keep them engaged. Replicating the same drill daily does not help the brain generalize the skill to the unpredictable conditions in a game.

Overall, within the SPORT framework, as coaches increase specificity of training tasks, mental load will increase while tedium decreases. Progression relies on understanding each player's optimal challenge point rather than assuming the entire team is at an equal learning stage. Load can be added to training through physical, mental, or tactical constraints. And by increasing progression and variability, reversibility will be managed.

"The reason we went with this approach is purely to engage the coaches," said Farrow. "The history of physical preparation and periodization is something that coaches have seen for a long time. So we thought: Why not use a common construct to talk about how to develop cognitive skills?"[18]

While this type of practice regimen is useful at all levels of skills coaching, Farrow knows firsthand that small wins in training can have lasting impact, especially among amateur coaches and developing athletes. When asked for his one-minute pitch to everyday coaches on how to design practice, Farrow offered simple advice. "Have the coach step back and get out of practice," he said. "My example there is the coach who stands at the top of the line feeding a ball to the player who passes it back to the coach, then runs around to the end of the line. With ten kids in line, the coach gets ten repetitions and the players each get only one rep. So step out of the drill and let the kids do all of the practice. Especially for volunteer coaches, typically parents who are just trying to do the best they can with whatever coach education they have received, use your best small-sided game with limited rules and just let the kids play. Kids are very good at observing and imitating their heroes. Give them maximum engagement, maximum ball touches, and maximum enjoyment of the practice time." [19]

Of course, this advice works for parents who are not professionally trained coaches. The theories of deliberate practice assume expert coaching at just the right moments to continue to stretch an athlete's comfort zone by increasing progression and overload. "Getting skilled coaches with youth at the right time is currently the big gap in Australia," said Farrow. Volunteer coaches are still essential to keep large numbers of kids playing sports. Still, even with the same quality of instruction, the same environment, and relatively the same physical size and strength, there can often be a gap in the skill achievement and rate of improvement, even among teammates. Just like students in a classroom, some kids get it and some struggle when mastering a new task. But why? "Two things, both from a research perspective," Farrow explained. "First, we have a post-doc student here at Victoria, Dr. Tim Buszard, whose research is looking at working memory capacity in children learning sport skills. What we're seeing there is that children who have a lower-capacity struggle to hold immediate sources of information about their surroundings and instructions from the coach—whereas kids with higher capacity working memory are able to quickly put the instructions into practice."

Indeed, Buszard, Farrow, and others from Victoria found that explicit coaching instructions during a basketball shooting drill helped some players improve but actually hindered others. They tested the working memory and attention of ninety eight- to ten-year-olds using standard neuropsychology exams. Next, two groups, the highest-performing twenty-four kids and the lowest-performing twenty-four kids, entered into a series of practice sessions designed to improve their shooting, with the remaining kids sent home. A pre- and post-test of twenty shots each plus a retention test given one week later measured any progress from the twelve practice sessions given over three consecutive days. However, before each twenty-shot practice, the kids were asked to read aloud five coaching instructions that were given to them:

1. Bounce the ball on the ground twice before each shot.
2. Start with your elbow under the ball.
3. Use both hands to hold the ball but shoot with only one hand.
4. Extend your arm fully when shooting.
5. Finish the shot by pointing the shooting hand toward the rim.

The idea was to fill their brains with tips for shooting better right before the task, much like a coach does, to see if they could use their working memory to remember and actually utilize the information to make more shots. Both technical form and actual shooting percentage was tracked. As expected, the higher working memory group not only could remember the instructions but improved their form and their accuracy from pre-test to post-test to retention test, while the group with lower working memory saw their performance decline when repeatedly exposed to explicit coaching tips.

"Previous research has highlighted the strong relationship between working memory capacity and the ability to implement instructions in a classroom setting, but this is the first study, to our knowledge, that has included a learning element," the researchers indicated. "Much like the studies that assessed the ability to carry out instructions in a classroom, we found that the provision of multiple technical instructions, which seemingly placed high demands on working memory, hindered motor learning for children with lower [working memory] capacity." [20]

While there are some interventions to improve overall working memory, the easier solution is to understand that not all young athletes can absorb rapid-fire, machine-gun coaching instructions delivered continuously.

"Good coaching that keeps it simple helps those with lower working memory capacity to grasp concepts. Invariably, what we find is that volunteer coaches think the best thing to do is talk more." [21] So while some variation in motor skill learning rates can be partially explained by cognitive hardwiring, considering each athlete as a separate learner with different thinking machinery can go a long way in engaging them.

Speaking of engagement, Farrow has also found firsthand that kids who absolutely love the game strive to play more, which only reinforces learning. "I coach my daughter's under-twelve Australian football team," Farrow told us. "With the recent growth of the game on the women's side, I've got all of these girls at twelve years old playing football for the first time. So I'm teaching a group of novices who are playing on a weekly basis. What I've noticed is that they all come to training, they all get the same instruction. I try to run the best training session I can, knowing what I do about skill acquisition. [E]very week there are the same girls who are getting better and better. But then there are other girls who are not improving. The big difference is that some of the girls are absolutely engaged and they love the sport. They are the ones who leave training and go accrue all of this extra deliberate play outside of the ninety minutes they spend with me. These are the ones with intrinsic motivation that are improving their skills each week, which I believe is what Ericsson has observed."

Training the Athlete Cognition Cycle

A few years ago Farrow created a learning environment for an AFL team that, in our opinion, captures the entire athlete cognition cycle of search, decide, and execute. As we've mentioned before, the ultimate environment to build playmaker skills is the actual game. But when trying to advance cognitive capabilities without taxing the body, a simulated world that still couples perception and action can be a great substitute. To create a virtual kicking world, Farrow and his colleagues first captured a series of video clips of actual footy players from a first-person, down-on-the-field point of view. Instead of overhead, TV-style game film, this angle drops a player right into the action to give him the realistic complexity of live play. Next, they projected the video clips onto life-sized screens rather than computer monitors. If that defender is six feet tall in real life, then it would be best to show him six feet tall during training. Then they gave the player a real football to kick at the screen once the best option has been found. Connecting the genuine sport motor skill with the perception process enhances the learning process better than clicking a mouse or mashing controller buttons. And don't worry about the screen: like the ones used in golf simulators, it can absorb the impact of the ball. Finally, the player wears eye-tracker glasses to record exactly where his eyes focus multiple times per second. Did they actually see the open man downfield? The eyes don't lie.

As Farrow plays the first video sequence, the player watches the action with ball in hand. Scanning the screen, watching for the runs of teammates and the coverage of the defenders, he picks out the best option. Combining the sensory input from the scenario and the tactical awareness that coaches have imprinted on his memory, while taking the first, best option, he simultaneously calls out the direction of his kick while executing it. After a series of kicks, Farrow can provide instant feedback on the decisions made by reviewing the eye-tracker data revealing the key focus points leading up to the action point.

"They'll tend to search left to right, which is probably quite traditional in our culture, given we read books left to right," said Farrow. "Probably the most significant visual behavior is attraction to movement. That's probably the thing that makes coaches pull their hair out more than anything else: if they're caught up looking at the movement when the best decision-making option might be a player somewhere else standing a little bit more quietly, a little bit more discreetly."[22]

With virtual reality systems being adapted to sports spheres, Farrow believes these simulations will only become more realistic: "Probably the big limitation at the moment with the system that we have is that we have pre-planned patterns that execute and they're not at all influenced by the participant who's kicking the football. And so, as technology does evolve, we will try and improve the immersiveness of the situation, and that's what I think virtual reality systems do allow."[23]

By creating training that represents the game and then tracking game data per player, teams can finally accelerate their skill growth rate while linking practice with performance. Farrow's practice design, together with Robertson's post-match analytics, can show signs of transfer from the training ground to the stadium. "Data analytics has provided us with a transfer test to put in experimental terms," said Farrow. "From large volumes of data on decision-making in games, we're able to start making some recommendations [about] the way that coaches might want to change the way they train."

So, did Farrow and Robertson's work with the Bulldogs contribute directly to one of the biggest upsets in AFL history? "Without giving away the competitive secrets that we can't talk about, there was a particular set of numbers that the analytics generated early on that Sam was able to uncover that influenced the way coaches structured training," Farrow said. "It seemed to have a noticeable impact within a week or two and was a defining feature in their play. The numbers said, 'This is how we're practicing, but *this* is how the game is being played,' exposing a gap between training and game day. While the analytics and subsequent shift in practice did not cause their victory, it was one of many things that contributed to their performance throughout the season."

Maintaining that success season after season is the toughest task for any team. Just as the Bulldogs may have used a mix of neurology, psychology, and technology to get an edge, their competitors don't sit still very long. "That's our challenge, and it's hard to look beyond this, but sustainability would be great," Luke Beveridge said after last year's historic win. "That's our next mandate: to see if we can pull that off."

Indeed, Beveridge's Bulldogs ended their 2017 season in tenth place, just four points outside the eight-team AFL playoffs. Meanwhile, Longmire's Swans are playing in the postseason for the eighth straight year.

DOC Z'S BRAINWAVES PART 2: BUILDING THE ATHLETE COGNITION CYCLE

While most undergraduate education curriculums, including mine, provide a good understanding of child and adolescent development, educational psychology, pedagogical strategies, human anatomy, and physiology, there is often little exposure to the core of cognitive neuroscience. In the late 1960s and into the 1970s, when I was training to be a teacher and coach, there was a dearth of knowledge about mechanisms involved in brain development and function, so it was rare to see it taught in education or psychology departments. In graduate school, I made a point to study neuroanatomy, believing it was the key to finally cracking the playmaker code. Dr. Liberato DiDio, a South American professor teaching at the Medical College of Ohio, instilled in me the importance of studying neural mechanisms directly, in addition to psychological signposts, to truly get a glimpse of how the brain regulates our thoughts, emotions, and motor responses.

Even at BU's School of Education, I assumed they would surely embrace the idea that future teachers and coaches should understand the developing brain, the central nervous system, the autonomic nervous system, and the implications for learning. But this was a hard sell, not only in Boston but nationwide. Educators stuck to the basics of traditional reading, writing, and arithmetic instruction using "old school" drill and practice. The brain was still thought to be a "black box" where information goes in, magically transforms, then exits as knowledge. Finally, in 1999, the Learning & the Brain Foundation sponsored a conference entitled "Learning and the Brain" in an attempt to connect neuroscientists and educators so that both professions could better understand human learning and brain function. Convened first at Harvard University, the foundation continues to organize conferences across the country to bring teachers and neuroscientists together.

Beyond teachers, wouldn't it be refreshing if a leading professional coach argued on behalf of the idea that all coaches should study and understand athlete brain development and cognition, using evidence-based science to train players? That's exactly what Mike Sullivan did at that USA Hockey coaching symposium, as we detailed earlier.

A coach needs to understand how growing athletes learn skills, as well as understand what is happening in their brains as they acquire sport skills. Sullivan introduced the coaches to what myelin in the nervous system was all about, explained how elite athletes chunk massive amounts of information, and taught them cognitive neuroscience concepts like neuroplasticity. It will take championship coaches with credibility, like Mike, to help move the science of coaching into the next generation.

On Aussies and Sport Science

Our emphasis on Australian rules football may be new to you, but our choice was purposeful. In a nutshell, the Australians are simply the best in the world at applying sport science, including the neurocognitive domain. Since 1981, when they opened their world-class Australian Institute of Sport (AIS), I have been impressed by how passionate the Australians are about sporting excellence, especially with their two most popular sports, Australian rules football (aka "footy") and cricket.

While I am still trying to understand cricket, I learned a great deal about footy by spending time with Coach John Northey, who was with the Melbourne club at the time. Footy requires superb motor skill execution and quick decision-making skills, but it also demands incredible cardiovascular endurance. It is not uncommon for a player to run fifteen kilometers (over nine miles) during the course of an eighty-minute match.

In part because of the outstanding contributions of the AIS and sport science researchers at various universities, the Australians are significantly ahead of most countries in state-of-the-art sport science. For example, GPS tracking of athletes started in Australia in the early 2000s, and it is just now getting traction in North America.

You might be asking: Why haven't coaches and scientists paid attention to training the brain in the same way they paid serious attention to training the body some five decades ago? As I stated earlier, the brain, until recently, was the unknown "black box." Those who did believe that cognitive skills could be trained simply did not know how to do it. Fortunately, the rapid advancement of technology has changed this thinking.

Decide or Get Run Over

So what do we know today about training athlete decision-making? Can we train an athlete to make decisions more quickly and accurately? Or, at the least, train athletes to be decisive, right or wrong? Which reminds me of that wonderful expression, "The road of life is paved with flat squirrels who couldn't make a decision." Success or failure on the part of an athlete depends on what took place during her search for cues, making that quick, correct decision, then executing it on the field exactly as she had practiced it in her mind.

Track-and-field athlete David Hemery, CBE, used imagery during the last hour prior to his gold medal run in the Mexico City Olympics. He simply lay down and imagined the upcoming final, from his lane, in the greatest sensory detail possible, fully relaxed, running his fastest. Now, how hard is that? Yet, not enough athletes think about systematically engaging in visual imagery to train and prime their brains, despite all the available scientific evidence of its effectiveness. Today, with mobile devices, athletes can assist their imagery by also looking at their "highlight" videos that have been stored on their devices. Likewise, meditation and mindfulness techniques calm the body and mind, helping athletes to focus. Music also serves to prime the brain for many athletes. Heart rate variability (HRV) apps that teach you how to slow down your breathing and heart rate are readily available free or at low cost.

While working with the Vancouver Canucks, I used sophisticated biofeedback/neurofeedback technology as part of our Mindgym laboratory. While relaxing in a recliner, players learned how to control muscle tension, skin conductance (for anger management), HRV (for relaxation and post-game recovery), and brain activity through EEG sensors attached to the scalp. The players enjoyed being able to learn self-regulation skills using software that was challenging yet gamelike. Biofeedback training is gaining traction around the world as coaches and athletes finally accept the crucial role of the brain in performance.

Training the athlete cognition cycle has also taken a leap forward with temporal occlusion training, a video-based tool that shows game action up until the moment of decision (temporal), then it is blacked out (occluded). The athlete needs to make a decision immediately about the best option available: swing at a pitch, throw to a receiver, or step correctly at an attacker. In fact, Dr. Bruce Abernethy and his colleagues at the University of Queensland published a series of articles in the 1980s using temporal occlusion as a method to examine "novice" versus "expert" performers.[24] With today's technology, occlusion is being used as a cognitive training tool in fast-paced sports such as tennis, squash, football, and baseball. The training protocol used by the Western Bulldogs directed by Dr. Farrow is an excellent example of occlusion training combined with virtual reality.

A typical video-based occlusion task in baseball has a batter viewing a video display of a pitcher throwing a pitch that is cut off (occluded) at various points at or shortly after the release of the pitch. With this method, the batter does not swing a bat but rather identifies the type of pitch (e.g., fastball, curveball, changeup) and location (strike versus ball) through verbalization, key press, mouse click, or touch screen as quickly and accurately as possible.[25]

In 2008, Professor Jocelyn Faubert, a researcher at the University of Montreal, developed a method for training visual perception that used 3D-Multiple Object Tracking (3D-MOT), in which athletes watch a large screen and track multiple moving balls while trying to keep their eyes on just a few "target" balls. Because the methodology is evidence-based, we used it in the Canucks' Mind Gym to help train decision-making and also used it to "prime the brain" prior to a game.[26] Since 2010, 3D-MOT has been used globally by the NHL, NBA, NFL, EPL, Top 14 Rugby, military, and thousands of individuals.

In recent years, virtual reality (VR) systems for training elite athletes have established a strong presence, despite their expense. Because of eye-catching presentations, it intuitively seems that this form of simulation should be effective. Unfortunately, the hype has gotten ahead of the science, as there is a lack of hard evidence of transfer from training to competition. The potential is there for VR but requires more research and development.

Transcranial direct current stimulation (tDCS) is an emerging tool in which an athlete wears a headset that transmits a small electrical current into the parietal and frontal lobe regions of the brain. A number of U.S. athletes competing in the 2016 Olympic Games in Brazil used tDCS to help them with performance.

On Confidence, Self-Efficacy, and Dr. Albert Bandura, the Psychology Playmaker

Every playmaker we interviewed cited confidence in her abilities as critical to her success. Every coach we have talked to characterizes the playmaker as having high confidence in herself as well as her teammates. Perhaps a better term in the sports context is "self-efficacy," as proposed by Dr. Albert Bandura, professor emeritus at Stanford University.

If there was a playmaker among psychologists in the world, it would be Professor Bandura. Although as a young student I had read a lot of his influential studies, I did not meet Dr. Bandura until 1987 at a conference in Seattle. It was there that I learned we had a few things in common, like growing up on a farm in Northern Alberta in a hardworking Ukrainian immigrant family and starting school in a one-room schoolhouse.

Dr. Bandura drew the distinction between self-confidence and self-efficacy to emphasize the need for action to affect change in a situation. In his 1997 classic *Self-Efficacy: The Exercise of Control*,[27] he wrote, "It should be noted that the construct of self-efficacy differs from the colloquial term 'confidence,' . . . Confidence is a nondescript term that refers to strength of belief but does not necessarily specify what the certainty is about. I can be supremely confident that I will fail at an endeavor.

Perceived self-efficacy refers to belief in one's power to produce given levels of attainment. A self-efficacy assessment, therefore, includes both the affirmation of capability and the strength of that belief. Confidence is a catchword in sports rather than a construct embedded in a theoretical system. Advances in a field are best achieved by constructs that fully reflect the phenomena of interest and are rooted in a theory that specifies their determinants, mediating processes, and multiple effects. Theory-based constructs pay dividends in understanding and operational guidance. The terms used to characterize personal agency, therefore, represent more than merely lexical preferences."

Relating self-efficacy to sport means having confidence in the ability to exert control over one's specific fundamental motor skills, fitness, sport technical and tactical dimensions, as well as decision-making skills, rather than a vague feeling of superiority over an opponent.

Bandura would say that the process of processing information, making split-second decisions, and executing flawlessly would not be possible if the playmaker did not have high "self-efficacy." He viewed perceived self-efficacy as the cornerstone of human motivation and action.

Personal self-beliefs reflect one's confidence, but they are situation- and task-specific. For instance, based on your mastery or lack of it, you as a basketball player may have high confidence in your ability to hit foul shots but low confidence in your ability to hit three-point shots. And as an athlete you may have high confidence in your soccer skills but low confidence in your baseball skills.

Bandura lists four sources to build self-efficacy:

1. **From mastery experiences.** In sport, successful previous performance breeds confidence and further success, whereas failure undermines confidence. Confidence in your ability to be resilient following adversity also requires experience in successfully

overcoming obstacles through persistent effort. So when you are trailing in a game late in the fourth quarter, effort and belief in your own abilities and those of your teammates will likely result in successful performances.

2. **From social modeling.** Our observation of people around us, particularly those we consider as role models, builds self-efficacy. As Yogi Berra supposedly stated, "You can observe a lot by just watching." By attending carefully to what they do, drawing from your memory bank, and being motivated, you will undoubtedly raise your self-efficacy.

3. **From verbal persuasion.** Advice and encouragement from a knowledgeable and credible source like a parent, teacher, coach, or teammate provides you with a reinvigorated source of confidence and effort to succeed.

4. **From physical and emotional states.** Physiological and affective states can directly affect your ability to self-regulate your emotions. Can you maintain slow breathing, decelerate your heart rate, stay cool under pressure? When your emotions and physiology are under control, you will have confidence. Conversely, stress reactions or tension expose you to poor performance.

Psychologist James Maddux has suggested a fifth route to increased self-efficacy through "imaginal experiences," or the art of visualizing yourself performing effectively in a given situation. From my experience, visualization can be enhanced if you have a short video clip of your successful sporting performance.[28]

Neuroscience research on cognitive functioning came late in Dr. Bandura's career, but I am certain he would have appreciated learning about brain mechanisms in the development of self-efficacy. Is that happening? Indeed, it is at the Cold Spring Harbor Laboratory in New York, where a team of scientists led by Dr. Adam Kepecs have been attempting to quantify confidence in the brain. At this time there appears to be a brain region for confidence, called the orbitofrontal cortex (OFC), an area known to be involved in making predictions and decision-making confidence. Even now, in his nineties, Dr. Bandura still enjoys discussing the latest research built on his groundbreaking theories.

PART THREE

THE PLAYMAKER'S COMMITMENT

CHAPTER 8

How to Prepare: Mindset, Grit, and Greatness

Kawhi Leonard is, in my opinion, the best player in the league right now. He's the best two-way player, and does it all with such class, it's impressive."[1] Gregg Popovich, head coach of the San Antonio Spurs, is not known for dishing out superlatives, especially to individual players, so his high praise for his young playmaker was conspicuous. After closing out their first-round series of the 2016–17 NBA playoffs, the San Antonio Spurs head coach declared to the world that his twenty-five-year-old small forward had not only been handed the baton from Spurs legend Tim Duncan but was ready to take his place among the league's elite.

David Fizdale, head coach of the Memphis Grizzlies, who lost to the Spurs in six games, agreed with his counterpart about Leonard. "The thing that just makes him different is, I just don't know many possessions that he takes off because he plays both ends of the floor so well," Fizdale said in his post-game press conference. ". . . I mean, the guy, he just keeps coming and keeps coming and keeps coming and he finds a way to make a play, a winning play, whether it's a steal, a block, a rebound, a drive, pass."[2]

For Leonard, it's all about the work. Everyone wants to be the best but few understand and commit to the sacrifice required. Many get fooled by the early shiny objects of fame: being a starter in high school, playing in a D1 program, getting drafted by a pro team. But Leonard has always had his eyes fixed far down the road. "He wants the greatness badly," Popovich declared. "He doesn't give a damn about the stardom."[3]

Becoming a playmaker is a marathon not a sprint. The so-called overnight superstar often spends years getting to a place where he is finally noticed. He has to navigate a labyrinth of paths including selecting a sport, joining teams with effective coaches, practicing efficiently, and learning from life's trials. Family, environment, physical maturation, genetics, and a mix of psychological traits all play a part in the eventual success of every young athlete. At any point along the journey, the athlete can declare the search over, satisfied that the target destination had been reached. For some it ends with a high school state title, while others won't stop until they have championship rings or Olympic medals.

"To the outer world, it appears that he has suddenly emerged as an All-Star or an MVP candidate," said Chad Forcier, a former Spurs assistant coach, on Leonard's ascent. "It seems like he has suddenly showed up and all of a sudden, 'Wow. This guy's really good.'

"I don't see it that way," Forcier continued, "and what the outer world can't see is truly, like, how much time and actually how slow the process was in terms of the work and the sweat and the commitment and the desire and the day-in-and-day-out process or multiple seasons before we really got to see him grow in terms of the opportunity that Pop began to start to give him."[4]

Being drafted number fifteen overall in 2011 was just another step on the road to greatness for Leonard. It's not often that a storied coach and franchise trade one of their starters to take a chance on a talented but untested rookie with only two years of college experience. But the Spurs did just that on draft night, sending George Hill to the Indiana Pacers in exchange for Leonard. Popovich and his staff knew they had a project on their hands, but one that had a potential franchise-defining payoff. "We were scared to death sitting in the room," said Popovich. "I think it was the fifteenth pick, if I remember, and when we got to 11, 12, 13, Danny Ferry, our CEO, and I were looking at each other saying, 'Are we really going to do this?'" [5]

But for a young man who, as a teen, worked twelve-hour shifts alongside his dad at the family car wash, then accepted a scholarship from the first and most persistent program to recruit him (San Diego State), earning a spot in the Spurs starting lineup was just the next milestone in his journey. In his first five professional seasons, he was voted Defensive Player of the Year twice, All-NBA first team twice, and both an All-Star and Finals MVP. In 2016–17 he added a three-point threat to his arsenal of weapons, culminating in strong consideration for league MVP.

Besides his Spartan training regimen and the endless court time working on his technical game, Leonard also builds his knowledge base. "I look at film," he told *Sports Illustrated*, "but more than watching individual players, I'm trying to watch a team's whole offensive scheme. I'm trying to know their tendencies so I can . . . guess. That's what it comes down to, really, making the best guess. I'm trying to change up their scheme." [6]

It's the whole package: commitment, humility, work ethic, and practice toward a visualized level of play. In today's sound-bite, quick-fix world, parents and coaches often grab onto trending science that, usually to the scientist's irritation, turns an interesting research study into a miracle athlete development concept. In this chapter we will examine a few of these over-promised concepts to see where they fit into the future playmaker's future. We'll also examine narratives from great athletes that reveal the preparation paths they chose along the way, hoping we can straighten the road a bit for future superstars wanting to be the next Kawhi.

The Talent Development Soup

Wrapped inside of Joyner-Kersee's motivational statement about preparation are the key ingredients to a secret success sauce—a talent development soup, if you will. Separately, having a definition of success and an ultimate goal will not define the playmaker or the champion. But when combined with intentional practice, environmental advantages, genetic gifts, and, yes, a bit of luck, the developing athlete has a chance to achieve greatness.

> "Achieving success . . . in athletics has less to do with wins and losses than it does with learning how to prepare yourself so that at the end of the day . . . you know that there was nothing more you could have done to reach your ultimate goal."[7]
>
> —JACKIE JOYNER-KERSEE, THREE-TIME OLYMPIC GOLD MEDALIST

In September of 2009, UK Sport, the high-performance development organization for British athletes, sought out that ideal recipe for finding and developing young athletes that would, quite simply, produce the most Olympic medals at Rio 2016 and beyond. Specifically, they asked academic experts and experienced coaches to "research and understand elements of identification and development, to ultimately inform the prediction of future elite sporting talent" and "conclude unique recommendations from the research that highlight key accelerants and retardants in the pathway development of elite performers."[8] Dr. Lew Hardy, research professor of sport, health, and exercise sciences at Bangor University, Wales, took up the challenge by recruiting a who's who of sports performance leaders to make sense of the current landscape of athlete development.

"With the competition for medals at Olympics and World Championships intensifying, there is greater investment than ever in sporting systems and structures to identify and develop exceptionally talented athletes," wrote Hardy et al. ". . . With so much information and opinion across many sub-disciplines of the sports sciences, so many models and frameworks, so many levels of performer, such varied levels of empirical knowledge and much apparent truth, popular wisdom and controversy, the task of generating a clear understanding of the development of the world's best sporting talent was challenging." [9]

Their plan had two parts: an exhaustive search for relevant research to understand the current state of knowledge on high-performance preparation, followed by real conversations with those select British athletes who had actually achieved the dream of becoming Olympic or international champions. Studies done in labs with multiple variables on diverse sets of athletes can provide some insight into narrow hypotheses. Moreover, sitting down with the "super-elite," as they were called in the study, to quiz them on their backgrounds, motivations, challenges, and preparation patterns can reveal hidden insights into what actually works.

First, Hardy and Dr. Tim Rees of Bournemouth University, along with their all-star roster of experts, affectionately known as the RAT (Research Advisory Team), took a comprehensive look at the existing literature to get a snapshot of what we know. With a reference list of almost three hundred articles and studies, they developed a framework to break down the performance universe into ten possible contributing factors in three broad categories: the performer, the environment, and practice/training. The athlete cohort of each study was classified into four performance levels: non-elite (athletes not competing at a national level), junior elite (young athletes competing at junior national or international levels), elite (athletes on senior national teams or competing at world championship levels), and super-elite (Olympic or world championship gold medalists).

The end product, quite candidly, represented the most thorough review to date of what we know about athlete preparation. By rating each study according to research quality, consistency, and relevance to developing athletes, Hardy and Rees also offered recommendations to coaches and parents on each element. Starting with the performer (i.e., the athlete), four factors—birth month, genetics, physiology, and psychology—have sparked plenty of recent debates about what truly leads to elite status.

Often, when young athletes are picked for select travel teams, being born in the first three months of the year can be an advantage, as they may have a head start in physical maturation and coordination compared to those born late in the year. As an example, if the earliest eligible birthday for a specific age group is January 1, those kids born in January are eleven months older than those born in December of the same year. According to NCAA research,[10] bigger, stronger, and faster kids get noticed earlier and selected by coaches, starting a self-fulfilling loop of more access to better teams and better competition, especially in hockey, baseball, and soccer.

However, after reviewing many studies on this "relative age effect," Hardy and Rees found that the early advantage is often nullified by the time an athlete rises through the ranks. "The evidence suggests that any advantage associated with being born in the first two quarters of the year may disappear by the time athletes reach elite level," they concluded.[11]

Picking the right parents, however, does seem to be good tongue-in-cheek advice for future superstars. Genetic gifts are useful—not necessarily for sports to choose athletes but rather to help athletes choose the right sports. In fact, Hardy and Rees showed that physiological and anthropometric factors like height, weight, VO2 max, limb length, and bone density produced the highest correlation with becoming an elite athlete. "It would appear no longer a case of whether there is a genetic component to sporting performance, but rather which genetic profiles make the greatest contribution," wrote Hardy and Rees.[12] ". . . The most obvious issue for talent identification researchers in sport to solve is the problem of predicting adult performance from adolescent anthropometric and physiological data."

If fact, predicting the future physical growth of young athletes may be the easier task when compared to judging the inner drive and persistence of an adolescent. Whether it be 10,000 hours of deliberate practice or ten years of sacrifice, reaching the apex of a sport often requires an athlete to adopt a lifestyle that is different, single-minded, and more difficult than the 99 percent of their peers who stop somewhere along the way. Putting an all defining name on this special ingredient has become a fascination in popular science and produced a clash of competing concepts that, by themselves, don't quite grasp the complex psychological makeup of a champion.

Grit and Growth

Pete Carroll knew it right away. "When I first heard her on a TED Talk, I thought she was talking about our stuff. I was really enthused, because it just gave a new look and new language to add to something we've been trying to explain and work towards all along," he said about Dr. Angela Duckworth's 2013 TED presentation on grit,[13] now with over 10 million views.

"Striving is what competing is all about—striving for excellence, striving for knowledge," said Carroll, head coach of the

Seattle Seahawks and one of only three coaches to win a Super Bowl and a college national championship. "It has nothing to do with winning or losing. It's about a mentality and a mindset that does give us direction in creating a culture." [14]

To be sure, "grit" is a wonderful word. Literally meaning small particles of sand or stone, it has come to represent rigid resolve in the face of adversity, as in "grit your teeth and bear it." Its close cousins, perseverance, hardiness, and conscientiousness, just don't have the same punch as grit. John Wayne did not star in a movie called *True Fortitude*. So it's not surprising that the word and the concept behind it have struck a chord with many coaches, parents, and teachers. When an athlete is described as "gritty," we instinctively know that she will fight through long practices and grueling games.

"When I say grit, I don't just mean old-fashioned mental toughness—in some athletic circles, that's what grit means," said Duckworth in a forum presentation alongside Carroll. ". . . It's not just that. When I talk about grit, I really mean this combination of perseverance and passion for what you're doing over the long term. It's not just being mentally tough in the moment, it's all the other moments, it's all the practice that goes into being truly world-class in what you do. It's actually being kind of preoccupied by what you do. When I look at individuals who have grit, it is invariably a characteristic that I find in high achievers in every domain that I've studied." [15]

Since that video introduction of grit to the world, Duckworth has expanded her research and written a book on the subject: *Grit: The Power of Passion and Perseverance*.[16] Technically, she defines grit as "passion and perseverance for long-term goals." While other factors are necessary for athletic success, Duckworth feels that grit is essential. "Talent and luck matter to success. But talent and luck are no guarantee of grit. And in the very long run, I think grit may matter at least as much, if not more." [17]

To take grit from being a fuzzy, feel-good concept to a comparative data point, Duckworth created the Grit Scale,[18] currently a ten-question survey available to anyone, which calculates a baseline score from 1 to 5. Of course, with test statements like "I am diligent, I never give up" and "I finish whatever I begin," the scale is easy to game and requires honest introspection. With a grit score in hand, the real question for developing playmakers is whether it can be grown over time. If you score a 2.5 at age fourteen, are you doomed to a life of sports mediocrity? Even Duckworth admits she and her research team are still learning: "I don't know that anybody's totally figured out how to teach it: What do you do exactly, even when we do have insights from research?" [19]

That hasn't stopped several school districts from trying to measure and improve grit in students, or at least what are called "noncognitive" areas for improvement (e.g., social skills). Always honest about grit's early learning curve, Duckworth is skeptical about teachers being asked to pilot new programs. "I do not think we should be doing this; it is a bad idea," she told the *New York Times* about attempts to quantify and measure kids. She and colleague David Yeager wrote an opinion paper [20] on the potential pitfalls, especially in the rudimentary measurement tools, which may include her own Grit Scale. "Our working title was all measures suck, and they all suck in their own way," said Duckworth.[21]

Other researchers have been quick to question grit's contribution to the field. In 2016, Marcus Credé, an assistant professor of psychology at Iowa State University, and his colleagues published a meta-analysis [22] of eighty-eight studies of grit involving 67,000 people. The fact that there were already eighty-eight grit studies confirms its rapid ubiquity. His conclusions were that grit has been overstated as a contributing factor to success and that, as a concept, it's not that much different from conscientiousness, a long-studied trait. Rather than a singular focus on one characteristic, he prefers to think of talent development as a puzzle with many pieces. "Nobody wants to hear that success in life is made up of many small factors that all add up. It's your education, it's how hard you work, it's your conscientiousness and creativity— all these little pieces that add up," Credé said. "We want to be told here's one big thing that explains everything."[23]

When Hardy and Rees cross-indexed their large collection of performance studies, they found that, indeed, athletes who have climbed the ladder to elite status have displayed higher levels of several psychological factors, including motivation, confidence, mental toughness, anxiety control, and resistance to "choking" (performing worse than expected). In addition, individual personality traits of conscientiousness, optimism, and adaptability to changing conditions were evident in top performers.

However, this brings us to the chicken-or-egg problem of which came first, a strong, striving personality (as Carroll described it) or early success in sports that built their self-confidence over time. Hardy and Rees leave that issue on the table for the next batch of studies: "Key questions for future research include examining the *causes* of exceptional levels of motivation, resilience and mental toughness, including assessing whether and how psychological skills at junior level influence long-term adult elite/super-elite performance."

"I Think I Can, I Think I Can"

To execute the "Just do it" mantra of grit, an athlete needs to believe that change is possible and achievement is not predetermined. That optimistic attitude has been given another sound bite–ready label, a growth mindset. As with grit, the common-sense allure of a growth mindset, as opposed to a fixed mindset, reinforces the life advice that hard work toward a goal will eventually be rewarded. Carol Dweck, professor of psychology at Stanford University, is widely credited for her research on mindsets as an answer to the question, "Where does ability come from?" As she explained in a sporting context for TeamUSA's *Olympic Coach* magazine, "Those with a fixed mindset believe that their talents and abilities are simply fixed. . . . In this mindset, athletes may become so concerned with being and looking talented that they never fulfill their potential.

"People with a growth mindset, on the other hand, think of talents and abilities as things they can develop—as potentials that come to fruition through effort, practice, and instruction," Dweck continued. "They don't believe that everyone has the same potential or that anyone can be Michael Phelps, but they understand that even Michael Phelps wouldn't be Michael Phelps without years of passionate and dedicated practice. In the growth mindset, talent is something you build on and develop, not something you simply display to the world and try to coast to success on."[24]

She admits that abilities are "always a product of nature and nurture" but that, all else being equal, those athletes with a growth mindset will believe in the future payoff of years of practice and commitment. To uncover a fixed mindset, Dweck suggests measuring agreement with statements like "You have a certain level of athletic ability, and you cannot really do much to change that" and "You can learn new things, but you can't really change your basic athletic ability." Just like athletes, coaches can also have fixed mindsets. Believing that top athletes have predetermined abilities, they would stress talent identification as their top priority, while growth mindset coaches emphasize talent ID combined with athlete development to build out additional skill sets.

As with grit, knowing your mindset is helpful, but can it be converted from fixed to growth over time? "Mindsets can be fairly stable, but they are beliefs, and beliefs can be changed," said Dweck.[25] Again, as Duckworth discovered, such a common-sense concept (work hard and believe that you can improve) can't always be proven and replicated with science. Specifically, a 1998 study[26] by Dweck and Claudia Mueller while both were at Columbia University showed that fifth-graders who were praised after a test for their effort (growth mindset) rather than their intelligence (fixed mindset) were more likely to take on harder tests and strive to learn new subjects. The message to parents and teachers was to change their comforting verbal reinforcement from ability to effort. "Well-meant praise for intelligence, which is intended to boost children's enjoyment, persistence, and performance during achievement, does not prepare them for coping with setbacks," the researchers concluded.

Several researchers have tried to re-create the results that Dweck and Mueller found in their early research. In three related studies of a total of 624 fifth-graders, Timothy C. Bates and Yue Li of the University of Edinburgh, using methods similar to Dweck's, concluded that the type of praise just didn't matter to kids. "Mindset theory states that children's ability and school grades depend heavily on whether they believe basic ability is malleable and that praise for intelligence dramatically lowers cognitive performance. . . . Praise for intelligence failed to harm cognitive performance and children's mindsets had no relationship to their IQ or school grades. Finally, believing ability to be malleable was not linked to improvement of grades across the year. We find no support for the idea that fixed beliefs about basic ability are harmful, or that implicit theories of intelligence play any significant role in development of cognitive ability, response to challenge, or educational attainment." [27]

Even without strong empirical support, there is nothing inherently wrong with encouraging kids to work hard and believe in themselves. However, just as Duckworth discouraged overreaching with grit, she feels that some practitioners have gone a little too far in promoting the concept without really understanding it, creating what she calls a false growth mindset. "A false growth mindset is saying you have [a] growth mindset when you don't really have it or you don't really understand [what it is]," Dweck recently clarified. "It's also false in the sense that nobody has a growth mindset in everything all the time. Everyone is a mixture of fixed and growth mindsets." [28]

So, going beyond idle praise for effort, the most effective feedback may be to focus on effort that leads to improvement. "A lot of parents or teachers say praise the effort, not the outcome," said Dweck. "I say [that's] wrong: Praise the effort that led to the outcome or learning progress; tie the praise to it. It's not just effort, but strategy . . . so support the student in finding another strategy." [29]

The Nurturing Environment

Besides obvious physical abilities and technical talents, coaches also look for these character skills in their recruits. Sue Enquist, the legendary UCLA softball player and coach, identified five traits that she looked for during her twenty-seven years finding the players who won ten national championships: growth mindset, high accountability, recovery from failure, independence, and time management. "There are many little pieces of evidence that build up," said Enquist. [30] "If an athlete has the ability to think positively, use their words positively and have a positive reaction to failure, they will be a person of great character. Think, speak and act. But it's one of the most difficult things to do with all the noise around us."

And while parents think they are helping their kids by being very involved, Enquist feels they need to back off to allow independence to grow. "It's difficult, because in highly competitive sports, it appears that the helicopter parents get more and create more for their athletes," she noted. "But in the long run, they do a disservice to their athlete. . . . I challenge every parent to have their kid organize their day and their week." [31]

As can be expected, Hardy, Rees, and their colleagues found that the support of families and coaches does have a direct impact on the growth and development of their young athletes but in subtle ways that are not quite clear. "There is still a relative lack of knowledge with regard to the influence of early family experiences, and we need to know more about the role of the family (parents, siblings, inter-relations) more generally with respect to who reaches super-elite level in sport." [32]

Rather than total immersion in a sport-specific setting, Hardy and Rees reported that athletes who grew up in a small- to medium-sized city (30,000 to 100,000 residents) were more likely to succeed than those with the assumed advantages of large cities.

That leaves the two final areas that Hardy and Rees reviewed, practice and specialization. So much has been researched and written about these topics that we are giving them their own chapter, so we invite you to jump there. As with the performer and the environment, the takeaway is the same: somewhere in the middle. There is no simple formula for practice hours per year or the age at which future playmakers need to commit exclusively to their sports of choice. The answer is a mix of dedicated focus in the primary sport but with the chance to play other sports, with emphasis on the word "play."

"The probability of attaining elite or super-elite level may be enhanced by the *coupling* of a large volume of intensive, organized specific training/practice in the main sport with appreciable amounts of organized training/practice and competitions in other sports and/or non-organized play in the main or other sports," concluded Hardy, Rees et al.[33]

Been There, Done That

"If you want to become educated about what great looks like, you need to see it up close and personal," advises UCLA's Sue Enquist.[34] When the lights are on and the game starts, we love to watch our favorite superstars perform. As fans, we expect near perfection even though we know we could not duplicate their feats. What we don't see is the life journey of each player to get to this point in time. Each athlete has her own story of her chosen path, including the dead ends. But it is those stories that young playmakers need to hear, so that they can relate to the inevitable bumps in the road.

Visiting with those rare athletes who have been to the top of the mountain was the next assignment from UK Sport for Hardy and Rees, along with colleagues Matthew Barlow, Lynne Evans, Tim Woodman, and Chelsea Warr, in a grand endeavor known as the Great British Medalists project. Beyond their meta-analysis of past research, they shifted gears to proactively go out and interview the one-percenters across multiple sports: sixteen former British athletes who had won multiple Olympic or world championship medals, with at least one gold, and sixteen additional athletes that ended up just below that level—still world-class, having competed at international tournaments, but not podium finishers. The goal was to find the last piece of the puzzle, the last ingredient in the soup that took a well-trained, talented athlete to the pinnacle of sport.

Overall, forty-three questions were asked in one-on-one interviews with each athlete, along with their parents and coaches. Over 1,400 hours and 2.4 million words later, several similar themes were uncovered separating the two groups. The questions related to the athletes' psychosocial development have been reported,[35] while questions on their coaches, training environment, demographics, practice, and competition will be summarized in future papers. Using word content analysis techniques, the researchers pieced together the athletes' answers, stories, and descriptions to tease out where the careers of champions diverged from their less successful peers. Before revealing Hardy and Rees's results, let's take a look at a very similar analysis that had already been done by one of Great Britain's super-elites.

The Search for Sporting Excellence

Thirty years before UK Sport authorized their introspective narrative research, another great British medalist began his quest to answer the same puzzling questions about human performance.

Going into the 1968 Olympic four-hundred-meter hurdles final, David Hemery's personal best time was sixth among the eight finalists. Two American runners, Geoff Vanderstock and Ron Whitney, were ranked first and second in the world and were the clear favorites. An hour before the final, on an unusually cold and damp day at Mexico City's Estadio Olímpico Universitario, Hemery felt like a fish out of water.

"I had done my eight-hundred-meter jog and was changing over into spikes to do some sprints and go over the hurdles," Hemery recalled to us. "While I was sitting on the side of the track just putting the other shoes on, my attention was drawn out of the corner of my eye to someone who was moving extremely fast. It was one of my top competitors [Vanderstock] going over the first three hurdles around the bend and he absolutely flew. My heart hit my throat, thinking, 'Am I supposed to be running faster than that? How do I get back under control into something where I have the feeling of strength in running?' " [36]

He remembered back to his senior year at Boston University, when he was recovering from an injury, jogging on a stretch of beach at Powder Point, next to Duxbury Bay. "Because of the injury to the hamstring I had, I ran in about six inches of water, which was to cushion the landing," said Hemery. "I was only running like a trotting horse. You have to lift the knee up to be able to get it out of the water and then step out. I decided I would pick it up to 4 × 400-meter relay pace. I held that for what felt like five minutes, and felt unbelievably good with the sun on my back and just wearing a pair of shorts and nobody else there. So I thought, 'I'm going to sprint,' and I ran as hard as I could. After about, what felt like half a minute at least, finally I felt like I'm going to cruise down here. And with the water splashing up into my face, I thought, 'Gosh, that felt fabulous.' I remembered that session while sitting on the side of the track [in Mexico] in this apprehensive state."

While his competitors huddled with their tracksuits on, Hemery took advantage of the afternoon shower that had dampened the infield grass. He took off his spikes and started a slow barefoot jog, letting his wet feet remind him of that feeling of being unstoppable. "Within about twenty to thirty meters, Vanderstock had gone and I was feeling the flow of water under my toes, being under control, and feeling the best that I had experienced in terms of running and flow and power."

From the opening gun to the finish line, Hemery dominated the field, winning by almost a second—an eternity in this race—

and smashing the world record (held by Vanderstock) by eight-tenths of a second. Standing on the podium to receive his Olympic gold medal, Hemery began thinking. "One [feeling] was a sense of relief I hadn't blown it, because I was actually intending to win," he said. "The second thing, obviously with the euphoria, is that you actually achieve the dream of getting a world record and gold at the same time."

"The guy standing to my left, John Sherwood [U.K. teammate and bronze medalist], he and I were equal slowest on paper going into the final by about half a second, which is about four meters, behind the American co-favorites. To wind up winning by seven meters and John standing beside me made me question why do some people under pressure get very close to fulfilling potential and others for some reason blow it?"[37]

That question sparked years of education and research for Hemery, culminating with a doctorate in education and social psychology from Boston University while coaching the BU track team alongside fellow Olympic champion Joan Benoit Samuelson. From his own experiences and those of his athletes, he searched for the difference maker—or, as we like to call it, the playmaker's advantage.

"It is too easy to say, 'Oh, they're just naturals, they were born with the genetic gifts to do it' or, 'Oh, he or she is a born leader.' We know that's not the whole story; it cannot be," Hemery wrote in his classic book, *Sporting Excellence: What Makes a Champion?*,[38] which was based on his dissertation, supervised by Len. "What do successful international performers do to hold together so well under intense competitive pressure? Is it something in their background or personality? What are they thinking about? Does it come naturally or can it be learned? The bottom line question is: what makes a winner?"

So Hemery asked fifty-three world-class athletes these and

other questions, eighty-eight altogether, over several years. The list included fellow Olympic champions Sebastian Coe, Carl Lewis, Edwin Moses, Jayne Torvill, and Christopher Dean; tennis champions Stefan Edberg, Chris Evert, Billie Jean King, and Rod Laver; golfers Nick Faldo and Arnold Palmer; and team sport legends Bobby Charlton, Bryan Robson, and Wayne Gretzky, to name just a few.

Everything from sport specialization to coaching relationships to team leadership to dealing with pressure was covered by Hemery's survey. Tellingly, across these great athletes, the typical age of single-sport specialization was sixteen, while two-thirds identified themselves as late bloomers, both physically and emotionally. Through the interviews, the champions pleaded with parents to allow kids to sample several sports and then, in the end, let the child choose their favorite. Once the young athlete's body and mind have matured and a sport is chosen, it's time for work—lots of hard work. The champions reported years of planned, intense, dedicated training, for which there is no substitute.

Still, staying enthused for those long years requires not only a life balance to prevent burnout but also a clear vision of a goal worthy of the work. "We simply don't often dare to dream what we might achieve in our lives," wrote Hemery. "Doubt is our greatest crippler." [39]

It is that dare to dream that inspires Hemery's "Be the Best You Can Be" program for youth at his charity, 21st Century Legacy,[40] started at the request of his friend, Lord Sebastian Coe, four-time Olympic track champion, leading up to the 2012 London Games. Beyond just sport, the program has touched more than 200,000 kids with the simple vision "that all young people, through coaching, are enabled to achieve their full physical, intellectual, social and spiritual potential as responsible individuals, citizens and members of their communities."

"As an educator, I want to find a way of inspiring our young-sters to be the best they can be in anything using the Olympian virtues of excellence, respect and friendship and the qualities all champions I have met possess—self-awareness and responsibil-ity," said Hemery. ". . . [W]e need to challenge the youngsters there to tell us what their dreams are, sporting or otherwise, and to be the best they can be and get some of the established 'names' or simply their peers, acting as mentors.

"Young people need to be inspired and to have mentors. How many of you out there were ever told you were great at something when you were young? We are poor at that. There is greatness in everybody and we need to turbo charge those early years." [41]

David Hemery is certainly both a "super-elite" athlete ac-cording to Hardy and Rees's definition as well as a great British medalist. Across the work of both research projects, the clues of greatness were almost identical, painting a portrait of the cham-pion playmaker's personality and preparation.

"The Super-Elite athletes typically experience some sort of foundational, negative, critical, life event during their devel-opmental years in close temporal proximity to a positive sport related event," concluded Hardy and Rees. "They also have a stronger need to succeed, are more selfish and ruthless in their pursuit of their sport, and more obsessive and perfectionistic with regard to that sport than Elite athletes. They attach rela-tively more importance to sport than other aspects of their life, adopt a dual outcome and mastery focus, and maintain high lev-els of performance under pressure." [42]

In other words, they just want it more, often after a "foun-dational, negative, critical, life event." Unfortunately for Kawhi Leonard's family, that type of event became a reality that changed the course of his life. On January 19, 2008, as a seventeen-year-old junior, he scored seventeen points for his Martin Luther King

High School (Riverside, California) team, less than twenty-four hours after learning his dad, Mark Leonard, had been shot and killed in front of the family car wash in Compton. "Basketball is my life, and I wanted to go out there and take my mind off it," he said after the game. "It was real sad. My father was supposed to be at the game."[43]

Six years later, on Father's Day, he was named the NBA Finals MVP after his Spurs clinched their fifth franchise title with a game five win over the Miami Heat. "It's a very special meaning for me, knowing that he's gone and I was able to win a championship on Father's Day," Leonard said. "But I mean, I'm just happy just winning the championship."[44]

Kim Robertson, Leonard's mom, knew her son had attained the complex psychosocial, gritty, growth mindset of a winner. "Kawhi just wants to get better and better and better. He does not want to be a superstar. He does not want to be in the limelight. He just wants to be good at what he loves to do."[45] Using Hardy and Rees's terminology, having a "stronger need to succeed," being "more obsessive and perfectionistic" while maintaining a "high level of performance under pressure," seems to be the secret recipe for the preparation of Leonard and future playmakers.

WHAT IS A PLAYMAKER?

Steven Kotler, New York Times *bestselling author, journalist, and the cofounder/director of the Flow Genome Project:*

I think, one, someone who is in control of their consciousness. Two, someone who can be creative in 360 degrees. To me, anything else is almost irrelevant. Mastery allows you the fullest range of creative expression—both the skill to be able to head in whatever direction you want, and the creative problem-solving to be able to recognize that new direction in the first place. I think that's critical here. Third, someone with that very nebulous quality that allows a playmaker to be somebody who lifts everybody up as well.

To me, it's possibly a cascade effect. If you have control of your consciousness, you're in the right state of mind to be able to express yourself and your skill in 360 degrees, and if done properly, this lifts everybody up. To me, a lot of this is actually the question of how quickly can you recruit dopamine and a few other neurochemicals to your situation. I am a little neurochemically biased, but if you can move the neurochemicals, everything else seems to follow. And once they're in your system, the results are big.

You're taking in more information per second and you're finding more patterns in that information. That, to me, is the ability to see things that other people aren't. Being able to be innovative, being able to make people around you better doesn't happen without a lot of pattern recognition. To get that pattern recognition, if you really want the wide-search database, you also have to be able to manage fear, technically manage cortisol and norepinephrine, because too much of those and they will shrink the size of that search database.

CHAPTER 9

How to Practice: Keeping It Real

Despite a Hall of Fame NBA career, Allen Iverson will forever be remembered for his 2002 end-of-season press conference where he expressed his disdain for practice, saying the word dismissively twenty-two times in a two-minute answer.[1]

Gary Payton, his friend and fellow Hall of Famer, later explained that he had told Iverson that his coach, George Karl, no longer required Payton to practice to preserve his energy for games.[2] Iverson liked the idea of reducing wear and tear on his mid-career body, so he cut back on his practice schedule. After a few losses and comments by his head coach, Larry Brown, the media caught wind of the plan and jumped on the story as a reason for the team's slump. A.I. was having none of it: "We're talking about practice, not a game . . . Not the game that I go out there and die for and play every game like it's my last . . . When you come to the arena, and you see me play, you see me play, don't you? You've seen me give everything I've got, right? But we're talking about practice right now."[3]

Ironically, despite his infamous rant, Iverson is revered as the ultimate playmaker by today's NBA superstars. Considered the best point guard in today's NBA, Chris Paul of the Los Angeles Clippers wears number 3 on his jersey in honor of Iverson. "He was my favorite player," said John Wall, All-Star point guard of the Washington Wizards. "I don't know anyone who didn't love A.I. He was a role model for me, and I just loved everything about him."[4] Breakout star Isaiah Thomas, point guard for the Boston Celtics and equally undersized, said, "I definitely wanted to be like Allen Iverson."

"Pound-for-pound, probably the greatest player who ever played," said LeBron James, four-time NBA MVP and three-time NBA champion.[5] "I didn't want to be Michael or Magic, I wanted to be Allen Iverson."[6]

Little did Iverson know back in 2002, but the infatuation with practice was just getting started. In fact, visit any sideline of parents and ask them to explain the "ten-thousand-hour rule." There is a good chance that you'll not only get a definition but also an update on their own child's progress toward the elusive target goal. At its most elemental level, the ten-thousand-hour rule has been interpreted as a finish line. Just survive the skill development marathon, log the hours, and you are guaranteed a winner's medal or an athletic scholarship when the practice odometer hits 10,000.

The concept represents all that is good about having a goal, putting in the work, and realizing your dream. But then up pops the devil with all of his dreaded details. What, exactly, is included in the 10,000 hours? What level of expertise (college, pro, international) will this lead to? How do different teammates, coaches, opponents, and geography affect the path to greatness? What role do natural, genetic abilities play in achieving greatness? So many articles, books, and presentations have been devoted to explaining and/or debunking what was previously an obscure piece of research on musicians that it is time we clear the air and move on.

"There is a lot of confusion about the ten-thousand-hour rule that I talk about in *Outliers*," commented Malcolm Gladwell about his 2008 bestselling book that started the debate. "It doesn't apply to sports. And practice isn't a *sufficient* condition for success. I could play chess for 100 years and I'll never be a grandmaster. The point is simply that natural ability requires a huge investment of time in order to be made manifest. Unfortunately, sometimes complex ideas get oversimplified in translation."[7]

In his examination of how extraordinary performers, aka outliers, distinguish themselves, Gladwell concluded that abilities, environment, and, yes, years of hard work all contribute at varying levels to each person's ultimate success. Certainly, LeBron James, at six feet eight inches and 250 pounds, has physical gifts that provided an instant head start in basketball, while Allen Iverson, listed at a generous six feet tall and 165 pounds soaking wet, learned to accentuate other abilities to play in a big man's sport. What he did with those abilities is the rest of the story.

"No one succeeds at a high level without innate talent, I wrote: 'achievement is talent plus preparation,'" said Gladwell. "But the ten-thousand-hour research reminds us that 'the closer psychologists look at the careers of the gifted, the smaller the role innate talent seems to play and the bigger the role preparation seems to play.' In cognitively demanding fields, there are no naturals."[8]

10,000 Hours: Give or Take

Based on the highly cited 1993 research[9] (cited over 7,300 times to date) of K. Anders Ericsson, Ralf Krampe, and Clemens Tesch-Römer that focused on violinists, Gladwell painted a portrait of the practice habits of the top 1 percent, not necessarily in sports, but in music, chess, and other "cognitively demanding fields." While both Ericsson and Gladwell agree on the importance of years of practice, it's that pesky number of hours that became over-interpreted by the dozens of commentators and interpreters of the original message.

"First, there is nothing special or magical about ten thousand hours," Ericsson clarified. ". . . [A]lthough Gladwell himself didn't say this, many people have interpreted it as a promise that almost anyone can become an expert in a given field by putting in ten thousand hours of practice. But nothing in the study of the Berlin violinists implied this." [10]

In fact, Ericsson's intended message was one of hope to those who feel they did not win the genetic lottery. "In pretty much any area of human endeavor, people have a tremendous capacity to improve their performance, as long as they train in the right way." [11]

And there is the key phrase: "train in the right way." Mindless hours of throwing a ball against a wall or dribbling through cones won't create the complete playmaker. What is needed is something Ericsson calls "deliberate practice," which exists on a sliding scale between game competition and pure play.

"In contrast to play, deliberate practice is a highly structured activity, the explicit goal of which is to improve performance," wrote Ericsson and his colleagues in their 1993 paper. "Specific tasks are invented to overcome weaknesses, and performance is carefully monitored to provide cues for ways to improve it further. We claim that deliberate practice requires effort and is not inherently enjoyable." [12]

In an engaging conversation, Ericsson told us, "I'm basically arguing that when you look at a lot of the practice that I've seen, visiting all sorts of different teams, very little of that is actually even getting close to this idea of individualized deliberate practice where somebody's doing something that is uniquely appropriate for them to improve some aspects of their performance basically in some more individualized context." [13]

Strong mental representations of a sport's playing patterns seem to be the cognitive advantage of playmakers, beyond the requisite motor skills involved. Much like a master chess player recognizes opportunities based on a memory of thousands of previous board positions, a playmaker can see available choices as they present themselves, seeing them faster than her opponents.

"I think, from all my discussions with athletes, the really good athletes have those representations where they see options and then they basically are making efforts to realize a particular option. They can also diagnose afterwards, if they were unsuccessful, what the source of the problem is and then ideally finding practice conditions that would be able to increase their control over their execution such that they would be able to realize the goal much more reliably in the future."

Mastering technical skills while being physically fit is of no value to an athlete if he can't achieve the desired outcome during a game. By studying musicians, Ericsson knows that many of them can play the notes but few can make music.

"If you take something like playing the piano, just hitting the keys in sequence—that's really not a musical skill. What you need to be able to do in order to give a musically pleasing performance is that you have an idea about what music that you want to make and then you need the representations to be able to realize that or at least try to realize it. Then you need to be able to actually listen to what it sounds like when you're actually producing those notes. Otherwise, you don't have a feedback loop that will allow you to be able to play things that you can hear in your head that you ultimately want the audience to hear when you're actually performing." [14]

It is this intentional, purposeful practice that Ericsson heard about in his interviews with world-class experts. In trying to improve your jump shot, compare an hour spent randomly shooting baskets in the driveway to a practice that is structured, focused, supervised, and unpleasant. What specific type of shot? From where on the floor? Catch and shoot or off the dribble? What teaching points and feedback will your shooting coach provide? Do you even have a coach watching? How does fatigue affect shooting accuracy? How will success be measured in this specific drill, so we know how you did and when it can end?

Actually, it is a basketball coach that Ericsson holds up as one of the best examples he has seen of a deliberate practice teacher. "I've been looking for examples of coaches that actually have had an influence on their players in a very consistent way," he said. "I think one of the coaches that emerges as a very nice example here is the shooting coach of the [San Antonio] Spurs." [15]

That coach, Chip Engelland, has transformed a string of otherwise talented players from being mediocre to consistently excellent jump shooters. Using Ericsson's plea for individualized, focused practice with expert feedback and adjustments, Engelland, better known as "the Shot Whisperer," [16] has boosted the shooting percentages of everyone from Steve Kerr to Tony Parker to Kawhi Leonard. As a player at Duke, Engelland shot over 55 percent from the three-point arc his senior year.[17] It is rare, however, for an athlete with a solid skill to become a coach who can teach that same skill. But Engelland knows it just takes a feedback loop of knowledge, practice, and adjustment. "When you start working with a player, you're writing the script," he said. "I'm helping, but the work that they put in and the confidence they have behind it . . . you can go one page of the script a day or you can move quickly." [18]

One of his many admirers is Kerr, a hired marksman as a player and now a two-time NBA champion head coach of the Golden State Warriors. "It was very subtle," said Kerr, "but before I started working with [Chip], the ball rolled more off my middle finger than my index finger. He taught me to spread my hands out a little wider on the ball and use my index fingers more. . . . He understands that a big part of shooting is the shooter's mind." [19]

The three-point shot was the missing skill from Leonard's game when he joined the Spurs as a rookie out of San Diego State. Enter Engelland and his eye for technique tweaks. "I had a good shooting form, but he brought my release a little lower and helped my follow-through," said Leonard. "But they were just little adjustments Chip had seen. I just believed in it and worked on it from there." [20] While improving his three-point percentage from 25 percent in college to 38 percent in the pros, Leonard made a career-high 147 three-point baskets in the 2016–17 season, a whopping 258 percent improvement over his rookie season.

Engelland's formula is a repeating cycle of observation, adjustment, and repeated practice for a specific skill of a single player. Beyond the angst of how many hours of practice, Ericsson would like to move the discussion from the athlete to the coach, hoping to duplicate Engelland's attention to detail and specific, repeatable learning sessions.

"I would argue that it starts out with questions about how can you actually measure how good a coach is. We would argue that the way you measure it is the way you measure other kinds of teachers, doctors, or even psychotherapists," he said. "You're basically looking at their ability to improve somebody's performance."

"The next step, which is something that we're just starting to look into, is what is it we can learn by examining what these expert teachers with better teaching outcomes do that is different and potentially something that other teachers might be taught to do that would actually improve their students' improvement during the year," he added. [21]

One of Engelland's many fans is his old boss, Jeff Bzdelik, former head coach of the Denver Nuggets. "He'll work with an 8- or

9-year-old at an Air Force Academy camp with the same intensity he would with a guy like Tim Duncan or Carmelo Anthony or Andre Miller," said Bzdelik. "There's integrity there." [22]

Playmakers Need More Than Just Practice

"No one disputes that practice is important," said Professor Hambrick, professor of psychology at Michigan State University. "Through practice, people get better. The question is whether that is all there is to it." [23] Indeed, the key phrase for this debate is "necessary but not sufficient." There is no need to pick one extreme or the other; skill acquisition and mastery happens somewhere inside the three dimensions of heredity, environment, and training.

Inside Hambrick's "Expertise Lab" on MSU's East Lansing campus, he and his team have been battling the ten-thousand-hour misconception for years. Luckily for them, there is an abundance of studies looking at deliberate practice in sports, music, dance, chess, and even memorizing long sequences of digits. From this rich collection of data, Hambrick and his longtime collaborator, Brooke Macnamara, psychology professor at Case Western Reserve University, created two significant meta-analyses, the first on multiple talent domains and the second targeted specifically at sports.

They started with this fundamental question: "Why do so few people who take up an instrument such as the violin, a sport such as golf, or a game such as chess ever reach an expert level of performance?" Next: "How much of the total variance in performance is explained by the accumulated amount of deliberate practice?" [24] Finally, in addition to training, Hambrick, Macnamara, and others have started to identify what else matters besides just training.

In a 2014 study, [25] starting from a staggering potential list of

9,331 research articles, a final subset of 88 studies were included across 5 domains, (music, games, sports, professions, and education), including more than 11,000 participants. Reporting on actual practice time over the years is a tricky exercise in itself. Researchers typically have two options, interviews with the athletes or some type of log recorded by the athlete, coach, or device. Because memories can become fuzzy over time, daily records of training time are preferred. Ericsson argues that the rigors of practice sessions vary greatly, so it's difficult to compare apples to apples. Still, Hambrick and Macnamara were able to select studies that had significant effect sizes from the correlation of accumulated quantity of deliberate practice and eventual performance.

Across the entire analysis, practice did, in fact, have a direct impact on performance. However, it only accounted for 12 percent of the variance in performance across all of the domains. In other words, 88 percent of "what matters" was left unexplained. When the individual domains were broken out, things got even more interesting. Across games (like chess), music, and sports, deliberate practice contributed 26 percent, 21 percent, and 18 percent of the difference, respectively. When studying education, as in learning new subjects, deliberate practice explained just 4 percent of success, while within the professions, like surgery or tax accounting, less than 1 percent of performance came from training.

Part of the differences between domains is tied to the predictable nature of the tasks required. For example, so-called CGM sports—those measured in centimeters, grams, or seconds—benefit more from deliberate practice than a complicated task like learning algebra or playing point guard. Cognitively complex tasks demand additional abilities that are still being identified.

"Don't get me wrong. Practice is important," Macnamara

said. "It's just not as important as many have thought. What does count for the skills is still unknown."[26]

Next, Hambrick and Macnamara drilled down further with another analysis of thirty-three studies focused solely on sports.[27] While Ericsson's original work avoided sports, the fascination of parents and coaches with the concept has generated more interest and research than any of the other domains. Also, by digging deep into sports, several other variables were evaluated, including team versus individual sport, externally paced (think basketball) versus internally paced (like bowling), ball/puck sports versus non-ball sports, and between open skills (playing basketball) and closed skills (shooting a basketball free throw). The characteristics of the players in the studies were also compared: youth versus adult and elite versus non-elite.

Once again, in surprising consistency, only 18 percent of performance gains were explained by deliberate practice alone. As it turned out, differences between young and old, ball or no ball, and open versus closed skill did not vary by a statistically significant amount. However, performance in an internally paced sport that allows a player to determine when the skill starts (like diving or golf) showed a larger effect from deliberate practice. This makes sense, as rehearsed repetitions seem to benefit those athletes who have the luxury of time to gather their thoughts and prepare their brain prior to skill execution.

One of the most fascinating findings was that among elite athletes—those that compete at national or international levels—deliberate practice only accounted for 1 percent of performance gains, while non-elite athletes saw a 19 percent correlation. "In other words, although there is evidence that deliberate practice is one factor that contributes to performance differences across a wide range of skills, it may not contribute to performance differences at the highest levels of skill," the researchers wrote.[28]

And since Hambrick and Macnamara had access to all of this data, they looked at one more relationship, the age that athletes started serious training in their major sport and whether they achieved elite status. Logically, as single-sport-specialization advocates would argue, starting at a younger age would provide that many more years of accumulated hours to add to the skill piggy bank. But the data showed that no such correlation existed: elite athletes across the thirty-three studies did not, on average, begin at a younger age.

The Talent Identification Myth

Indeed, at the 2016 Youth Athlete Development Conference hosted by Singapore's National Youth Sports Institute, Dr. Arne Güllich dropped a bomb on talent identification programs around the world. "Junior success is a poor indicator of long-term senior success. Their success at the age of 10 had a zero correlation with their success as a senior. Same was true with their success at ages 11–14, [and] 15–18. We have a zero correlation. That means, those who were better at a young age were not those who were better at an older age."[29]

Güllich, head of the Department of Sport Science and director of the Institute of Applied Sport Science at Kaiserslautern University of Technology, was summarizing his research from both the extensive network of German soccer development academies as well as German Olympic team athletes across all sports.

The purported vision of long-term athlete development is talent identification—finding the unpolished diamonds lying among the acres of ordinary rocks—so that dedicated coaches, trainers, and programs can spend their time productively with the best prospects in a process known as talent development. With the assumption that world-class athletes require roughly ten years to blossom, the sooner the better for committing to a program of skill refinement, according to existing LTPD philosophy. The only problem is that the data on real athletes does not agree with the premise.

In a 2014 study,[30] Güllich, along with Manuel Hornig and Friedhelm Aust, interviewed fifty-two soccer players who were members of Bundesliga teams (Germany's top tier and one of the world's elite leagues) as well as fifty amateur players who were in the fourth- to sixth-tier German leagues to understand their training histories and sport participation throughout their lives. They wanted to understand the different age points at which the athletes first played soccer, both organized and non-organized; other sports they played and when they stopped in favor of full-time soccer; and the "microstructure" of training, including strength and conditioning, skill drills, and actual gameplay.

The Bundesliga professionals, those that reached the pinnacle of German soccer, averaged about 4,300 hours of what would be considered deliberate practice before debuting at the top level. Those who went on to make the German national team averaged about 4,500 hours before their first starting appearance. Before age thirteen, compared to their amateur, age-matched counterparts, the professional players played more leisure, non-organized soccer and more sports in general. In fact, the earlier that players joined select, dedicated soccer academies, the less likely they were to make the senior teams.

"Of those who were recruited at an age of under 11 or under 13, at the age of under 19, only 9 percent are left," Güllich said in his presentation. "On the other hand, those who made it to the national A team of Germany, those we see in the World Cup, for example, were being built up gradually across all age stages." In fact, Güllich found that the annual mean turnover at these elite soccer schools was 41 percent, with only a 7 percent probability of lasting five years.

The results across other sports were no different. In a 2016 study,[31] matched pairs of German Olympic athletes—eighty-three who had medaled (including thirty-eight gold medalists or world champions) and eighty-three who had never medaled—were interviewed similarly to the soccer players. Across the board, the medalists started participation in their primary sport at an older age, accumulated less deliberate practice time during their preteen and early-teen years, but also played a wider variety of sports both as kids and well into their teen years.

"The world-class athlete differs from those who made it only to national class, not by having engaged in more sports specific training in their main sport, this was indifferent, or they even trained less at a young age at their later main sport, but consistently, they engaged in more activity in other sports," said Güllich.[32]

For today's obsessive youth sports culture, letting kids be kids is counterintuitive. Parents want to provide every opportunity that their checkbook can afford, and coaches—especially those who profit from early specialization—are eager to work with ever-younger athletes. Ironically, playing different sports may actually improve their preferred, main sport. Exercising different muscle groups as well as expanding perceptual-cognitive skills will build the whole athlete while preventing burnout.

The truth is brutal, but experts like Professor Güllich will continue to preach it: "Future 'top athletes' cannot be predicted reliably by way of young-age talent identification. Particularly early talent development programming is neither necessary nor beneficial but correlates negatively with long-term senior success."[33]

Dr. Peter Vint has had a rare vantage point on athlete development. As a senior sport scientist with the United States Olympic Committee for a decade, he contributed to the success of dozens of Team USA athletes in both individual and team sports.

Dealing with these elite performers required tweaks of seconds or inches or marginal improvements that made the difference between a medal or a trip home empty-handed. Transitioning to the world of English Premier League soccer as the youth academy director of Everton Football Club offered him a chance to work with budding superstars at an earlier stage in their development. From this unique set of perspectives, he sees the dangers of over-aggressive training programs.

"At Everton, the Academy was strongly influenced by a document called the EPPP, or the Elite Player Performance Plan," Vint told us in an interview. "It was a set of guidelines laid out by the Premier League to help improve the quality of the training environment and the support for Academy players. Interestingly, as rationale for a substantial increase in on-field, coach-led training time, the EPPP directly referenced the expertise literature, including Ericsson's concept of deliberate practice and Gladwell's ten-thousand-hour rule. It also contrasted historical Academy training hours with examples from other high-performance organizations like the Yehudi Menuhin Music School, the Royal Ballet School, British Cycling, the Lawn Tennis Association, and the English Cricket Board.

"It implied that, based on what has been done in the game traditionally, other schools with elite sports teams were falling woefully short in terms of on-field, coach-led training hours and that was possibly one of the reasons they were not producing more players for the professional game. So, these schools needed to change that. Specifically, they needed to substantially increase on-field, coach-led training time. The challenge is that when you literally interpret the EPPP framework against the actual contact time you have with players, you can end up with multiple two-a-day sessions per week for kids between twelve and eighteen years old. There is very little research related specifically to the physical, cognitive, and emotional load and recovery requirements for young athletes. As a result, it was difficult to find and maintain an appropriate balance between achieving the aggressive requirements of the EPPP with the periods of recovery and rejuvenation we felt were important to support the healthy and holistic long-term development of the young athletes/people in our care.

"I see kids training really hard, day in and day out, and I see them giving what I think is probably their very best effort. It is physical and it is tough. Over time and on competition days, particularly, it can be incredibly demanding, and that goes for any sport, any of the top youth sport programs I've seen. I see parallels in youth sport to professional game performance in that players have gotten bigger, they've gotten stronger, they've gotten faster, and therefore the games at these other developmental levels have gotten progressively tougher.

"So, to withstand those loads and to be even on the field, I think the level of athleticism and the general level of athlete development has probably improved. I think there's way more room to go in terms of more appropriate methodologies of instruction, better application of the principles of skill acquisition and motor learning, creating better and more meaningful balances between competition and training. And, I would say certainly there exists a vast opportunity to improve athlete performance, health, and well-being through a more complete utilization of applied sport science and medicine. I don't think that I've seen the perfect athlete development environment yet."[34]

Reinventing Practice

"Is it not possible, through the brain, to bring players to a higher level?"[35] That was the nagging question that Michel Bruyninckx brought to his first class at his soccer academy at the University of Leuven in Belgium over fifteen years ago. Having gained some notoriety for his work with younger players, the Belgian Football Federation invited him to work with 130 promising players whose potential had been recognized but who just weren't making the progress expected of them. "We need to stop thinking football is only a matter of the body," said Bruyninckx. "Skillfulness will only grow if we better understand the mental part of developing a player. Cognitive readiness, improved perception, better mastering of time and space in combination with perfect motor functioning." [36]

Trained as a teacher and now a certified UEFA A–licensed coach, Bruyninckx borrowed from his educational theory training, especially a pedagogical method known as brain-based learning, to reinvent how players can fuse processing in the brain with body movements. Creating playmakers who can increase the throughput from eyes to brain to body, the core purpose of what he calls CogiTraining.

> "You see with your brain, not with your eyes."
>
> —DR. PAUL BACH-Y-RITA, PIONEER IN NEUROPLASTICITY

"I think everybody begins to understand that the football game at the highest level is no longer based on athletic potential and ability but that the brain ability and potential has got an enormous influence," said Bruyninckx, who has worked with top professional teams over the last twenty years, including Belgian clubs RSC Anderlecht, KRC Genk, and Standard Liège, as well as FC Metz, AC Milan, and the Aspire Academy in Qatar. "Faster moving and decision-making can only be achieved through brain anticipation processes." [37]

In invasion-type sports, like soccer, hockey, rugby, and basketball, speed is measured more in decisions per second than meters per second. Since no two play sequences are the same, it is the processing speed of the brain, reliant on a supporting network of neurons, that must constantly create a micro movement plan on the fly. Without the right decision at the precise moment, the opportunity is lost.

"I think that coaches either forget, or don't even realize, that football is a hugely cognitive sport," said Kevin McGreskin, another Union of European Football Associations (UEFA) A–licensed coach and educator on cognitive training. "We've got to develop the players' brains as well as their bodies but it's much easier to see and measure the differences we make to a player's physiology than we can with their cognitive attributes." [38]

While Bruyninckx believes the ten-thousand-hour theory gives false expectations, he does advocate for young players to obtain 500,000 annual "touches" of a soccer ball. Using repetitive sequences of "pass and move" with the ball, Bruyninckx teaches a team to develop an internal timing and rhythm that emphasizes constant one-touch passes, allowing minimal time for overthinking a situation. The dizzying geometry of motion keeps defenders a step behind.

"Football is an angular game and needs training of perception—both peripheral sight and split vision," Bruyninckx explained. "Straight, vertical playing increases the danger of losing the ball. If a team continuously plays the balls at angles at a very high speed it will be quite impossible to recover the ball. The team rhythm will be so high that your opponent will never get into the match." [39]

But practicing one drill over and over is like playing computerized brain-training games. Performance on that one drill or computer game will improve over time but it won't transfer to the real world, where an infinite combination of patterns exists. By overloading the cognitive circuits during training, a player's neural network is better prepared to compute new solutions to one-of-a-kind, in-game situations.

"You have to present new activities that players are not used to doing. If you repeat exercises too much the brain thinks it knows the answers," Bruyninckx said.

"By constantly challenging the brain and making use of its plasticity you discover a world that you thought was never available.

"Once the brain picks up the challenge you create new connections that gives remarkable results." [40]

Practicing with Purpose

Despite its complex reality, most coaches will try to convince their players that their sport is a simple game, not to be overanalyzed. "Keep it simple," "Just let the game come to you," and "Don't

> "Playing football is very simple, but playing simple football is the hardest thing there is."
>
> —JOHAN CRUYFF,
> DUTCH SOCCER LEGEND

try to do too much" are all coaching clichés that try to calm the chaos going on in an inexperienced athlete's brain. Executing technical motor skills while mastering the principles and tactics of the game can quickly overwhelm young players. So, rather than eat the whole elephant, coaches break down the game into bite-sized chunks, compartmentalizing offense, defense, positional play, conditioning, and technical skill development, hoping that the sum of the parts will equal the whole. Training sessions are divided into timed portions across allocated days of the week.

Some sports lend themselves to more segmentation, with clear delineations between phases of the game. In baseball you're either on offense or defense, with transitions only happening at the half inning. While the flow of American football can flip with a turnover, the play resets with the appropriate units on the field after the whistle.

However, team sports with continuous flow (e.g., soccer,

hockey, lacrosse, basketball, rugby, and even volleyball) all consist of two states, offense or defense, and two transitions, offense to defense and defense to offense. Playmakers are those players who understand their roles under each condition and can instantly switch modes. Logically, not only should training sessions emphasize these game moments, but there is a growing paradigm shift in coaching that practice should be exclusively dedicated to these states.

"There is no attacking football or defensive football," said Vitor Frade. "When you have the ball, you have to think about what will happen when you lose it. When you do not have it, you need to know what you will do when you get it back." [41]

As a lecturer at the University of Porto, in Portugal, and a coach, although never a head coach, for FC Porto, Vitor Frade has become a growing cult figure among coaches worldwide, especially in his beloved sport of soccer. Leading the revolution is none other than the self-proclaimed "Special One," José Mourinho. In ten seasons managing some of the top clubs in the world, his teams have won eight league championships in Portugal, England, Italy, and Spain while capturing two Champions League trophies. He credits his compatriot, Frade, for his winning training methodology.

"We can differentiate among traditional analytical training where the different factors are trained in isolation, the integrated training, which uses the ball but where the fundamental concerns are not very different from the traditional one; and there is my way of training, which is called Tactical Periodization," said Mourinho. "It has nothing to do with the previous two even though many people could think so." [42]

Developed by Frade over thirty-five years of playing and coaching, tactical periodization aims to make every minute of training directly related to the objectives of a game. Longtime Portuguese author and soccer analyst Luís Freitas Lobo explains that this type of practice "never separates the physical, the tactical, the technical—the skills—and the mental in the work. Physical preparation doesn't exist by itself. It's integrated with the tactical game. You don't do any physical exercises without transferring them to the game."[43]

Team sports are made up of individual actions on the field, court, or ice. Each of those actions requires the four cornerstones of preparation (tactical, technical, physiological, and psychological). It starts with a tactical decision to execute a technical motor skill based on physiological foundation influenced by the psychological emotions of the moment. This combination is always interconnected, but coaches often disassemble these components during training, assuming it will help athletes learn faster. In one of these typical, traditional sessions, chalkboard discussions describe tactics, skill drills hone technical movements, and strength and conditioning focus on physiological development, while psychological stress is often absent. But that's not how the game is played.

"Preparing teams to win games is not a physical challenge, it is a holistic performance challenge," said Dr. Fergus Connolly, performance director of University of Michigan Football. ". . . You must train the team sport athlete to execute skills in a complete holistic manner, combining tactical, technical, and psychological qualities, not physical alone. . . . In team sport, you have the combination of tactical and physical abilities, which can only be trained effectively in a gradual integrated manner, not separately."[44]

Gameplay is continuously changing, so a coach can't script, duplicate, and test every possible decision. Instead, to help simplify the myriad choices, the coach can define the team's game model, a set of principles of play and desired behaviors that gives a player some generalized rules and guardrails for their decision-making. Ultimately a player is accountable to the coach, so it's the coach who defines the framework that the team must follow. What tactical formation should we play? How should we transition from offense to defense? How should we attack when we get the ball back? Second by second, individual creativity is still required, but the game model guidelines reduce the universe of options for a player to process. Instead of strict "If this happens, then do this" rules, the game model calls for a more flexible logic model, with variations like "If this happens, then do this. Otherwise, do this until this happens." This expands the set of possible choices, giving players room to create on the fly.

Linking the game model to every training activity every day is the key to tactical periodization. "For me training means to train in specificity," said Mourinho. "That is, to create exercises that allow me to exacerbate my principles of play." [45] Without this principle of specificity, random drills, inconsistent messaging, and isolated physical conditioning don't support the game model. If preferred behaviors and style of play are not constantly reinforced during practice, a coach can't expect it during a game.

How many times late in a game has a poor decision been the cause of a loss? Maintaining concentration until the final whistle doesn't just happen, it necessitates repeated attention, according to Mourinho: "Concentration needs to be trained. It can be done by training according to a specific philosophy. I cannot dissociate training intensity with the concept of concentration. When I say that soccer is made by actions of high intensity, I also refer to the need of permanent concentration; it is implicit to the game." [46]

Similar to Atlético's Ortega and Real's Pintus, Frade's methodology calls for the right type of fitness for game situations rather than just elite but non-sport-specific fitness. If the game requires rapid-fire decision-making while fatigued, then why separate that cognitive complexity from physical preparation in training? Recognizing and appreciating the brain's dominance in performance is the new differentiator for today's coaches.

One of the top performance specialists in the world, Valter Di Salvo, agrees that the cognitive generation is here. "I think the new frontier is this one," he told us in a recent interview.[47] For fifteen years Di Salvo was the fitness coach for SS Lazio, a perennial contender in Italy's Serie A league. From his success in Rome, he was lured away to Real Madrid in 2003 to run their fitness performance program, working with legendary players Beckham, Raúl, Ronaldo, Figo, and Zidane (now the manager). Impressed by his work with the Galácticos of Madrid, Sir Alex Ferguson named him Manchester United's head of fitness in 2004 for the next three seasons.

At Old Trafford, home of Manchester United, Di Salvo met a young Cristiano Ronaldo and was struck by the ambition of the rising playmaker. "I was training with him for four years and I'll tell you something about the power of his mind," he told us. "When he was twenty-three, he was improving, but I said, 'Come on, let's go. You can be the best player in the world this year.' He replied, 'No, I want to be the best player ever!'" Once Ronaldo finished second in the voting for the Ballon d'Or, the soccer world's MVP award, in 2007, he went on to win the award a record five times and finished second five times, all in the last eleven years.

In fact, in 2007, Real Madrid invited Di Salvo to return to the club as director of TEC, its football high-performance center, which he designed and created, just in time to welcome Ronaldo to the Santiago Bernabéu in 2009. According to Di Salvo, integration of tactical, technical, physiological, and psychological preparation has been the key to Ronaldo's success. As a perfect example, Di Salvo points to Ronaldo's second goal in this year's

Champions League Final, a one-touch finish from a diagonal pass into the six-yard box from the end line by Luka Modrić.

"Look what happened in three seconds," Di Salvo said. "Ronaldo reads the game to make a sprint into the box—a tactical decision followed by speed. He is in the right place at the right moment. He has the physiological capacity to do these movements, then finishes with a technical skill, maintaining his emotional control in front of the goalkeeper at the moment of shooting. All four components in three seconds. The future goal must be the capacity to develop, in an integrated and holistic way, all the activity that happens in that three or four seconds." [48]

Train for the Last 20 Minutes

Since Eddie Jones took charge of the England national rugby union team in late 2015, the Lions have outscored their opponents by eighty-three points in the last quarter of their games. "How many games out of our last 15 wins have we won in the last 20 minutes? That's not by coincidence," the Australian-born coach commented recently. "It's because we train to win those last 20 minutes." [49]

Because of the similarities between soccer and rugby, he brought it to Japan's national team in 2013 and has relied on it ever since. "Every day we train a specific parameter of the game," Jones explained. ". . . We don't do any extra fitness. It's all done within those training sessions. Because of that we've improved our fitness enormously." [50]

Imagine the training schedule as a matrix of fitness on one axis and tactical lessons across the other. On the fitness continuum, each day of the week emphasizes a physiological component (e.g., Mondays are endurance, Tuesdays are strength, Wednesdays are speed, and so on). By focusing on different physical demands throughout the week—what Frade calls the principle of horizontal alternation in specificity—players have a chance to recover from the previous day's work.

"We train fast and it's not just helter-skelter or unstructured," said Dylan Hartley, born in rugby-crazed New Zealand to an English mother and now Jones's team captain. "It's all planned and researched. It gives us confidence knowing we have trained to a greater intensity." [51]

Within each daily training session, a coach will stress the principles or sub-principles of play that need special emphasis by designing activities that combine the tactical lesson with that day's fitness focus. For example, if the team needs to improve its counterattack transition from defense to offense while training its speed, they may plan a drill that teaches proper passing channels with repeated breakout sprints. This principle of conditioned practices is the daily core of tactical periodization.

"We must teach our players to be self-reliant and not puppets on the end of the coach's strings," said Dave Hadfield, a veteran mental-skills coach who has worked with elite New Zealand rugby teams for over twenty years. "Rugby is an interactive, combat sport. The Chinese think it's the ideal sport to prepare for warfare, because it involves endurance, explosiveness, physical toughness. It's chess on a field that requires creating and recognizing space. It involves preplanning but also responding to what you see in the moment. It's a fascinating sport from a decision-making point of view." [52]

From working directly with players and coaches, Hadfield knows that quick, automatic decisions are generated and triggered from an instinctual region of our brain. "You play rugby with your subconscious mind. Your cue recognition, your decision-making, and your skill execution is done without thinking in the normal way. Our conscious mind runs our eyes and our ears and is responsible for picking up cues in an ever-changing, complex, interactive game where people are trying to knock your block off."

It seems complicated, but Frade's vision makes sense. There's a quote from the nineteenth-century British Baptist pastor Charles Haddon Spurgeon: "Begin as you mean to go on, and go on as you began." [53] Tactical periodization encourages players to practice as you mean to play, and play as you've practiced.

"A chameleon changes color," said Frade, "but never forgets it is a chameleon."

WHAT IS A PLAYMAKER?

K. Anders Ericsson, Conradi Eminent Scholar and professor of psychology at Florida State University:

In most teams, there's some organization where you actually have a structure. It's a little bit like in surgical teams. There's the surgeon who basically would take input from other people, but he or she is sort of the major decision maker. If it really comes to a critical phase, they are more or less taking over, and also may be held responsible for the outcome.

I would argue that in basketball or soccer there are certain types of positions that are localized in such a way that the person who has that playmaking role would basically be located in a way that would have maximal options available to him. Whereas if you penetrate too much, then the number of options that you can actually consider at a single time is going to be much more restricted than somebody who is playing closer to their offensive zone and basically can observe the movements of all the various players.

Basically, that's what I would associate with being a playmaker. I'm fine with everyone being playmakers, but at least in the teams that I've looked at, you really do have kind of an assignment of being a playmaker. It's a little bit of a hierarchical structure where some individuals seem to be given the opportunities here of making more of the decisions for the players on the team.

CHAPTER 10

How to Compete: The Clutch and Choke of the Performance Engine

Mark Newman has watched a lot of baseball but he had never seen anything like this. "Over the twenty-six years I was with the Yankees, we trained shortstops, at every level in the organization, to be there on that play," Newman, the team's recently retired senior vice president of baseball operations, said in an engaging conversation. "[Derek Jeter] was. Many others weren't. I'm not sure if he was trained any differently than the other twenty-five shortstops. His ability to pay attention, be in the moment, and respond to his environment was superior. That play's an example of it." [1]

That play is, of course, "the Flip," which defined Derek Jeter as the quintessential playmaker. Down two games in the 2001 American League Division Series, the Yankees were protecting a 1–0 lead in the seventh inning on the road at the Oakland Coliseum. With two outs and Jeremy Giambi on first, Yankees pitcher Mike Mussina gave up a sharp line drive down the right-field line. Outfielder Shane Spencer chased the ball into the corner and heaved it toward home plate, over the heads of both of his cutoff men. "I let it go and it took off on me," said Spencer. "I had a little too much on it." [2]

Surprisingly, Ron Washington, the A's third-base coach, waved a charging Giambi home for a play at the plate. Jeter instinctively knew where he needed to be. Sprinting to the first-base line, he fielded Spencer's overthrow with both hands and then made a forty-foot backhanded flip to catcher Jorge Posada, who tagged Giambi a split second before his right foot touched home plate. The Yankees held on to their 1–0 lead to win the game and then the series.

"It was my job to read the play," said Jeter after the game.[3]

"The kid has great instincts and he holds it together and that was obviously the play of the game," said manager Joe Torre about his twenty-seven-year-old shortstop.[4]

Newman has seen thousands of ballplayers in his career, not only with the Yankees but in eighteen years as a college coach at Southern Illinois and Old Dominion. He likes the label of "playmaker" to describe that something extra that differentiates the Jeters of the world from players with talent alone.

"Derek is an extraordinary example of a playmaker, someone who takes talent and skill and is able to use them in game situations," he told us. "There's a big difference when you've scouted and signed as many good players as we did with the Yankees. Many players who we thought were gonna be good and weren't. You become acutely aware of the difference between talent and performance. That bridge is the link of all those skills that allow a young player to go from being a prospect to a performer. That's what distinguishes the playmaker from the one who aspires to be a playmaker."

Newman joined the Bronx Bombers in 1989 as an instruction coordinator, then was promoted to vice president of player development and scouting in 1997. During his tenure the Yankees made the playoffs eighteen times, appearing in seven World Series and winning five of them. Beyond the well-known "five tools" of baseball talent—hitting for average, hitting for power, speed, throwing, and fielding—Newman and his scouts were always looking for that sixth tool, which was hard to describe but obvious when they saw it.

"In baseball, the old-school guys will call it instinct. As we thought more about it, we knew it's more than instinct; that term wasn't good enough to describe it. We wanted something with more specificity. Something to allow us to go out and search for this in the environment. Of course, we're always trying to identify the things that we need to sign, versus the things we can develop. How much of this stuff is innate or what particular things might be more innate versus what things we can develop?

"That's a huge part of the effective marriage of coaching and scouting or coaching and evaluations: understanding what the coaches can improve; what's more easily teachable and what's more difficult to teach. Beyond that is cognitive development: the ability to mentally and emotionally be tuned in to the environment and respond appropriately to it."[1]

That's the intrigue and thrill of team sports. Individual players who respond to the moment under the pressure of competition. Make enough plays when your team needs you, and your nickname becomes "Captain Clutch," as Jeter is known. Failure to manage the stress leads to a performance beneath expectations and with it a much different label, "choker." The capacity to compete sits squarely in the brain, relying on physiological and psychological processes that are still a mystery. But science is starting to scratch around the edges to reveal how playmakers rise to the occasion. Let's take a look.

Clutch Versus Choke: The Extremes
of Competitive Performance

Great comebacks in sports are the worst of times followed by the best of times. With eight minutes and thirty-one seconds left in the third quarter, Tom Brady and the New England Patriots trailed the Atlanta Falcons by twenty-five points in Super Bowl LI. The post-game stories were already being written: Was this the end of the Brady-Belichick golden era? Were we witnessing the final game of one of the greatest quarterbacks in league history? Not if it was up to Brady. After Atlanta's early-fourth-quarter touchdown, he stomped up and down the Patriots' sideline, pleading with his teammates, "We've got to play harder! Harder and tougher! Everything we've got!"[6] While the words he used were rather obvious, it was the intense urgency in his voice that defined the turning point in the game. His team needed to believe the unbelievable and he was the only one who could convince them that they could. "We just needed to execute one drive, and after that drive we'll come to the sidelines and we'll talk about the next drive," Brady told sportswriter Peter King a week later.[7]

After that exhortation from their leader, on four consecutive drives, the Patriots scored a touchdown, a field goal, and two more touchdowns, each with two-point conversions, to tie the game and force the Super Bowl's first overtime. A coin-flip win and one more touchdown drive confirmed the greatest comeback in NFL championship history if not all of sports. At the post-game press conference a smiling Brady had nothing but praise for his coaches and teammates, but they knew it started and ended with their playmaker QB.

"He's the best ever. I promise we don't try to do this but he deserves so much credit because he knew at halftime that there were a lot of eyes on him," said Josh McDaniels, Brady's offensive coordinator and close friend. "There was no flinch in Tom and really, that goes for our whole team." [8]

With experience comes confidence, and confidence enables clutch performances. The physical aspect of the game takes a backseat as the brain takes over. If prepared properly, then subconscious intuition and automaticity provide the solutions with a sense of calm.

"I have the answers to the test now," said Brady. "You can't surprise me on defense. I've seen it all. I've processed 261 games, I've played them all. It's an incredibly hard sport, but because the processes are right and are in place, for anyone with experience in their job, it's not as hard as it used to be. There was a time when quarterbacking was really hard for me because you didn't know what to do. Now I really know what to do, I don't want to stop now. This is when it's really enjoyable to go out." [9]

Even Dan Quinn, the Falcons' head coach, admitted after the game that experience matters: "You know, I think that one could say that regarding the experience, but the only fight that matters is the one you're in. So, we can't draw back from experience we didn't have." [10]

During those rare moments of perceived superiority, athletes can experience two different psychological states, flow and clutch, according to Dr. Christian Swann, sports psychology researcher at the School of Health and Human Sciences at Southern Cross University, in New South Wales, Australia. "Flow is a state of effortless excellence, in which everything 'clicks into place,' " said Swann. "We perform on autopilot, are totally confident in our abilities and fully absorbed in what we are doing without really thinking about it." [11] Most of us have experienced the wonderful passage of time in a flow state when we are totally immersed in an activity, cranking tasks out at a surprisingly high level of quality. Swann has interviewed dozens of elite athletes who describe just "letting it happen" like the flow of a river downstream.

As Jeter and Brady know, playing in a flow state is helpful but sometimes they have to ratchet it up to take over a game. "The Flip" was an intentional, intuitive reaction by Jeter to a real-time situation. The fourth-quarter focus by Brady united an acute sense of mission with a belief of being unstoppable. Swann describes this dominating desire to win as "making it happen" during what he calls a "clutch state."

"Clutch states share a core of similarities with flow, but are more effortful, deliberate, consciously controlled and intense," said Swann. "In this state, athletes are much more aware of the importance of the situation, what's at stake, the potential consequences, and what's required to achieve a successful outcome. In clutch, athletes describe being conscious of the pressure, and feel the pressure, yet are still able to perform at their peak." [12]

Through his research, Swann has been looking for a unified model of performance that helps explain the two outcomes of high-pressure events, succeeding and failing. First, he led a group of researchers at the University of Lincoln in the U.K. that distilled seventeen existing studies on flow in athletes trying to tease out the actual experience, how these states occur and could flow be controlled. Across 1,194 athletes, both elite and beginners, covering multiple sports, Swann found varying levels of flow described that matched the original nine dimensions defined by Mihaly Csikszentmihalyi, the godfather of flow and professor of psychology at Claremont Graduate University. Included in the nine dimensions are flow conditions, prerequisites for flow to occur, and flow characteristics, what the athlete actually feels during this state.

The tricky part of studying flow is asking athletes to describe it after a particular event that included outstanding results. Some researchers prime the athlete's knowledge by showing descriptions of the characteristics, then asking if they felt something similar. Conversely, they are presented with a questionnaire, or flow scales, that ask about the event. For example, on a scale of "never" to "always," they may be asked to rate "My attention is focused entirely on what I have to do" or "Things just seemed to be happening automatically." Trying to remember exactly what they were feeling during a time when they were actually carefree and completely focused can be difficult.

In the systematic review[13] sample, athletes reported experiencing about five of the nine flow dimensions during any one event. As each experience is unique to each individual, there may never be a definitive "flow tracker" tool that details each occurrence. As to how an athlete enters flow, one of studies concluded, "It is one thing to know, for example, that a flow experience is accompanied by focused concentration, feelings of control, and clear goals. It is quite another to know why or how the flow experience actually occurred [and] the mechanisms underlying the experience."[14]

Finally, creating flow on demand is the ultimate dream for athletes and coaches. In fact, if it was easy to "switch on" to this super-productive state, why would you ever turn it off? Every training session would multiply skills, while every competition would be personal bests. In fact, almost two-thirds of the athletes included in the meta-study were convinced that they could initiate and control flow. "Just because these factors are perceived to be controllable as well as related to flow does not mean that they cause flow to occur, or guarantee its occurrence," wrote Swann and his colleagues.[15]

And while Csikszentmihalyi's original description and framework of flow is considered the gold standard, some of the researchers advocate for letting the data lead the search in new directions if they don't match exactly with the traditional dimensions, at least in the sports context.

Kobe Bryant, a five-time NBA champion with the Los Angeles Lakers, is no stranger to being "in the zone" of flow. During his twenty-year career, he scored forty points in a game 135 times, third all-time highest behind Wilt Chamberlain and Michael Jordan, with twenty-six of those games being over fifty points. But it was his eighty-one-point game in a 2006 victory over the Toronto Raptors that added to his legacy as a playmaker. Clearly, Bryant was in a flow state that night, but it was his demeanor that was a telltale sign for his teammates that he had entered the zone. After the Raptors took an eighteen-point lead early in the third quarter, Bryant ignited scoring fifty-one more points for the comeback win. "He was ticked off," said Lamar Odom. When asked what Bryant talked about during time-outs, he said, "Nothing. That's when you know it's bad."

Even Kobe finds it hard to be specific about how he gets in that ultra-competitive zone. But he knows when he's there that it's best to just shut up and "make it happen."

"When you get in that zone, it's just a supreme confidence that you know it's going in," said Bryant. "It's not a matter of if it's going in. Things just slow down. When that happens, you do not try to focus on what's going on, because you could lose it in a second. Everything is just one noise. You're not paying attention to one noise or the other. You become oblivious to everything that is going on. You don't think about the surroundings or what's going on with the crowd or the team. You have to really try to stay in the present and not let anything break that rhythm." [16]

Through several recent research efforts, Swann and his collaborators are starting to outline this sensation of stepping up when the competitive moment demands it. Working with ten professional golfers, Swann interviewed each within a few days after a significant tournament win. They reported becoming aware of their flow state at different points in the tournament. One golfer commented, "You get so focused on the process and staying in the present and focusing on what you want to do with the golf ball, then that can help you click into it . . . You start hitting some good shots . . . and your confidence rises up a little bit . . . And when you have that confidence you can just get in the zone and start making everything . . . [I]t's just a ton of confidence." [17]

Other phrases, like "Nothing can go wrong . . . you feel things going your way" and "Everything seems to fall into place," signaled entry into the flow zone. But at some point the competitive realization hits an athlete, driving them to excel. Flow helped them play well and now they realize they are in contention to win. This situation awareness led them to create structured, fixed goals on the fly. Kobe was not happy being down by eighteen just as Brady was not willing to accept losing by twenty-five points. One golfer remembered thinking, "I only had three holes left of the tournament to play . . . the three [most] important holes . . . This was it, this was my time now. This is where I can win." This time-limited challenge shifts the athlete's mindset into intense focus knowing they can win.

"It just feels like I'm so focused and nothing else is around me . . . [I]t's just me and the ball . . . [T]hat's it, I don't think about anything else . . . [N]othing else was happening as far as I was concerned," said another golfer.

Feeling like they were onto something, Swann and his team expanded their interviews to athletes in different sports, both team and individual, and at different expertise levels, Olympians to recreational.[18] Similar to the golfers, two different experiences were described. When things are going well, beyond what was expected, athletes spontaneously enter a flow state that reinforces itself with increasing confidence. But when the game is on the line, an athlete who knows she's performing well takes it on herself to get the job done, to "come through in the clutch." While flow can be energizing, clutch efforts can be exhausting. Flow focuses on open goals ("I want to see how fast I can run five kilometers"), while clutch zeroes in on a closed goal ("We must make up a twenty-five-point deficit before the clock expires to win the game").

"Interestingly, athletes also report that they can experience both of these states during the same performance," said Swann. "In some cases, they start well and build into flow, which continues until they realize they can achieve exceptional outcomes and then transition into clutch—consciously giving everything to have the best chance of achieving that outcome." [19]

Swann admits that the discovery of this clutch state was not anticipated but rather emerged as an unexplainable variation from the accepted definition of flow during his athlete interviews. In an interview, we asked him what his reaction was to the data. "It totally took me by surprise. It took a lot of thought and deliberation and critical thinking in order to actually really even see it, to be honest. When analyzing the data, I was saying, 'Okay, there's some similarities here with what I kind of expected.' Then there's the odd thing that doesn't quite match up, and until you reach a tipping point with that, you naturally almost set it aside and focus on what does match up with your expectations. Then it really became that moment where you say, 'Hold on a second there might actually be something else happening here.'

"In fact, we took a pretty rigorous process with it, but it was absolutely not the case that we had any suspicion that this thing [the clutch state] even existed. I was very much a flow researcher and doing a PhD on flow, and to end up with a PhD which proposed something else was a surprise. It feels kind of good that we were able to do that and obviously very interesting for us to actually find out more about it." [20]

But what about that comeback of the century in Super Bowl LI? Was that the ultimate clutch performance? Interestingly, Swann said he saw both clutch and flow from the Patriots, but it hinges on the perspective of the athletes: "I would expect that it absolutely was clutch and it's almost inevitable," he said, interpreting the Super Bowl from afar. "The one thing I come back to is the idea of the objective versus the subjective perceptions of performance. Objectively, yes, it would match up that, according to the definitions, one team choked and one team entered the clutch state.

"From the interviews that I've done with athletes who have won, my best guess is that the Patriots experienced a clutch state followed by a flow state," he continued. "Once they were so far behind with time running out, they have that feeling of urgency that 'we just need to score, we need to get something on the board and get the ball rolling.' I can see how the clutch state would help really drive that initial push to get the first touchdown. Then flow involves this gradual buildup of things that go well. The initial clutch state gives a team a bit of a boost, an injection of confidence, and then once they've got that, it leads into the next phase of play and that goes well. And then another thing goes well, and then all of a sudden they're building momentum, which is again something we see in reoccurrence of flow, to the point that it's almost not in doubt that they're going to win."

Remember Brady's comment to Peter King? "We just needed to execute one drive, and after that drive we'll come to the sidelines and we'll talk about the next drive."

"They build up so much confidence that the performance is going so well that subjectively that experience is much more likely to be a flow state," Swann explained. "If you talk to them about the last five to ten minutes of that game, whether it was really intense pressure and consciously demanding or it was loads of fun with a totally confident feeling like you were going to do it, I would suspect the latter.

"So my take is that once you dig down underneath the objective performance [e.g., the scoreboard], then in situations like that you can get a really cool dynamic perspective of what the experience is actually like. I would speculate that it was that initial push for clutch and then they got themselves into a flow state." [21]

From his research to date, Swann has found that athletes do transition between flow and clutch states. "We consider clutch and flow states as being shortly distinct in that you can't experience both at the same time," said Swann. "Our data so far suggests that it's either one or the other, and we think that because of the situational context in which they occur, so the dynamics of the situation, like I mentioned before, and also the experiential descriptors of the states suggest to us that they are very distinct and can't be experienced at the same time. It's either one or the other. We do see athletes transitioning from one into the next." [22]

Being Creative in 360 Degrees

While Csikszentmihalyi provided the core research on flow decades ago, the concept took on a second life thanks to author Steven Kotler. His 2014 *New York Times* bestselling book, *The Rise of Superman: Decoding the Science of Ultimate Human Performance*,[23] ignited a renewed interest in the use of flow states in sports, specifically action sports in which the consequences of indecision are severe. "To me the greatest example of that is an extreme ski competition," Kotler told us.[24] "These guys hike up this hill, then stand on top of a mountain for hours, in the freezing cold. The chances of them going to the hospital on their way to the bottom of the hill are high. I'm famous for telling people that it's not a sport unless you can break bones on a regular basis. This kind of skiing—no question about it—is a real sport."

Describing a playmaker, Kotler combined the obvious technical skill required with the proper state of mind. "It's similar to the question of 'What is mastery?' Three things come to mind when you say 'playmaker.' First, it is someone in control of their consciousness. Second, the ability to be creative in 360 degrees—not just that they have expertise, but also the ability to use that expertise extremely well. Third, being a playmaker is that very nebulous quality, that ability, in team sports, to lift everybody else up.

"To me, it's possibly a cascade effect. If you have control of your consciousness, you're in the right state of mind to be able to express yourself in 360 degrees and, done properly, this lifts everybody up."

Kotler tries to keep his explanation grounded in neuroscience. "To me a lot of this is actually the question of how quickly can you recruit dopamine and a few other neurochemicals to your situation. If you can move the neurochemicals, everything else seems to follow. It's never as simple as I'm describing it, of course. What I'm giving you is a hacker's view of the mechanism."

After studying skiing, surfing, and other high-speed, high-risk competitions, Kotler agrees there is a victory-focused state that top athletes can switch on. "There is something about clutch performance that is absolutely true. Top performers are in flow so much, they're not bedazzled by it. They know how to use it. There's a lot of information that comes in via that state. That has to be processed completely to be effective. On top of that, there is this ability to turn it on at that moment."

Perhaps the key ingredient to a clutch state is a little more ferocity, the energy to trigger a higher level of performance rather than trying to force the flow state. "The gateway to flow can often be aggression," said Kotler. "You have to be able to tap into that. I think athletes screw this up by taking risks. They choose risk rather than aggression as the gateway into performance. I think you can see that in team sports when athletes will start trying to take bigger chances. Consider basketball players trying to find the rhythm coming down the court. They're not in flow, so they shoot a ridiculous three-point shot just to see if, by taking a big risk, they get lucky and flow is triggered."

The clutch moment may actually be a buildup of years of competitive pressure and a desire to win. Maybe being the 199th pick in the sixth round of the 2000 NFL Draft continues to be a huge chip on the shoulder of Tom Brady. That refusal to succumb to the moment may be at the heart of a clutch breakthrough.

"Just about all successful people are running from something just as fast as they're running toward something. It's this combined motivation that seems to underpin their drive to win," Kotler observed. "Again, it's the habit of ferocity. It's learning to take that thing that is chasing you and use it as motivation. I don't know how to quantify that. It's a different way of processing fear. Top athletes can reframe fear almost automatically as challenged."[25]

In Kotler's latest book, *Stealing Fire: How Silicon Valley, the Navy SEALs, and Maverick Scientists Are Revolutionizing the Way We Live and Work*,[26] written with his longtime collaborator Jamie Wheal, he shares our premise that athletes and their coaches need to understand the brain as the next frontier to train future playmakers. "If you're really interested in high performance, you are going to require a certain level of cognitive literacy, meaning you have to understand what is going on in your brain and your body when you're performing," he said. "We keep trying to train up so-called twenty-first-century skills, like high-speed decision-making, cooperation, and creativity. We can't unlock them by traditional skills training. It doesn't work that way. Instead, we need to be training states of consciousness. That's how you do this."

Avoiding the Chokehold

And then there is the dark side of thrilling victories: the agony of defeat. As part of his recovery process from the Falcons' second-half collapse against the Patriots, head coach Dan Quinn sought some solace from his coaching peers who had similar scars. His support group included Steve Kerr, whose Golden State Warriors squandered a 3–1 series lead in the 2016 NBA Finals to the Cleveland Cavaliers (only to beat the Cavs in 2017); Terry Francona, manager of the Cleveland Indians, victims of the Chicago Cubs' storybook comeback to win the 2016 World Series; and Pete Carroll, head coach of the Seattle Seahawks and Quinn's old boss. In fact, Quinn was on the sideline as Seahawks defensive coordinator during the 2015 Super Bowl when the Seahawks infamously chose to pass from the one-yard line, only to have Malcolm Butler intercept Russell Wilson to seal a Patriots win.

"I wanted to hear their opinion how they handled their team going into the next year," Quinn said. "How do you find a place to put some things mentally where it's hard to find space for a really difficult loss at times?"[27]

Indeed, as victims of remarkable comebacks by their opponents, players and coaches are often labeled "chokers," a harsh term that fans use when describing inexplicable losses, whether they are major mistakes on a single play or a disappointing performance in a series-ending loss. But researchers who study human performance prefer to reserve the word for a specific type of poor result. Dr. Sian Beilock, current president of Barnard College and formerly head of the Human Performance Lab[28] at the University of Chicago, helped define choking in sport in a classic 2001 paper with Dr. Thomas Carr, psychology professor at Michigan State University.

"Choking, or performing more poorly than expected given one's level of skill, tends to occur in situations fraught with performance pressure," they wrote.[29] In other words, your past results would indicate that you have all of the skills necessary for the big game. But when the heat was on, something went wrong, causing you to make mistakes and underperform. This is different from being in a slump, which is a longer-term period of poor results that are not tied to a pressure-packed moment.

So, when the game is on the line, performing above expectations is perceived by the player as a clutch state, but failing to execute to your potential ends in this frustrating, anxiety-ridden choke state. At halftime of Super Bowl LI, quarterback Matt Ryan and the Falcons must have been feeling pretty confident if not in a full flow state with their surprising control of the game. In the Patriots locker room, however, a sense of choking surely was in the air, even though none of the players would admit it after the game. To watch players and teams flip-flop so dramatically within a sixty-minute timeframe provides a microcosm of the clutch/choking continuum.

Looking at the tale of two halves in that game, according to the scoreboard, it would seem that choking and clutch states are polar opposites on the game performance scale. But Dr. Swann suggests that it is the athlete's perspective that is the key caveat. "One critical difference that I see is really about how performance is defined. So choking is obviously worse performance under pressure. Clutch performance typically is considered to be better or enhanced performance under pressure. Talking to athletes, really the most important thing for them and for the experience of these states is the subjective perception of their performance. It's not the objective things that go on a scoreboard that matter in terms of them experiencing some clutch." [30]

But what causes this meltdown of motor skills? More important, can athletes and coaches take steps to avoid it? Maybe because of the negative consequences of poor performances, there is an abundance of theories and research trying to identify where the breakdown occurs. As skill acquisition studies have taught us, elite playmakers are master multitaskers, monitoring their environment at a higher cognitive level while the ongoing operation of technical skills is managed by automated processes. It's how we're able to hold a conversation, think about next week's game, and sing along with the radio—all while driving a car. The micro adjustments to the steering wheel, acceleration, braking, and navigation all happen at a subconscious level, freeing up our attention and focus for higher-order tasks.

Similarly, dribbling a basketball, stick handling a puck, and keeping a lacrosse ball in the webbing happen without our continuous awareness. Adding tactical decisions to the mix also becomes a well-practiced neural mechanism. A quarterback working through his progression of available receivers, or a midfielder "checking her shoulders" to monitor the locations of teammates and opponents, is preprogrammed, almost mechanical, in emotionless scrimmages during the week.

Then it's game time. Add the distractions of the fans, the expectations, the fear of failure, and the pressure to win to the mix, and a player's brain can be quickly overloaded with external stimuli and internal noise. Think of driving 70 miles per hour on an open freeway versus 15 miles per hour in stop-and-go city traffic. Cruising along frees up the brain's capacity to think, while congestion forces full attention to the whims of aggressive drivers surrounding your car. Your brain's available bandwidth must be divided between competing tasks. In fact, according to one theory, it is these distractions associated with game situations that can cause athletes to split their attention between the tactical/technical mix they need to execute and the interference coming from the outside, competitive environment. This so-called distraction theory of choking centers on the role of working memory in the brain and its finite capacity to hold information for a short time. If a hockey player is charging up the ice, managing the puck, and searching for passing options while eluding defenders, chances are that his working memory is near capacity. But then if a coach, fan, or parent shouts at him or he allows the memory of a bad pass five minutes ago to enter his consciousness, his working memory will be split, reducing his attention and possibly causing a mistake.

On the other hand, if we believe that sports skills become ingrained in our neural networks to the point of being automatic, then the need for working memory during a game should be minimized. "Specifically, the types of high-level motor skills that have been the subject of the majority of choking research in sport (e.g., well-learned golf putting, baseball batting, soccer dribbling) are thought to become proceduralized with practice. Proceduralized skills do not require constant online attentional control and are in fact thought to run largely outside of working memory,"[31] wrote Beilock with Rob Gray, PhD, associate professor of human systems engineering and director of the Perception and Action Lab at Arizona State University.

They proposed an alternative and opposite theory of choking, claiming we actually focus too much on the task when we're under pressure. Indeed, the "explicit monitoring theory" says that game pressure takes us out of this well-practiced state, making us nervous that the penalty shot or free throw or field goal will be missed. Instead of a fluid, practiced free-throw motion, a stressed basketball player may now start thinking about her grip on the ball or choose a different focus point on the rim or observe her arm angle at follow-through. This "dechunking" of the composite skill sets her back to when she was a novice just learning the correct form, along with a novice's success rate.

"Explicit monitoring and distraction theories essentially make opposite predictions regarding how pressure exerts its impact," Beilock and Gray noticed. "Whereas distraction theories suggest that pressure shifts needed attention away from execution, explicit monitoring theories suggest that pressure shifts too much attention to skill execution processes."[32]

Beilock actually put the two theories head-to-head in a soccer ball dribbling experiment.[33] Skilled players were asked to dribble around cones under two different skill conditions. First, while managing the ball at their feet, they needed to monitor an audio cue, causing a working memory split as proposed in distraction theory. Then they were asked to keep track of which side of their feet most recently touched the ball, forcing them to focus on a component part of their dribbling meta-program. As predicted by the explicit monitoring theory, the players performed poorly in the second test when they disrupted their internalized skill routine. Splitting their working memory by listening for an audio cue did not affect their dribbling skill.

Gray, a pioneer in baseball hitting research, tried the same experiment with collegiate players at the plate.[34] First, while swinging during a batting exercise, they were asked to monitor a tone and report if it was high or low frequency, an external dual task. Next, a tone would play randomly during their swings and the batters had to report if their bats were moving upward or downward when the tone sounded, a skill-focused condition. As with the soccer players, the hitters' performance remained unchanged from the baseline in the external dual task situation but declined when they were asked to think about their swings.

But what about the pressure variable? Choking is below-par performance under stressful conditions. In an intriguing twist, Gray tweaked the competitive nature of these Division 1 athletes by adding what every broke college athlete needs, a monetary incentive. Half of the players were told that they had been partnered up with another player, and if the two of them combined could improve their hitting success in the two drills by a certain amount, they would both get a nice little payout. To add the joys of peer pressure, each player was told that his buddy had already hit the improvement target and now it was up to him. Compared to the control group, who were not put under any competitive pressure, the batting performance of the test group dropped significantly after being given the incentive. In other words, they choked. (And don't worry, NCAA, no one earned the small cash reward.)

While this inward focus can affect sport-specific technical skills, it can also degrade athlete cognition, including pattern recognition, reaction time, and decision-making. A confident quarterback decides and executes a pass instantly on instinct, but when under pressure he may focus inward, second-guessing himself even for a split second and causing an ill-timed interception. In a downward spiral of errors and uncertainty, the performance throughout the game deteriorates into choking.

So what's the Heimlich maneuver to save choking athletes? Practicing like they play, including the pressure element, allows developing athletes to learn to deal with the urge to refocus their attention. Simulating crowd noise, introducing competitive incentives, and filming scrimmages help them adapt to life in a fishbowl, making the transition to game day less abrupt. But what if the initial skill acquisition process could avoid this reliance on step-by-step instruction altogether? If stressful situations cause athletes to backtrack to thinking about individual pieces of a skill, then what if they learned the whole movement naturally? When we learned to walk, our parents didn't instruct us on right-left-right-left, proper arm swing, and balance. We just kept trying the whole process. When we first rode a bike, we relied on our brains to orchestrate pedaling, balance, and direction without explicit instructions or disassembled processes. This implicit learning depended solely on trial and error of the composite skill set: either you stayed upright on your bike or you crashed. But once you experienced the joy of conquering the task, it was never forgotten.

"In this type of learning, the goal is to keep performance 'automatic' throughout the entire skill acquisition process as deliberate efforts are made to limit controlled processing during execution; e.g., by reducing the availability of information-processing resources through the use of secondary task loading," Gray writes.[35]

Despite a hectic academic schedule of research and teaching at ASU, Gray has created a fascinating resource for athletes and coaches to explore so many of the topics we discuss in this book. Celebrating its two-year anniversary, the Perception Action podcast[36] gets today's sports science research out from behind journal paywalls and into an understandable context where it can be used by those who need it most. When we caught up with Rob, we asked him if the explicit monitoring theory of choking was still the leader in the clubhouse.

"Yes, most of the data we're seeing still agrees with that side. It's not just monitoring movements; there's more to it with different levels of components. Becoming self-conscious of what you're doing motivationally, emotionally, and cognitively in terms of motor performance seems to be a better fit with the data on why athletes choke. Some researchers are beginning to argue that the dichotomy between the two [explicit monitoring and distraction] theories is not the best way to think about it, but I still believe that's what is happening. We take this well-learned automatic skill and then try to exert this control over it because the situation is so important."

Instead of thinking of a clutch state as the opposite of choking, Gray argues that clutch performances are simply doing what is expected under pressure. "I believe that clutch is doing the same thing that you always do. Clutch is being normal and not choking. The hardest thing that an athlete has to learn, and why teams may have to get to the playoffs a few times before they succeed, is to not do anything different in big games. There's a reason you got there. So there's no elevation of performance, just maintaining it."

By not panicking or trying to do too much, the Patriots were able to rely on their experience and collective skills to eventually reach their expected level of excellence. In the end, they learned how to compete.

"We just kept trying to find a little crack in the armor and keep plugging away," said head coach Belichick. "Our team showed great mental toughness throughout the game, never really flinched even though the score was_____ I guess for so long that we just kept plugging along, just kept fighting, just kept trying to make plays."[37]

DOC Z'S BRAIN WAVES PART 3: KIDS HAVE EMOTIONS, TOO

In Part Two, we introduced the athlete cognition cycle of searching, deciding, and executing as part of the playmaker's cognition. Now, in Part Three, we need to discuss a related component of cognitive neuroscience: the playmaker's commitment, what some would term "emotional neuroscience," when different brain mechanisms operate. However, it is important that we recognize that these two neuro processes are intricately linked. In fact, our thoughts have an influence on our emotions, and our emotions have an influence on our actions or, in the case of sports, our motor skills. We can all think of instances when a single thought got us excited with feelings of either love or hate. These feelings then impact on what we do or how we act. Our actions can then give rise to different thoughts that may perhaps alter our feelings or emotions. This rather simplified feedback system repeats continuously throughout our day but certainly within an athlete's competitive life.

The neural mechanisms by which the brain communicates with the central and peripheral nervous systems, the autonomic nervous system, and the muscular system involves electrical impulses that signal the release of neurotransmitter substances such as acetylcholine, dopamine, noradrenaline, adrenaline, histamine, and serotonin. In addition to having neurotransmitters impacting our thoughts, feelings, and actions, we have circulating hormones such as testosterone and cortisol that have reciprocal interactions with our thoughts, feelings, actions, and motor responses.

Concepts like mindset are not distinctly part of the thinking portion of the brain nor uniquely part of the emotional part of the brain. Nevertheless, it is important to point out that the "emotional brain" goes a bit deeper into the human brain and is part of the brain anatomy we call the limbic system, with the main processing center being a small organ called the amygdala. The rather recent popular ideas of "positive psychology" championed by Martin Seligman at the University of Pennsylvania, and "emotional intelligence" popularized by Daniel Goleman, are excellent examples of a healthy integration of the cognitive and emotional systems of the brain. Although the constructs of positive psychology and, in particular, emotional intelligence have been criticized in academic circles, they have gained substantial traction in sport leadership development as well as athlete training.

In 2009, while at Boston University, I was approached by a mental-skills trainer from an English Premier League soccer club, an NCAA head soccer coach, and an American venture capitalist to provide advice on how it might be possible to accurately measure Carol Dweck's recent portrayal of "mindset" and the important concept of "mental toughness" in young athletes aspiring to become world-class soccer players. Their start-up company was convinced that mental toughness and mindset were the primary psychological discriminants of future playmakers in young athletes. I agreed that they were important psychological attributes for young athletes; however, they were not the only psychological constructs in this complex world of cognitive neuroscience.

Briefly, this endeavor led to a doctoral dissertation by Dr. Mark Stonkus.[38] Mark developed a new "mental toughness" scale called the Inventory of Mental Toughness Factors in Sport (IMTF-S) that consisted of four factors measured by forty-eight items. The IMTF-S had high overall reliability as well as excellent concurrent, construct, and predictive validity. I subsequently did further analysis of the data to specifically measure mindset, something that had not been done previously.

In my position as psychologist and sport scientist with the Vancouver Canucks, I measured both mindset and mental toughness with approximately two hundred eighteen-year-old hockey players eligible for the 2011 and 2012 NHL draft. I used the IMTF-S inventory, which included a mindset factor. Examples of statements that the players rated were "I need to be born with talent to be successful at hockey" and "Hard work involving planning will always develop me at hockey." Players were asked to rate their opinion on a Likert scale using these five descriptors: strongly disagree, disagree, neutral, agree, and strongly agree. I would also ask this simple question, "Athletic ability is ____ percent natural talent and ____ percent effort/practice." These data were then shared with Dave Gagner, director of player development, as well as the Canucks scouting staff in preparation for profiling players for the NHL draft.

You can appreciate why the Canucks were looking for eighteen-year-old hockey players with a self-reported growth mindset that I later confirmed through interviews. They wanted athletes who genuinely believed they could grow their abilities rather than being fixed by their genetic heritage. They embraced challenges as opposed to avoiding them. They persisted in the face of setbacks rather than give up. They saw effort as the pathway to mastery. They learned from constructive criticism rather than ignoring it. And they found inspiration in the success of others rather than feeling threatened by the success of others.

Some of what makes up the construct of mindset is clearly related to mental toughness or what Dr. Angela Duckworth popularized as "grit." Others, like Dr. Suzanne Kobasa, use the term "hardiness" to describe a personality characteristic that enables some individuals to put high-stress situations into perspective and cognitively interpret them as less threatening.

Several years after Mark and I worked at defining and measuring mental toughness, Dr. Duckworth published her book *Grit: The Power of Passion and Perseverance* (2016), as well as the "Grit Scale." "Grit" has historically been a term used by coaches and athletes in the world of sport. But it is merely a four-letter word used to describe another equally used term: mental toughness. Today, the IMTF-S continues to be used as a research tool and as an assessment of mental toughness in athletes. Although some educators and psychologists argue that "mental toughness" cannot be trained, Stonkus and I both contest this position. Since nobody has discovered a gene for mental toughness, we maintain that mental toughness can indeed be trained. As director of performance at Saint Andrew's School in Boca Raton, Florida, Mark has successfully implemented mental toughness training with his students as well as with elite and aspiring elite athletes.

Ed Viesturs, a seven-time conqueror of Mount Everest and successful author on mountaineering, is someone I brought to Vancouver to share his mental toughness stories with the Canucks. Viesturs accurately sums up Duckworth's book with this quote: "Grit teaches that life's high peaks aren't necessarily conquered by the naturally nimble but, rather, by those willing to endure, wait out the storm, and try again." [39]

So, whether we call this grit, mental toughness, hardiness, or some other term, the reality is that we are referring to the ability to self-regulate or control your stressors, maintain concentration, believe in yourself, be determined, handle pressure and failures, stay motivated and committed, and have a growth mindset. That's it!

On Practice

We were delighted to speak with my friend and colleague Dr. K. Anders Ericsson of Florida State University, who coined the term "deliberate practice" over thirty years ago. As we try to explain, the main message from his research is that the practice of any skill needs to be "deliberate": highly structured, specifically designed to improve performance, increasingly challenging, and requiring a great deal of effort that takes the performer out of her comfort zone. Whether the process and progression to world-class status takes 1,000 or 10,000 hours is a red herring. It is the method of practice and training that produces results at different rates across different athletes.

After years of observing and spending hours talking to the great basketball coaches, like Arnold "Red" Auerbach and John Wooden, I am convinced that they used deliberate practice principles but just didn't have a name for it at the time. For example, Coach Wooden shared with me the story, told to many, of how he had his UCLA Bruins "deliberately practice" putting their socks on as they prepared for their first practice. Now this is indeed pretty deliberate but this "sock skill" enabled his athletes to engage in intense practice sessions and not develop blisters.

Wooden, building on his planning skills as an English teacher in Indiana, wrote detailed lesson plans for his practices and kept them in a file so he could look back at them a season or two later. How many coaches are that deliberate in structuring their practices? But it was this precise planning and expertise as a teacher that made John Wooden teams consistently great. "The Wizard of Westwood," as John Wooden was affectionately described, won ten NCAA basketball championships in his twelve years at UCLA, including seven in a row with an .804 winning percentage. This record of success plus his other impeccable credentials rightfully earned him the title of "Coach of the Century."

Ericsson's deliberate practice research has heightened our sensitivity to the importance of practice in achieving outstanding performance. But several questions remain: What do we practice? How do we design practices? How frequently should we practice? How long do we practice? Do we really have to practice 10,000 hours to become world champions? Is that all there is? When discussing long-term athlete development, sport organizations around the world often write about "pillars" that need to be developed in athletes. These pillars include: technical (ball handling, tackling), tactical (patterns of play), physical (strength and conditioning), mental (performing under pressure; controlling anxiety), and leadership. Deliberate practice design can span all of the pillars as a foundational concept.

Almost thirty years ago I was a director of coaching for a youth hockey organization in Massachusetts. Recently, one of the coaches in the program was cleaning out his attic and found a folder of coaching documents, many of them copies of memos I sent to coaches and parents. And there to refresh my memory were detailed explanations about team selection procedures, fundamental skills the coaches would be teaching, as well as the rationale for all of it. Nowhere did I mention tactical strategies such as how to kill penalties, exploring breakout options, or how to coach the power play. Rather, emphasis was placed on improving skating skills and puck handling skills by using cross ice, tight areas during practice.

I urged them to use "over-speed training," a concept developed by Dr. Jack Blatherwick, a physiologist and hockey coach from Minnesota who has had a strong influence on many hockey coaches at all levels.[40] Youngsters were asked to do drills, skating as fast as they could to the point where they fell down (from loss of balance, not exhaustion). Falling was not viewed as failure but rather a realization and awareness of what their body could do at that time. With further over-speed practice, the youngsters would master hockey moves at their highest possible speed. I recall parents objecting to what for them were strange and unusual practices that they had never witnessed before. But Coach Mike Sullivan of the Pittsburgh Penguins recently told me he experienced similar parental objections when he coached his son in a youth hockey program on Boston's South Shore. Today's USA Hockey coaching guidelines for long-term player development utilize most of the deliberate practice concepts I tried to introduce over thirty years ago, with only modest success. Eventually, sound principles, based on science, for coaching youth player development will become the standard.

For preteen athletes, the goals of practice should be to emphasize fundamental movement skills followed by the specific motor skills essential to the sport they are playing. As they mature into their teen years, the emphasis of practice should gradually shift to learning more of the technical and tactical areas of the sport.

But where do we teach the cognitive and emotional pillar—or, more generally, psychology—of a sport, and how is this done? My early research[41] demonstrated that youth as young as six years old could effectively learn proper breathing techniques to self-regulate stress responses they experienced in competition. Coaches in youth sport programs should seize the opportunity to teach fundamental mental skills to this age group in a deliberate manner. Children love the exercises, already understand the pressure situations of youth sport, and soak up this information like sponges. Mastering mental skills at a young age through deliberate practice will help ensure mastery of the major pillars of athlete development. You do not have to be in high school or college to learn how to effectively use imagery, learn how to concentrate more effectively, develop self-confidence, and develop a growth mindset and mental toughness or grit. Simple concepts like over-speed training and imagery can be applied to develop the future playmaker's cognitive system.

On Competition

"Choking" is a term that may be misunderstood and overused by parents and coaches. For example, when an athlete loses a one-on-one battle, it does not necessarily mean they choked or performed below what was expected of them based on their past performances. Consider this game scenario: the bases are loaded, two out in the ninth inning, a 3-2 count, and the relief pitcher strikes out the batter. Some reporters and fans will say the batter choked, when in fact it was a perfectly located "clutch" pitch that was unhittable. Another example may be a penalty shot in soccer or hockey. If the player scored, some would say the goaltender choked. But again, it may have been a perfectly located shot.

Early in my career, I urged sport psychologists, coaches, and athletes to consider using biofeedback technology—sometimes referred to as applied psychophysiology—to help athletes self-regulate stress responses. Athletes, like all performers, experience stress and performance anxiety in competition, resulting in a performance that is below expectations. Biofeedback uses sensors placed on the body to record biological functions such as heart rate, respiration rate, muscle tension, skin temperature, sweat response, and brain wave activity. Without the use of recording sensors, an athlete has no idea what his heart rate or respiration might be. The sensors allow data to be collected and processors feed these values back (biofeedback) to the athlete through a visual or auditory display. The athlete, with practice, can now learn how to be in their optimal zone of physiological arousal.

The early psychophysiology research allowed us to learn a great deal about the role of the central nervous system and autonomic nervous system in athlete performance, but few of us actually engaged in practical clinical use of biofeedback in sport organizations. Colleagues like Dr. John Crampton in Australia and Dr. Sue Wilson in Canada were avid proponents of using biofeedback in their work with athletes. Dr. Bruno Demichelis, an Italian sport psychologist, developed perhaps the first large-scale application of biofeedback training for elite athletes at

AC Milan with his "MilanLab" and "Mindroom." He later followed coach Carlo Ancelotti to England and imported his Mindroom concept to Chelsea FC. But this applied science was ahead of its time, and too many of my sport psychology colleagues felt uncomfortable using it.

Fast-forward to 2012, when I was invited by the editor of the *Journal of Clinical Sport Psychology* to be a guest editor for a special volume we called *Psychophysiology and Neuroscience in Sport*.[42] My goal with this book was to educate sport psychologists and scientists about advances in the use of cognitive neuroscience tools and say, "Look at what you are missing."

The five research papers from this volume, plus rapid advances in micro technology, started an international movement that began to truly bring psychophysiology and cognitive neuroscience to sport. Shortly thereafter, the United States Olympic Committee hired one of my doctoral students, Lindsay Shaw Thornton, to bring psychophysiology training to Olympians at the USOC training facility in Colorado Springs.

Meanwhile outside the world of sport, the medical profession in particular jumped all over advances in neuroscience technology. The development of brain scanning or imaging technology brought wonderful revelations of brain mechanisms in disease and healthy states. No longer did we have to refer to the brain as the "black box." We could actually see, in real time, what was happening in the brain when we engaged in specific thoughts and emotions and executed a movement. In the 1960s we used computerized axial tomography (CAT) scans, followed by positron-emission tomography (PET) scans in the 1980s. Magnetic resonance imaging (MRI) scans arrived in the 1990s, while functional magnetic resonance imaging (fMRI) is now the standard brain-imaging tool.

In 2005, Dr. Hap Davis, a private practice psychologist in Calgary, Alberta, and head sport psychologist for Swimming Canada, developed a hypothesis that athlete affect or mood was directly related to performance. In fact, he believed that management of mood was the most important requisite for expert championship performance. His hypothesis developed from observations and assessments he made with swimmers who failed to make the 2004 Canadian Olympic team. A significant percentage of these athletes developed prolonged negative affects/moods to the point where he assessed them as being clinically depressed—not a condition you want with world-class athletes. He connected with two specialists in depression research: Dr. Helen Mayberg, who at that time was at McGill University; and Dr. Mario Liotti, at Simon Fraser University in Vancouver, British Columbia. Being neuroscientists, but with little familiarity in high-performance sport, they suggested that Dr. Davis do a study utilizing fMRI brain scanning. Generous supporters of Swimming Canada funded the research, and the results of this first study were published in *Brain Imaging and Behavior.*[43]

In the study, swimmers entered the full-body MRI scanner and viewed a neutral video of swimming as well as their own personal underperformance. Watching their disappointing swims triggered relatively high levels of activity in the prefrontal cortex and the amygdala, the emotional centers of the brain, as well as low levels of activity in the motor cortices, where movements are executed. Dr. Davis did a brief cognitive behavioral intervention with the athletes that consisted of slow deep breathing, which helped the swimmers control their emotions, and an analysis of what they had to do to improve their next performances. Now, brimming with renewed belief and confidence in their abilities, they returned to the fMRI scanner to be reassessed. The earlier decrease in blood flow to the prefrontal and motor cortices had reversed and the emotional centers returned to a more normal state.

Finally, sport researchers now had the opportunity to use state-of-the-art medical research tools to answer what previously were "black box" questions. Fascinated with this new approach, I invited Dr. Davis to do some follow-up research[44] with collegiate swimmers at Boston University, where an fMRI laboratory had just been created. Our goal was to confirm the relationship between mood and performance and that activation occurred in the prefrontal, anterior cingulate, amygdala, and limbic areas of the brain during negative moods.

As part of the fMRI protocol, swimmers viewed photos of themselves published in the university newspaper and directly below the photo, a list of positive or negative adjectives describing themselves (e.g., "confident" or "tense"). After rating their emotions, the athletes were asked to do a vertical squat jump that was measured by the Optojump apparatus, a simple device that gave accurate measures of jump height and energy output. We found that athletes identified as "successful" showed significantly more positive affect and greater jump height and power when they viewed images of themselves and focused on positive mood adjectives. So having a positive mood state rather than a negative one results in increased performance, even in a simple jumping task.[45]

Genetics and the Playmaker

Throughout the book we bring up the important question of how a young man or woman becomes a playmaker. The predominant evidence clearly points to the importance of athlete nurturance and less so to the impact of nature or genetic explanations.

However, after we told friends and neighbors unconnected with the world of academia and sports about this book, they still expressed the belief that genetic factors explain playmaker skills. They point to the examples of young, talented athletes with one or both parents excelling in sports, like the Howe family in hockey, the Griffey and Bonds families in baseball, the Long and Manning families in football, and the Curry and Irving families in basketball. But this is hardly scientific evidence in support of the athletic gene. During our discussions, I found that these fans failed to realize the incredible supportive nurturing environments these sons and daughters have by being part of a professional sport culture and the advantages this provides them over their peer groups.

Is it possible that there is a genetic explanation for athletic greatness? Are genes even a small part of the explanation? Yes, there is a possibility that inherited genes contribute to athletic excellence. We are not all born equally in so many ways, so we all start with different baselines of sporting ability: in physique, physiological capacity, motor control, and perceptual-cognitive abilities. But I base my opinion on the research of sport genetics researchers such as Claude Bouchard, Yannis Pitsiladis, and others. Pitsiladis, who has spent a lifetime searching for the sporting gene, wrote in the prestigious *Routledge Handbook of Sport Expertise*: "The first positive findings from ongoing genome-wide associated studies (GWASs) involving world-class athletes will provide the first tangible evidence of genetic predisposition to elite human performance."[46]

So, like Ponce de León's search for the fountain of youth, the search for the playmaker gene continues.

Epilogue: Preparing Future Playmakers

"The vision of a champion is someone who is bent over, drenched in sweat, at the point of exhaustion when no one else is watching."
—ANSON DORRANCE[1]

At the 2016 What Drives Winning Conference, a gathering of elite and emerging sport coaches trying to answer the question posed by the conference's name, Anson Dorrance told the story behind his famous quote about the "vision of a champion" that opens Mia Hamm's 1999 autobiography. As Hamm's head coach at the University of North Carolina (UNC) and the U.S. Women's National Team (USWNT), it was Dorrance who knew that Hamm was destined for greatness the first time he saw her playing in a Texas tournament when she was fourteen. Years ago he described her determination, after glimpsing it for the first time, as "an uncanny ability to go through defenders, as if by molecular displacement." Sure, the raw speed was there—"she had the best acceleration of any soccer player I had ever seen," Dorrance said—but she also had an assassin's calm demeanor: "She had skill and composure. I knew she'd be on the national team. It was just a matter of when."[2]

As a Hall of Fame college coach for the last thirty-nine years,

Dorrance has won more than eight hundred games, with a winning percentage of 90.7; twenty-two national championships; and the inaugural Women's World Cup in 1991.[3] Having mentored hundreds of young women over the years, it is Hamm whom he continues to hold up as the best example of the ultimate competitor and playmaker. During his conference talk, he described a remarkable encounter on one of his early-morning commutes to campus in 1994, Hamm's senior year at Chapel Hill. "It's late winter, early spring. It's cold out and I'm ripping through the park, and all of a sudden, out of the corner of my eye, I can see this figure going five and back, ten and back, fifteen and back, twenty and back, twenty-five and back, and this is our grueling fitness exercise that we call 'cones.' And I'm looking out there and I pull over and I'm just watching and I'm thinking, 'Oh my gosh, that's Mia.' And in between sprints, you can see her bent over and sweat is just flying off her brow, with hot air shooting from her lungs. And I was just so impressed with what I saw, I drove into work, I scribbled a note to her, and I forgot about it.

"Ten years later, after Mia had become world-famous, she wrote a book, called *Go for the Goal*, and she sent me that book. There in the breastplate of that book was the note that I'd written her. 'The vision of a champion is someone who is bent over, drenched in sweat, at the point of exhaustion when no one else is watching.' The final measure of athletic greatness is not what you do in the training session with your peers and teammates, it's basically what you do on your own . . . [Of] all the incredible gifts I've been given by my players over the years, this was the absolute most heartfelt."[4]

For today's generation of girls (and plenty of boys) who are more familiar with soccer stars like Abby Wambach, Alex Morgan, and Carli Lloyd, Mia Hamm was the first true superstar of women's soccer. In fact, in 2003, on the fiftieth anniversary of the Atlantic Coast Conference, known for its rich history of championship teams, its greatest male and female athletes were named, with Michael Jordan and Hamm topping their respective lists.[5] When FIFA, the world governing body of soccer, celebrated their one hundredth anniversary in 2004, they asked Pelé, the Brazilian legend, to compile a list of the 125 best players of all time. Hamm and Michelle Akers, her U.S. teammate, made Pelé's final cut as the only two women and the only Americans on the list. "When I came up with the names Mia Hamm and the midfielder Michelle Akers, everyone was a little surprised," he said. "But women's football in the world is very important."[6]

Unlike pure goal scorers, Hamm was the complete playmaker, even though she played forward for much of her career. Best known for her 158 international goals, which still rank her third all-time, more than a decade after her retirement, she is still the all-time career-assists leader. With 144 assists in 276 international games, she averaged more than one every two games over her seventeen seasons.[7] With four NCAA championships, two Olympic gold medals, two FIFA World Cups and two FIFA World Player of the Year awards, Hamm could be forgiven for enjoying her fame, but her teammates only talk about her team-first attitude.

"Everyone knows what Mia did as an athlete," said Julie Foudy, her longtime USWNT teammate. "You know about her successes and awards as the best female soccer player in the world. But it's her refreshingly sincere selflessness—in everything she does—that helped make her an icon. And that is the essence of Mia.

"This unselfishness, her willingness to deflect and graciously thank others, is what I will always cherish the most when I think of Mia's many qualities. Because her way of doing things showed her teammates, along with millions of girls and boys and grown-ups, that success is about working your tail off, motivating others to join you and celebrating others when the focus could be on you."[8]

Upon breaking Hamm's goal-scoring record in 2013, Abby Wambach said, "When I look in the mirror I don't see a person who's made the kind of impact that Mia Hamm made on the game. She's still my idol, the greatest player and the greatest teammate. She achieved so much in so many different ways. What she did for women's soccer can't be measured."[9]

Today, Hamm is teaching the next wave of playmakers through her aptly named Team First Soccer Academy, along with her longtime teammates and friends Kristine Lilly and Tisha Venturini Hoch. In fact, the three-pronged philosophy of their camps is to be a personality, a playmaker, and a factor: "Personality creates a player that knows how to excel individually but still be a team player. Playmakers play unselfishly and create for themselves and their teammates. When you become a factor on the field, you make a difference for yourself and for your team."[10]

Now, as a mom of three kids with former all-star shortstop Nomar Garciaparra, Hamm sees life as an athlete from a different perspective, the sideline. While she understands a parent's drive to help their kids succeed, she advocates letting them learn on their own. "Resist the urge to make excuses for your kids," she recently told an audience of sports parents. "They look up to you. They are so vulnerable after a defeat. They don't need to hear, 'Oh, my, if Suzie had just passed the ball to you.' Or, 'If that ref had a clue. Somebody needs to talk to him.'" Instead, she asks parents to set the right example about the joy of sports with encouragement. "'I'm so happy watching you play,'" suggests Hamm. "When they're extremely vulnerable, that is your opportunity to set a better standard for them. I think what you're trying to do as a parent is take the pain away, make them feel better. You kind of get locked into that rather than what example you are setting for them." [11]

Growing up, she was never singled out for her performance by her parents. "Nobody made me feel different or strange," she said. "That acceptance meant everything. I thought, 'This is normal. This is wonderful. Why not want to be as good as you can be?'" [12] Indeed, "that acceptance" is needed by every young player—by their coach, by their teammates, and by their parents. It helped Mia thirty years ago and it is still works with today's generation of playmakers. Meet Mallory and Christian.

The Next Mia Hamm

"My parents were always super supportive and helpful and understood everything that I was going through," said Mallory Pugh, who, at age nineteen, wears the thousand-pound yoke of being called "the next Mia Hamm." [13] For other promising players, the burden of high expectations has been too much to bear, but Pugh's parents, like Hamm's, know that a child's athletic talent is no different from their academic or artistic talent. Expose them to new opportunities and let them thrive in whatever direction their passion takes them. As we heard from Brad Stevens, the rush to specialize in just one sport before the age of thirteen is just not necessary and may be counterproductive to excelling later, "in large part, because I think that you figure out what your passion is truly for as you get older." The Pugh family followed that formula for both of their daughters. "They were little and you just tried everything, and [soccer] is what stuck," said Karen Pugh. "Like throwing spaghetti against the wall, it stuck." [14]

And just like her older sister, Brianna, who starred at the high school, club, and college levels, Mallory showed early interest in soccer. Always with a ball at her feet, she would offer unsolicited coaching advice to her sister's team from the sidelines or watch entire U.S. national team games on her Hello Kitty television, broadcast in Spanish on Telemundo. Even though her parents kept throwing that spaghetti at the wall, having their girls try basketball and track, it was soccer that lit the fuse, despite any parental preferences. "I loved watching her run track," said Mrs. Pugh, a former prep track star.[15]

Even at a young age, Mallory's playmaker qualities began to emerge, at least to a trained eye, but those elusive cognitive skills take time to develop. "Having done this for so long, you think there's potential there," said Jared Spires, her U11-to-U12 coach at Real Colorado soccer club. "You see special qualities but I don't think there was any way of envisioning she would do it quite like this."[16] Indeed, as we learned earlier, talent identification can be messy, unpredictable, and difficult to measure, which is why the love of playing needs to be allowed over the love of winning at those fragile young ages.

After leading her Mountain Vista High School team to a state championship as a freshman, Mallory exploded on the international stage with the U.S. U17 national team in 2013, then advanced up to the U20 team where she led all scorers and was named the best player at the 2015 CONCACAF (Confederation of North, Central American and Caribbean Association Football) U20 Women's Championship. At seventeen she captained the team at the 2016 FIFA U20 Women's World Cup, scoring two goals against some of the top female competition in the world, who were as much as three years older.

Having impressed Jill Ellis, the USWNT head coach, she was called up to the senior team for winter training. "There's ice in her veins," said Ellis about Pugh. Playing alongside women she had grown up idolizing, Pugh, still seventeen, was in awe. "This was different than what I was used to," said Pugh. "I was nervous, oh yeah. I remembered walking into the meal room and just seeing everyone and just thinking, 'oh my gosh, this is so weird.' " [17] But Ellis had seen the calm fury of a playmaker. "She doesn't get rattled, she's very competitive, always has a big smile on her face. She's having fun. She's enjoying it." [18]

Later that month, during the second half of a friendly game (a soccer euphemism for "non-tournament") against Ireland, Ellis substituted star forward Alex Morgan in favor of Pugh, making her the youngest player to play for the USWNT since 2005. In the eighty-third minute, Pugh made history again. The U.S. team was attacking with forward Christen Press slicing through the right side of the Irish defense. Nearing the end line, Press instinctively chipped the ball to the front of the goal, assuming that the precocious seventeen-year-old would probably be close by. Seeing the play develop in front of her, Pugh had already made the decision to make a diagonal run toward Press, splitting two defenders. Her forehead met the ball in flight, redirecting it 90 degrees to the left of the Irish goalkeeper and into the back of the net. Knowing that she had just joined the exclusive "first game, first goal" club, she raced over to Press to celebrate. "I don't really remember how the goal happened," said Pugh. "It was so fast, but I do remember not even looking to see if it went in. I just heard the crowd go crazy and I ran straight to Press. The fact that she scored on her first cap and I did too . . . I could just tell when I hugged her that she understood what had happened." [19]

Ellis took a calculated chance by adding Pugh to the reduced eighteen-player roster for the 2016 Rio Olympics. "On the field, she's still continuing to learn there, but because of her technique and her IQ, I think she's adjusted very quickly. Now it's just more and more experience against these top, top teams. She's special." [20] Others in the soccer world were starting to take notice as well. After watching her score a dazzling goal against Costa

Rica in a final tune-up game before heading to Brazil, none other than Mia Hamm tweeted, "Speed kills but technical speed absolutely annihilates defenders. Mallory Pugh is for real."[21] In Rio, Pugh delivered once again, playing almost two hundred minutes in three games and becoming the youngest U.S. woman to score in the Olympics.

Two weeks before her nineteenth birthday, Pugh announced her decision to go pro, leaving behind what would surely have been a stellar college career at UCLA, to play for the National Women's Soccer League's Washington Spirit. The irony was not lost on Spirit head coach Jim Gabarra that, sixteen years before, Mia Hamm signed her first professional contract with another D.C. women's pro team, the Washington Freedom. "The best way I can put it is that she is her own player, and it's kind of a blend of all those players that she sees herself in," said Gabarra. "She's different than Mia, but that might be the closest comparison given the pace. The stardom and the fans and the craze that Mia had, always feeling like you've got to provide some kind of protection for them because it can be too much, and it can be a distraction to them."[22]

Mallory Pugh is an aberration, a young playmaker who has developed the speed, technique, and cognition to be recognized at the highest level of her game. But being put on a pedestal has not affected her confidence or long-term goals. She still turns inward to motivate herself despite outside pressures. "I have expectations on myself, and I think that's really the only expectations I should put on myself," Pugh said. "I have to remember I am young, this is my rookie season, so I think it was a great learning experience for me and that's kind of the biggest thing I took out of it."[23] Sounds like a growth mindset to us.

The Number 10 Jersey

If ever there was a flashing beacon to highlight a team's top play-maker, it is wearing the number 10 jersey in soccer. While most sports don't have a logical order to their uniform numbering (with the exception of American football), soccer has long had an association between jersey numbers and their role on the field. Defenders typically wear low numbers, from 2 to 5, while mid-fielders usually wear 6 through 8. The star forward usually grabs number 9. But the number 10 jersey carries a legacy and responsibility that is instantly recognizable. Past legends Pelé, Maradona, Ronaldhino, Totti, and Zidane wore the number 10 shirt, while today's stars—Messi at Barcelona, Neymar at Paris Saint-Germain, Hazard at Chelsea, and Modrić at Real Madrid—have followed in their footsteps.

While new tactical formations have tinkered with the traditional positioning of a number 10 (no longer anchored to the middle of the field), the symbolism of the team's most creative playmaker still exists. Messi and Neymar are known for their goal scoring, but because of that threat they also have become disruptors who sense the open man when defenders flock toward them. Luka Modrić, a midfielder for Real Madrid who also captains his Croatian national team, is the calming presence in the middle of a team packed with world-class players. Yet, Zidane, his manager, lauds him as the linchpin that holds the team together. "It's his tranquility. It's his tranquility with the ball," said Zidane. "I have the best players and we could talk about any of them, but if you ask me about Luka, I have to talk about his calmness with the ball at his feet. *La tranquilidad*. That's what he gives to the team when he's playing well. He makes the rest play."[24]

Indeed, Modrić finished tied for third with Neymar for the 2017 World's Best Playmaker award given by the International

Federation of Football History & Statistics (IFFHS) based on the votes of soccer experts in ninety-one countries.[25] To no one's surprise, Messi won the title for the third consecutive year.

The double-edged sword of respect and expectation that comes with the number 10 jersey is reserved for the shoulders of a player that can handle the weight. So when Jürgen Klinsmann, former U.S. Men's National Team head coach, handed it to seventeen-year-old Christian Pulisic before a 2016 World Cup qualifier game, he knew the load that was being placed on the young playmaker. "The No. 10 has a meaning," Klinsmann said. "Ask him now how he feels with that heavy number on his back."[26]

That night, Pulisic responded brilliantly, scoring two goals and assisting on a third in just twenty-six minutes, making him the youngest U.S. player ever to score in a World Cup qualifier.

Even Bruce Arena, who's seen his share of promising prospects in his forty years of coaching at the college, pro, and national team levels, believes in Pulisic. "I think he is just a natural," said Arena. "The game's easy for him. He's got exceptional skill, vision, he's pretty smooth."[27] Wary of anointing him a savior too early, Arena did inch out on a limb when pressed: "It makes you think that this is going to be perhaps the first American superstar in the sport. You have to be hesitant about this but this is a very talented young man."[28]

Unlike Mallory Pugh, who has female American role models like Hamm, Akers, Foudy, and Wambach to follow, Pulisic is breaking new ground for American men. Other than goalkeepers, Pulisic is the rare U.S. player who is not just on the roster of a top European club but a regular starter and playmaker for Borussia Dortmund, a perennial contender in the German Bundesliga. Signed at age seventeen, he scored his first goal for the senior team that same season. For a five-foot-eight-inch kid from Hershey, Pennsylvania, performing in front of 80,000 loud, demanding German fans against some of the world's great players could be overwhelming.

However, like Pugh, Pulisic is grounded with his own expectations. "Of course, I hear about all the stuff people talk about, the hype and whatever, but I just try to keep it out of my mind as much as I can, because it doesn't really matter to me. I put enough pressure on myself. I don't need all this outside tension or whatever." [29]

Because both of his parents played college soccer at George Mason University, you would expect early pressure, even obsession, to have their kids excel at the game. But Mark and Kelley Pulisic purposely avoided the temptation to push too hard. "I just think what we did differently was made sure that we didn't put him in a structured environment all the time," said Mark. "He played for one team. He would practice twice a week and play a game on the weekend." [30]

But as Christian's skill became obvious and he moved up the ladder of competition, his parents instilled one word into his vocabulary. "He was always playing up against older kids so I said there was only one thing you can never lose—you always have to play with confidence," said Mr. Pulisic.

What are the early signs that you might be raising a playmaker? Much like Pugh, Pulisic showed an unusual early passion for perfection and for the game. "Everything he does has to be at a very high level," said Kelley Pulisic. "He doesn't like to fail. And he wants it to be perfect. When he was two years old he would color. And he would color out of the lines and just flip out. And that's his personality in a nutshell, at two years old he had to keep in the lines.

"He became obsessed with soccer and before he started kindergarten had mastered one of the sport's most difficult skills: playing with both feet. He'd play for hours in the yard."[31]

Also like Pugh, being undersized while playing against older players has forced Christian to rely not only on his physical speed but also on his brain processing speed. "As he was playing U12, U14, and U16, you could tell he watched," said Mark Pulisic. "He was trying things that he saw. He was tactically aware, and a lot of that came from seeing games."

"I had to use other ways," said Christian, "and try to out-think opponents even more."

Playing at a top club with so many stellar prospects provides the deliberate practice environment that Ericsson recommends for fastest growth. "In the U.S. it's very comfortable for players," the senior Pulisic said. "If you're successful as a young player, you're told that a lot. But are players being taken out of their comfort zone? That's how you improve. When you come to Germany and you're training every day in January in the wind-driven rain and freezing cold, you're fighting through that. You're becoming stronger and better as a player."[32]

So far, the new number 10 is living up to expectations. In an eye-opening stat that compared Pulisic's career prior to his nineteenth birthday to Messi and Cristiano Ronaldo at the same age, the American has played more games and scored more goals for both club and country.[33] Pulisic's performance last season in expected goals and assists for Borussia Dortmund was fifth-best among teenagers across all of Europe's top leagues in the last six years.[34]

These days, advice for young playmakers is everywhere: Join the right team, play in all the right tournaments, travel hundreds of miles, hire specialty coaches, and eat ultra-healthy performance diets. However, the Pulisics, just like the Pughs, know that you still need to let kids be kids while they find their way. "After games, we were more Slurpees and Doritos," said Mark Pulisic.[35]

Keeping a long-term perspective beyond the latest game helps coaches and parents to stay focused on the real purpose of sports, to teach life lessons. At the same 2016 conference, Coach Dorrance shared a quote from Amos Alonzo Stagg, the fabled head football coach at the University of Chicago for forty years. After winning the 1913 national championship game, Stagg was asked by a reporter what he thought of his team. "I'll tell you in twenty years," replied Stagg.

"It's perfect," said Dorrance. "He wasn't going to talk about the championship game because he knew, in the larger scheme of things, it was absolutely irrelevant. But what had huge value was the character of the boys he was coaching."[36]

And that may just be the Playmaker's Advantage. We wish you the best as you develop your future playmakers!

ACKNOWLEDGMENTS

When we decided that this book needed to be written, we knew it would create its own niche in the athlete training literature. Not exactly a sport-specific coaching book, not just a sports psychology book, we envisioned a deep dive into the athlete's brain in action. Of course, when authors venture out into new territory, they need a team who is willing to go along for the ride. We couldn't have asked for a better group of professionals to help us navigate.

It starts with Laura Yorke at the Carol Mann Agency. As an experienced and in-demand literary agent, Laura sees hundreds of book proposals but her intuition to find out more about our book was the beginning of the journey. We appreciate and thank her for taking the chance and for her guidance during the process.

Equally brave was Adam Wilson, Senior Editor at Jeter Publishing/Gallery Books at Simon & Schuster, who saw the possibility of what this book could be if given a chance. His curiosity about the brain and sports along with his keen eye for what our readers will want to know has shaped our rough manuscript into this polished book.

Finding out where the intersection of science and performance lies could not have been possible without the input of all of our interviewees, who were generous with their time and expertise. In addition, the many athletes, coaches, and scientists quoted throughout the book allowed us to put the pieces together.

But beyond the experts cited in this book there are many others, far too many to name, who made immense contributions as we searched for the playmaker's secrets. Len would like to give a special "thank you" to his academic colleagues at Boston University and beyond who challenged him to be a good scientist and a never-ending teacher. And "thank you" to the great student-athletes he had the privilege of working with over a forty-year period. And of course, thanks to the brilliant coaches whose mission was to develop playmakers: in particular, two respected Boston University coach colleagues, Jack Parker and Neil Roberts.

Finally, our wives and families are the ultimate playmakers, helping us get better every day to reach our full potential.

NOTES

Chapter 1: Setting the Playmaker's Foundation

1. "2015 U.S. Trends in Team Sports," Sports and Fitness Industry Association, sfia.org, 2017, https://www.sfia.org/reports/409_2015-U.S.-TRENDS-IN-TEAM-SPORTS-.
2. King, Bill, "Are the Kids Alright?" *Sports Business Journal*, Sportsbusinessdaily.com, August 10, 2015.
3. "Home," *ADM Kids*, 2017, http://www.admkids.com/.
4. ADM brochure, http://assets.ngin.com/attachments/document/0042/7978/ADM_Newspaper.pdf, 2017.
5. Da Silva, Matt, "New Era for US Lacrosse: Q&A With CEO Steve Stenersen," *US Lacrosse* (blog), August 26, 2016.
6. "The Case for Evolution—A Logical Progression," *Lacrosse Magazine*, 2017.
7. "Player Development and How They Learn with Mike Sullivan—Development Coach, Chicago Blackhawks," *YouTube*, 2017, https://youtu.be/IzNlsO_L-_0?list=PLFA6D04F5F6305B9A.
8. Werner, Sam, "Mario Lemieux, Wayne Gretzky Agree: Sidney Crosby Is the League's No. 1 Player Now," *Pittsburgh Post-Gazette*, January 28, 2017.
9. Jake Guentzel 2016–17 Scoring Log, https://www.hockey-reference.com/players/g/guentja01/scoring/2017.
10. Author interview with Jake Guentzel, 9/16/2017.
11. Wyshynski, Greg, "Jake Guentzel Lifts Stanley Cup as Rookie, Thanks to Sidney Crosby," *Yahoo! Sports*, June 12, 2017, https://sports.yahoo.com/jake-guentzel-lifts-stanley-cup-rookie-thanks-sidney-crosby-155653646.html.

12. Author interview with Sidney Crosby, 9/16/2017.
13. Ibid.
14. Ibid.
15. Ibid.
16. Ibid.
17. "AGM 2014—Long-Term Player Development 2.0," *YouTube*, 2017, https://youtu.be/ozjgmwaPYzE.
18. Farrey, Tom, *Game On* (New York: ESPN Books, 2008).
19. "Exclusive: Tom Farrey Interview Excerpt from SFIA U.S. Trends in Team Sports Report," *SFIA Insider* (blog), 2016.
20. "Project Play: Home," The Aspen Institute, 2017, *Project Play: Playbook*, http://youthreport.projectplay.us/.
21. "Exclusive: Tom Farrey Interview Excerpt from SFIA U.S. Trends in Team Sports Report."
22. Author interview with Brad Stevens, 7/20/2017.
23. Author interview with Avery Faigenbaum, 5/13/2017.
24. "Youth Fitness Manual," American Council on Exercise (ACE), acefitness.org, 2017.
25. "International Physical Literacy Association," IPLA, 2017.
26. Whitehead, Margaret, *Physical Literacy* (London: Routledge, 2011).
27. "Exercise Physiologist Wants Greater Emphasis Put on Physical Literacy," *CBC News*, 2017.
28. Author interview with Avery Faigenbaum, 5/13/2017.
29. "PLAY Tools—Physical Literacy Assessment for Youth," Play.physicalliteracy.ca, 2017, https://play.physicalliteracy.ca/play-tools.
30. Author interview with Avery Faigenbaum, 5/13/2017.

Chapter 2: The Road to Elite

1. Gladwell, Malcolm, *Outliers* (New York: Little, Brown, 2008).
2. Mann, Derek T. Y., A. Mark Williams, Paul Ward, and Christopher M. Janelle, "Perceptual-Cognitive Expertise in Sport: A Meta-Analysis," *Journal of Sport and Exercise Psychology* 29 (4) 2017: 457–78.
3. Chi, Michelene T. H., "Two Approaches to the Study of Experts' Characteristics." In K. A. Ericsson, N. Charness, P. Feltovich, and R. R. Hoffman (eds.), *The Cambridge Handbook of Expertise and Expert Performance* (Cambridge, UK: Cambridge University Press, 2006), 21–38.
4. Swann, Christian, et al., "Defining Elite Athletes: Issues in the Study of Expert Performance in Sport Psychology," *Psychology of Sport and Exercise* 16, January 2015.
5. Ibid.

6. Stone, Simon, "Kevin De Bruyne Second Only to Lionel Messi, Says Man City Boss Pep Guardiola," *BBC Sport,* September 17, 2017.

7. Ibid.

8. "Welcome, Beckman Institute Lifelong Brain and Cognition Lab," Lifelong Brain and Cognition Laboratory, Beckman Institute, University of Illinois, http://lbc.beckman.illinois.edu/.

9. Hillman, Charles H., Kirk I. Erickson, and Arthur F. Kramer, "Be Smart, Exercise Your Heart: Exercise Effects on Brain and Cognition," *Nature Reviews Neuroscience* 9 (1) 2008: 58–65.

10. "Health, Brain & Cognition Lab, Department of Psychological and Brain Sciences, College of Liberal Arts and Sciences, The University of Iowa," 2017, https://psychology.uiowa.edu/health-brain-cognition-lab.

11. Voss, Michelle W., "Understanding the Mind of the Elite Athlete," *Scientific American,* June 1, 2010.

12. Hillman, Charles H., Kirk I. Erickson, and Arthur F. Kramer, "Be Smart, Exercise Your Heart."

13. "Health, Brain, & Cognition Lab, Department of Psychological and Brain Sciences, The University of Iowa."

14. Voss, Michelle W., "Understanding the Mind of the Elite Athlete."

15. Mann, Derek T. Y., A. Mark Williams, Paul Ward, and Christopher M. Janelle, "Perceptual-Cognitive Expertise in Sport: A Meta-Analysis," *Journal of Sport and Exercise Psychology* 29 (4) 2007: 457–78.

16. Voss, Michelle W., Arthur F. Kramer, Chandramallika Basak, Ruchika Shaurya Prakash, and Brent Roberts, "Are Expert Athletes 'Expert' in the Cognitive Laboratory? A Meta-Analytic Review of Cognition and Sport Expertise," *Applied Cognitive Psychology* 24 (6) 2009: 812–26.

17. Ibid.

18. Ibid.

19. "Beckman Institute Illinois Simulator Laboratory," Illinois Simulator Laboratory, University of Illinois at Urbana-Champaign, 2017, http://www.isl.uiuc.edu/Labs/CAVE/CAVE.html.

20. Chaddock, Laura, Mark B. Neider, Michelle W. Voss, John G. Gaspar, and Arthur F. Kramer, "Do Athletes Excel at Everyday Tasks?" *Medicine & Science in Sports & Exercise,* 1, 2011.

21. "FIVB—Volleyball," Fivb.org., 2017, http://www.fivb.org/en/volleyball /VB_Ranking_M_2016–08.asp.

22. Alves, Heloisa, Michelle W. Voss, Walter R. Boot, Andrea Deslandes, Victor Cossich, José Inacio Salles, and Arthur F. Kramer, "Perceptual-Cognitive Expertise in Elite Volleyball Players," *Frontiers in Psychology* 4, 2013.

23. Yates, Diana, "Elite Athletes Also Excel at Some Cognitive Tasks,"

Illinois News Bureau, News.Illinois.edu., March 18, 2013, https://news
.illinois.edu/blog/view/6367/204860.

Chapter 3: What Gets Measured Gets Noticed

1. Bacharach, Erik, "Central's Justyn Ross Receives Invitation to the Opening Finals," Oanow.com, March 27, 2017.
2. Ibid.
3. "SPARQ, Analytics, and the NFL Draft," *Three Sigma Athlete* (blog), 2017, https://3sigmaathlete.com.
4. Ibid.
5. "Zach Whitman on Twitter," *Twitter*, 2017, https://twitter.com/zjwhitman/status/838798417904095232.
6. "Relating Athleticism to Production," *Three Sigma Athlete* (blog), 2017, https://3sigmaathlete.com/2015/02/16/investigating-the-relationship-between-athleticism-and-production/.
7. Ibid.
8. "Pro Football Statistics and History," *Pro Football Reference*, 2017, http://www.pro-football-reference.com/.
9. "Approximate Value," Sports-Reference.com, http://www.sports-reference.com/blog/approximate-value/.
10. Kloet, Jim, "Visualizing 16 Years of NFL Combine Data," *RotoViz*, February 20, 2017, http://rotoviz.com/2017/02/nfl-combine-trends-over-time/?hvid=3yNPul.
11. "Win Shares Sample," *Bill James Online*, 2017, Billjamesonline.com, http://www.billjamesonline.com/stats/win_shares_sample/.
12. "NBA Win Shares," Basketball-Reference.com, http://www.basketball-reference.com/about/ws.html.
13. Golliver, Ben, "Is Greg Oden Really the NBA's Biggest Draft Bust?" *Sports Illustrated*, November 17, 2016.
14. Moxley, Jerad H., and Tyler J. Towne, "Predicting Success in the National Basketball Association: Stability & Potential," *Psychology of Sport and Exercise* 16 (2015): 128–36.
15. Ibid.
16. "NBA.com/Stats: Draft History," Stats, NBA.com, 2017, http://stats.nba.com/draft/history/.

Chapter 4: The Endurance Thermostat

1. Honrubia, Guillermo, "Griezmann Promises Tireless Atlético in Final," UEFA.com, 2017, http://www.uefa.com/uefachampionsleague/news/newsid=2367206.html.

2. Walsh, Vincent, "Is Sport the Brain's Biggest Challenge?" *Current Biology* 24 (18) 2014: R859–60.
3. Noakes, Timothy David, "Fatigue Is a Brain-Derived Emotion That Regulates the Exercise Behavior to Ensure the Protection of Whole Body Homeostasis," *Frontiers in Physiology* 3, 2012.
4. Mosso Angelo, *Fatigue* (London: Allen & Unwin Ltd., 1915).
5. Author interview with David Epstein, 6/3/2017.
6. Heil, Nick, "Fatigue Is All in Your Head," *Outside Online*, September 19, 2016.
7. "Professor Samuele Marcora—School of Sport & Exercise Sciences—University of Kent," Kent.ac.uk, 2017, https://www.kent.ac.uk/sport sciences/staff/s-marcora.html.
8. "Endurance Fatigue: Perception Is Everything," Competitor.com, 2017, http://running.competitor.com/2014/05/training/endurance-fatigue-per ception-is-everything_9067#GSxJcftZBfcrZcd7.99.
9. Author interview with David Epstein, 6/3/2017.
10. "Atlético Madrid News: Diego Simeone Weighs His Players Daily to Ensure Their Fitness," Sportskeeda.com, 2017, https://www.sportskeeda.com/foot ball/atletico-madrid-players-follow-strict-rules-under-diego-simeone.
11. "Atlético De Madrid: Los Secretos Del 'Profe' Ortega," MARCA.com, 2017, http://www.marca.com/2014/10/13/futbol/equipos/atletico/14132 10304.html.
12. "Mauled: Rugby's Role in Atlético's Success," Inbedwithmaradona.com, 2017, http://inbedwithmaradona.com/journal/2016/5/10/mauled-el-profe -and-rugbys-role-in-atléticos-success.
13. Smith, Mitchell R., Samuele M. Marcora, and Aaron J. Coutts, "Mental Fatigue Impairs Intermittent Running Performance," *Medicine & Science in Sports & Exercise* 47 (8) 2015: 1682–90.
14. Ibid.
15. Ibid.
16. Smith, Mitchell R., Aaron J. Coutts, Michele Merlini, Dieter Deprez, Matthieu Lenoir, and Samuele M. Marcora, "Mental Fatigue Impairs Soccer-Specific Physical and Technical Performance," *Medicine & Science in Sports & Exercise* 48 (2) 2016: 267–76.
17. Ali, Ajmol, Clyde Williams, Mark Hulse, and Steve McGregor, "Reliability and Validity of Two Tests of Soccer Skill," *Journal of Sports Sciences* 25 (13) 2007: 1461–70.
18. Smith, Mitchell R., Aaron J. Coutts, Michele Merlini, Dieter Deprez, Matthieu Lenoir, and Samuele M. Marcora, "Mental Fatigue Impairs Soccer-Specific Physical and Technical Performance."

19. Smith, Mitchell R., Linus Zeuwts, Matthieu Lenoir, Nathalie Hens, Laura M. S. De Jong, and Aaron J. Coutts, "Mental Fatigue Impairs Soccer-Specific Decision-Making Skill," *Journal of Sports Sciences* 34 (14) 2016: 1297–1304.

20. Ibid.

21. "Atlético De Madrid: Los Secretos Del 'Profe' Ortega."

22. "UEFA Champions League 2015/16—History—Atlético-Bayern—UEFA .com," Uefa.com, 2017, http://www.uefa.com/uefachampionsleague/sea son=2016/matches/round=2000637/match=2015786/prematch/preview /index.html.

23. "NBA Basketball Player Stats—Minutes Played," Teamrankings.com, 2017, https://www.teamrankings.com/nba/player-stat/minutes-played.

24. "NHL Stats," Foxsports.com, 2017, http://www.foxsports.com/nhl/stats.

25. Stulberg, Brad, "8 Simple Tips to Live Longer and Healthier," *Outside Online*, 2017, https://www.outsideonline.com/2173721/outside-guide -life-extension.

26. Stulberg, Brad, "The Stranger-Than-Fiction Way to Cheat Fatigue," *Out- side Online*, 2017, https://www.outsideonline.com/1928691/stranger -fiction-way-cheat-fatigue.

27. Giovio, Eleonora, "Zidane Se Pone El Mono De Trabajo," *El País,* Janu- ary 2016.

28. Giovio, Eleonora, "Antonio Pintus, El Primer Fichaje De Zidane," *El País,* July 2017.

29. Bruña, Manuel, "Antonio Pintus, El 'Profe' Ortega De Zidane," *Mundo Deportivo*, 2017, http://www.mundodeportivo.com/futbol/real-madrid /20160720/403334340655/pintus-antonio-pintus-profe-ortega-zidane .html.

30. Giovio, Eleonora, "Zidane Se Pone El Mono De Trabajo."

31. "UEFA Champions League 2016/17—History—Real Madrid-Atlético Statistics," Uefa.com, 2017, http://www.uefa.com/uefachampionsleague /season=2017/matches/round=2000786/match=2019638/postmatch/sta tistics/index.html.

32. "Who Scored," Whoscored.com, 2017, https://www.whoscored.com /Statistics.

33. Giovio, Eleonora, "Antonio Pintus Aguanta al Real Madrid a Todo Gas," *El País,* May 2017.

34. Yael Beniamini, Joel J. Rubenstein, Leonard D. Zaichkowsky, and Mari- lyn C. Crim, "Effects of High-Intensity Strength Training on Quality-of- Life Parameters in Cardiac Rehabilitation Patients," *American Journal of Cardiology* 80 (7) 1997: 841–46.

35. American College of Sports Medicine, Position statement on the use and abuse of anabolic-androgenic steroids in sports, *Medicine & Science in Sports & Exercise*, 9 (4) 1977.

36. Faigenbaum, A., L. Zaichkowsky, W. Westcott, L. Micheli, and A. Fehlandt, "Effects of a Twice per Week Strength-training Program on Children," *Pediatric Exercise Science* 5 (4) 1993: 339–46.

37. Bertrand Russell, as quoted in "On the Recipe for Longevity," *Collected Papers of Bertrand Russell*, vol. 29 (2012).

38. Goleman, Daniel, *Emotional Intelligence* (New York: Bantam Books, 2006).

39. "Athletic Intelligence Measures," Athleticintel.com, 2017, http://www .athleticintel.com/.

40. MHS Assessments, TAIS™, https://www.mhs.com/MHS-Talent?prod name=tais.

41. SFU Beedie School of Business, "The Science (or Not) of Drafting Professional Hockey Players," *Ideas @ Beedie* (blog), http://beedie.sfu.ca/ideas /2013/08/the-science-or-not-of-drafting-professional-hockey-players/.

42. Morgan, W. P., and D. L. Costill, "Psychological Characteristics of the Marathon Runner," *Journal of Sports Medicine and Physical Fitness* 12, 1972: 42–46.

Chapter 5: Search: The Hunt for Opportunities

1. "Patrick Vieira at the Rubin: A Conversation with Neuroscientist John Krakauer," *YouTube*, 2017, https://youtu.be/Q4LSkSXckVc.

2. Ibid.

3. "Home Content," *Brain, Learning, Animation, and Movement Lab*, 2017, http://blam-lab.org/.

4. "What We Can Learn from the Minds of Olympic Athletes: Q&A with John Krakauer, M.D.," *Dana Foundation*, 2017, https://danablog.org /2016/08/08/what-we-can-learn-from-the-minds-of-olympic-athletes-qa -with-john-krakauer-m-d/.

5. Ibid.

6. Yarrow, Kielan, Peter Brown, and John W. Krakauer, "Inside the Brain of an Elite Athlete: The Neural Processes That Support High Achievement in Sports," *Nature Reviews Neuroscience* 10 (8) 2009: 585–96.

7. Ibid.

8. Ibid.

9. "Patrick Vieira at the Rubin: A Conversation with Neuroscientist John Krakauer."

10. "Collection—The Brain Series—The Motor System—Charlie Rose," *Charlie Rose*, 2017, https://charlierose.com/collections/3/clip/15387.

11. Ibid.

12. Ibid.

13. Gretzky, Wayne, and Rick Reilly, *Gretzky* (New York: HarperCollins, 1990).

14. *The Hockey News*, 1/16/1983.

15. NHL, "1982–83 NHL Summary: Hockey-Reference.com," Hockey -Reference.com, 2017, https://www.hockey-reference.com/leagues/NHL _1983.html.

16. Gretzky and Reilly, *Gretzky*.

17. Ibid.

18. Ibid.

19. Williams, A. Mark, and Paul Ward, "Anticipation and Decision Making: Exploring New Horizons," *Handbook of Sport Psychology*, 2012: 203–23, doi:10.1002/9781118270011.ch9.

20. Ibid.

21. "Paolo Maldini: The Defender So Good, He Didn't Even Need to Tackle," *The Sun*, 2017, https://www.thesun.co.uk/archives/football/169264/paolo -maldini-the-defender-so-good-he-didnt-even-need-to-tackle/.

22. Ibid.

23. Wolpert, Daniel, "The Real Reason for Brains," Ted.com, 2017, https:// www.ted.com/talks/daniel_wolpert_the_real_reason_for_brains/.

24. Ibid.

25. Aglioti, Salvatore M., Paola Cesari, Michela Romani, and Cosimo Urgesi, "Action Anticipation and Motor Resonance in Elite Basketball Players," *Nature Neuroscience* 11 (9) 2008: 1109–16.

26. "Collection—The Brain Series—The Motor System—Charlie Rose."

27. "Delis-Kaplan Executive Function System™," Pearsonclinical.com, 2017, http://www.pearsonclinical.com/psychology/products/100000618/deliska plan-executive-function-system-d-kefs.html.

28. "Psychological Testing May Predict Success in Soccer," *Sciencedaily*, 2017, https://www.sciencedaily.com/releases/2012/04/120405092919.htm.

29. "Xavi Assessment," *YouTube*, 2017, https://youtu.be/uwlVBQF3J5k.

30. "Former Results: IFFHS," *IFFHS*, 2017, http://iffhs.de/former-results/.

31. Ingle, Sean, "Are We a Step Closer to Being Able to Measure Football IQ?" *The Guardian*, 2017, https://www.theguardian.com/football /blog/2016/dec/04/barcelona-andres-iniesta-scope-embrace-brain-game -real-madrid.

32. Lowe, Sid, "I'm a Romantic Says Xavi, Heartbeat of Barcelona and Spain," *The Guardian*, 2017, https://www.theguardian.com/football /2011/feb/11/xavi-barcelona-spain-interview.

33. Pirlo, Andrea, Alessandro Alciato, and Mark Palmer, *I Think Therefore I Play* (Glasgow: BackPage Press, 2014).

34. "Beautiful Game. Beautiful Mind," ESPNFC.com, 2017, http://www.espnfc.co.uk/england/story/1071240/beautiful-game-beautiful-mind.

35. Uli Hesse, "Thomas Müller: The Modest Assassin," *The Guardian*, 2017, https://www.theguardian.com/football/2016/feb/23/thomas-muller-mod est-assassin-bayern-munich-germany.

36. Vestberg, Torbjörn, Gustaf Reinebo, Liselotte Maurex, Martin Ingvar, and Predrag Petrovic, "Core Executive Functions Are Associated with Success in Young Elite Soccer Players," *PLOS ONE* 12 (2) 2017.

37. "One Card—Cogstate," *Cogstate*, 2017, https://cogstate.com/cognitive -tests/one-card/.

38. Soccer Success in the Young Can Be Measured in the Brain," Sciencedaily .com, 2017, https://www.sciencedaily.com/releases/2017/02/17020909 1201.htm.

39. Ibid.

40. "Neuroscience Can Guarantee Your Team Wins the Euros," *Quartz*, 2017, https://qz.com/725122/neuroscience-can-guarantee-your-team -wins-the-euros/.

41. Williams, A. Mark, Nicola J. Hodges, Jamie S. North, and Gabor Barton, "Perceiving Patterns of Play in Dynamic Sport Tasks: Investigating the Essential Information Underlying Skilled Performance," *Perception* 35 (3) 2006: 317–32.

42. Ibid.

43. Smeeton, Nicholas J., Paul Ward, and A. Mark Williams, "Do Pattern Recognition Skills Transfer Across Sports? A Preliminary Analysis," *Journal of Sports Sciences* 22 (2) 2004: 205–13.

Chapter 6: Decide: Choose Wisely

1. Schuhmann, John, "Other Raptors Reward Demar Derozan for Making Right Reads in Game 5," NBA.com, 2017, http://www.nba.com/article /2017/04/25/toronto-raptors-teammates-reward-demar-derozan-making -right-reads-game-5.

2. Lowe, Zach, Bill Barnwell, Ben Lindbergh, and Brian Phillips, "Lights, Cameras, Revolution," *Grantland*, 2017, http://grantland.com/features /the-toronto-raptors-sportvu-cameras-nba-analytical-revolution/.

3. Goldsberry, Kirk, Bill Barnwell, Ben Lindbergh, and Brian Phillips, "Databall," *Grantland*, 2017, http://grantland.com/features/expected -value-possession-nba-analytics/.

4. Ibid.

5. "NYKTOR," *YouTube*, 2017, https://youtu.be/5Sq_Z6Um3UM.

6. Lowe, Zach, Bill Barnwell, Ben Lindbergh, and Brian Phillips, 2017, "Lights, Cameras, Revolution."

7. Ibid.

8. "Data-Driven Ghosting Using Deep Imitation Learning—MIT Sloan Analytics Conference," MIT Sloan Analytics Conference, 2017, http://www.sloansportsconference.com/content/data-driven-ghosting-using-deep-imitation-learning/.

9. "Deep Learning Is About to Revolutionize Sports Analytics. Here's How," *Xentaurs*, 2017, https://www.xentaurs.com/2017/05/27/deep-learning-is-about-to-revolutionize-sports-analytics-heres-how/.

10. De Bono, Edward, *Simplicity* (London: Viking, 1998).

11. Bar-Eli, Michael, Henning Plessner, and Markus Raab, *Judgement, Decision Making and Success in Sport* (Malden, MA: Wiley, 1998).

12. Staff, Investopedia, "Economic Man," *Investopedia*, 2017, http://www.investopedia.com/terms/e/economic-man.asp.

13. Klein, Gary, "Naturalistic Decision Making," *Human Factors: The Journal of the Human Factors and Ergonomics Society* 50 (3) 2008: 456–60.

14. Kahneman, Daniel, and Gary Klein, "Conditions for Intuitive Expertise: A Failure to Disagree," *American Psychologist* 64 (6) 2009: 515–26.

15. "Herbert A. Simon—Prize Lecture: Rational Decision-Making in Business Organizations," Nobelprize.org, 2017, https://www.nobelprize.org/nobel_prizes/economic-sciences/laureates/1978/simon-lecture.html.

16. Klein, Gary, "Naturalistic Decision Making," *Human Factors: The Journal of the Human Factors and Ergonomics Society* 50 (3) 2008: 456–460.

17. Kahneman, Daniel, *Thinking, Fast and Slow* (New York: Farrar, Straus and Giroux, 2015).

18. Ibid.

19. Lewis, Michael, *Moneyball* (New York: W. W. Norton, 2013).

20. Thaler, Richard, and Cass Sunstein, "Who's On First," *New Republic*, 2017, https://newrepublic.com/article/61123/whos-first.

21. Lewis, Michael, "How Two Trailblazing Psychologists Turned the World of Decision Science Upside Down," *The Hive* (blog), 2016, https://www.vanityfair.com/news/2016/11/decision-science-daniel-kahneman-amos-tversky.

22. Lewis, Michael, *The Undoing Project* (New York: W. W. Norton, 2017).

23. Kahneman, Daniel, and Gary Klein, "Conditions for Intuitive Expertise: A Failure to Disagree," *American Psychologist* 64 (6) 2009: 515–26.

24. Ibid.

25. Lowe, Zach, Bill Barnwell, Ben Lindbergh, and Brian Phillips, "Lights, Cameras, Revolution."

26. Johnson, Joseph G., and Markus Raab, "Take the First: Option-Generation and Resulting Choices," *Organizational Behavior and Human Decision Processes* 91 (2) 2003: 215–29.

27. Ibid.

28. Ibid.

29. Ibid.

30. Raab, Markus, and Joseph G. Johnson, "Expertise-Based Differences in Search and Option-Generation Strategies," *Journal of Experimental Psychology: Applied* 13 (3) 2007: 158–70.

31. "OpenMask," Openmask.org, 2017, http://www.openmask.org/images /handball-materiel1.png.

32. Author interview with Brad Stevens, 7/20/2017.

33. Author interview with Mark Newman, 6/16/2017.

34. Author interview with Dave Hadfield, 5/17/2017.

Chapter 7: Execute: Make It Happen

1. "We Want to Be Envied: Bevo's Plans for a Bulldog Dynasty," Afl.com .au, 2017, http://www.afl.com.au/news/2016-10-01/we-want-to-be-en vied-says-proud-beveridge.

2. "Extreme Disappointment for Swans," Dailytelegraph.com.au, 2017, http://www.dailytelegraph.com.au/sport/afl/teams/sydney/sydney-coach -john-longmire-says-he-feels-extreme-disappointment-after-losing-another -grand-final/news-story/291f1ce51b689fe803d460cc828c710f.

3. "AFL Tables—Coaches," Afltables.com, 2017, https://afltables.com/afl /stats/coaches/coaches_idx.html.

4. "Longmire a Coaching Genius Without Plaudits," Heraldsun.com.au, 2017, http://www.heraldsun.com.au/sport/afl/expert-opinion/jon-ralph /john-longmire-is-a-coaching-genius-and-has-elevated-a-team-few -believed-in-to-a-grand-final/news-story/da0e8f35f22f871afc68fcc724 46c54c.

5. Author interview with John Longmire, 8/20/2017.

6. Farrow, Damian, "Periodisation of Skills Training," *Clearinghouse for Sport*, 2017, https://www.clearinghouseforsport.gov.au/Library/videos /smart_talk_seminar_series/2017_presentations/periodisation_of_skills _training.

7. Seuss, Dr., *Green Eggs and Ham*, 50th Anniversary ed. (New York: Random House, 2006).

8. "Lecture 5 Damian Farrow Not All Practice Is the Same 1," *YouTube*, 2017, https://youtu.be/5rMqX36d-6c.

9. Farrow, Damian, "Periodisation of Skills Training."

10. Ibid.

11. Rowbottom, David J., "Periodization of Training," in Garrett, William E., and Donald T. Kirkendall, *Periodization of Training* (Philadelphia: Lippincott Williams & Wilkins, 2000), 499.

12. Farrow, Damian, and Sam Robertson, "Development of a Skill Acquisition Periodisation Framework for High-Performance Sport," *Sports Medicine* 47 (6) 2016: 1043–54.

13. O'Brien, See, "Artificial Intelligence Helped the AFL Champions End a 62-Year Famine, But Will We Ever See It in GAA?" *The42*, 2017, http://www.the42.ie/western-bulldogs-machine-learning-3213937 -Feb2017/.

14. Farrow, Damian, and Sam Robertson, "Development of a Skill Acquisition Periodisation Framework for High-Performance Sport."

15. Farrow, Damian, "Periodisation of Skills Training."

16. Author interview with Damian Farrow, 8/24/2017.

17. Farrow, Damian, "Periodisation of Skills Training."

18. Author interview with Damian Farrow, 8/24/2017.

19. Ibid.

20. Buszard, Tim, Damian Farrow, Simone J. J. M. Verswijveren, Machar Reid, Jacqueline Williams, Remco Polman, Fiona Chun Man Ling, and Rich S. W. Masters, "Working Memory Capacity Limits Motor Learning When Implementing Multiple Instructions," *Frontiers in Psychology* 8, 2017.

21. Author interview with Damian Farrow, 8/24/2017.

22. "Catalyst: Eye-Tracker—ABC TV Science," Abc.Net.au, 2017, http://www.abc.net.au/catalyst/stories/3515097.htm.

23. Ibid.

24. Abernethy, Bruce, and David G. Russell, "The Relationship Between Expertise and Visual Search Strategy in a Racquet Sport," *Human Movement Science* 6 (4) 1987: 283–319.

25. Fadde, P. J., "Interactive Video Training of Perceptual Decision-making in the Sport of Baseball," *Technology, Instruction, Cognition and Learning* 4, (3/4) 2006: 265–85. Larkin, P., C. Mesagno, M. Spittle, and J. Berry, "An Evaluation of Video-Based Training Programs for Perceptual-Cognitive Skill Development: A Systematic Review of Current Sport-Based Knowledge," *International Journal of Sport Psychology* 46 (6) 2015. Miller, B. T., and W. C. Clapp, "From Vision to Decision: The

Role of Visual Attention in Elite Sports Performance," *Eye & Contact Lens* 37 (3) 2011: 131–39. Muraskin, Jordan, Jason Sherwin, and Paul Sajda, "Knowing When Not to Swing: EEG Evidence That Enhanced Perception-Action Coupling Underlies Baseball Batter Expertise," *Neuroimage* 123, 2015: 1–10.

26. Faubert, J., "Professional Athletes Have Extraordinary Skills for Rapidly Learning Complex and Neutral Dynamic Visual Scenes," *Scientific Reports* 3 (1154) 2013. Faubert, J., and L. Sidebottom, "Perceptual-Cognitive Training of Athletes," *Journal of Clinical Sport Psychology* 6, (1) 2012: 85–102.

27. Bandura, Albert, *Social Learning Theory* (New York: General Learning Press, 1977).

28. Le Poole, Karen Clark, "Training with the Video iPod," *IMPACT Magazine*, 2007, pp. 84–85.

Chapter 8: How to Prepare: Mindset, Grit, and Greatness

1. "Gregg Popovich: Kawhi Leonard Is the Best Player in the League—Spurs Vs Grizzlies R1G6," *YouTube*, 2017, https://youtu.be/WfOSTXA FeZQ.

2. "David Fizdale Postgame News Conference—Spurs vs. Grizzles R1G6, April 27, 2017," *YouTube*, 2017, https://youtu.be/FktzzC40wJY.

3. Jenkins, Lee, "The Island of Kawhi Leonard," SI.com, 2017, https://www .si.com/nba/2016/03/15/kawhi-leonard-spurs-tim-duncan-gregg-popovich -tony-parker-manu-ginobili.

4. Abrams, Jonathan, "The Making of Kawhi Leonard, the Silent Superstar," *Bleacher Report*, 2017, http://bleacherreport.com/articles/2700 300-the-making-of-kawhi-leonard-the-silent-superstar.

5. Ibid.

6. Jenkins, Lee, "The Island of Kawhi Leonard."

7. Flegel, M. J., *Sport First Aid: A Coach's Guide to the Care and Prevention of Athletic Injuries*, 4th ed. (Champaign, IL: Human Kinetics, 2008).

8. Rees, Tim, Lew Hardy, Arne Güllich, Bruce Abernethy, Jean Côté, Tim Woodman, Hugh Montgomery, Stewart Laing, and Chelsea Warr, "The Great British Medalists Project: A Review of Current Knowledge on the Development of the World's Best Sporting Talent," *Sports Medicine* 46 (8) 2016: 1041–58.

9. Ibid.

10. NCAA, "The Birthday Effect in College Athletics," 2017, http://www .ncaa.org/sites/default/files/bdayXP_0.pdf.

11. Rees, Tim, Lew Hardy, Arne Güllich, Bruce Abernethy, Jean Côté, Tim Woodman, Hugh Montgomery, Stewart Laing, and Chelsea Warr, "The Great British Medalists Project."

12. Ibid.

13. Duckworth, Angela, "Grit: The Power of Passion and Perseverance," Ted .com, 2017, https://www.ted.com/talks/angela_lee_duckworth_grit_the _power_of_passion_and_perseverance.

14. Seattle Seahawks, "Seahawks Coach Pete Carroll and Dr. Angela Duckworth Discuss Grit in Town Hall Event," 2017, http://www.seahawks .com/news/2016/05/20/seahawks-coach-pete-carroll-and-dr-angela-duck worth-discuss-grit-town-hall-event.

15. Ibid.

16. Duckworth, Angela, *Grit: The Power of Passion and Perseverance* (New York: Scribner, 2016).

17. Duckworth, Angela, *Angela Duckworth Q & A*, 2017, https://angela duckworth.com/qa/#faq-125.

18. Duckworth, Angela, *Grit Scale*, 2017, https://angeladuckworth.com/grit -scale/.

19. "Interview With Angela Duckworth," Scholastic.com, 2017, http://www .scholastic.com/browse/article.jsp?id=3758297.

20. Duckworth, A. L., and D. S. Yeager, "Measurement Matters: Assessing Personal Qualities Other Than Cognitive Ability for Educational Purposes," *Educational Researcher* 44 (4) 2015: 237–51.

21. Zernike, Kate, "Testing for Joy and Grit? Schools Nationwide Push to Measure Students' Emotional Skills," *New York Times*, February 29, 2016.

22. Credé, Marcus, Michael C. Tynan, and Peter D. Harms, "Much Ado About Grit: A Meta-Analytic Synthesis of the Grit Literature," Academia .edu, 2017, https://www.academia.edu/25397556/Much_Ado_About _Grit_A_Meta-Analytic_Synthesis_of_the_Grit_Literature.

23. "No Evidence That Grit Improves Performance, Iowa State Analysis Finds—News Service—Iowa State University," News.Iastate.edu, 2017, http://www.news.iastate.edu/news/2016/05/18/grit-analysis.

24. Dweck, Carol, "Mindsets: Developing Talent Through a Growth Mindset," *Olympic Coach* 21 (1) 2009: 4–7.

25. Ibid.

26. Mueller, Claudia M., and Carol S. Dweck, "Praise for Intelligence Can Undermine Children's Motivation and Performance," *Journal of Personality and Social Psychology* 75 (1) 1998: 33–52.

27. Li, Yu, and Timothy C. Bates, "Does Growth Mindset Improve Chil-

dren's IQ, Educational Attainment or Response to Setbacks? Active-control Interventions and Data on Children's Own Mindsets," SocArXiv, July 7, 1998, osf.io/preprints/socarxiv/tsdwy.

28. Gross-Loh, Christine, "How Praise Became a Consolation Prize," *The Atlantic*, December 16, 2016.

29. Ibid.

30. Cooper, Garland, Director of Softball NCSA, USA Today High School Sports Jim Halley, and USA Today High School Sports Jason Jordan, "What an 11-Time NCAA Champion Coach Says About Evaluating Recruits," *USA Today High School Sports*, 2017, http://usatodayhss.com/2017/what-an-11-time-ncaa-champion-coach-says-about-evaluating-recruits.

31. Ibid.

32. Rees, Tim, Lew Hardy, Arne Güllich, Bruce Abernethy, Jean Côté, Tim Woodman, Hugh Montgomery, Stewart Laing, and Chelsea Warr, "The Great British Medalists Project."

33. Ibid.

34. Cooper, Garland, Jim Halley, and Jason Jordan, "What an 11-Time NCAA Champion Coach Says About Evaluating Recruits."

35. Hardy, Lew, Matthew Barlow, Lynne Evans, Tim Rees, Tim Woodman, and Chelsea Warr, "Great British Medalists."

36. Author interview with David Hemery, 5/4/2017.

37. Ibid.

38. Hemery, David, *Sporting Excellence* (London: Collins Willow, 1991).

39. Ibid.

40. "21St Century Legacy—Welcome to 21St Century Legacy," 21Stcentury legacy.com, 2017, http://www.21stcenturylegacy.com/.

41. Gallagher, Brendan, "David Hemery Helping Provide London 2012 With 21St Century Legacy," Telegraph.Co.uk, 2017, http://www.telegraph.co.uk/sport/olympics/2419124/David-Hemery-helping-provide-London-2012-with-21st-Century-Legacy.html.

42. Hardy, Lew, Matthew Barlow, Lynne Evans, Tim Rees, Tim Woodman, and Chelsea Warr, "Great British Medalists."

43. "Sondheimer, Eric, "Shooting Death of His Father Drives Riverside King's Leonard," *Los Angeles Times*, March 8, 2008.

44. Shelburne, Ramona, "Shelburne: Leonard Rises Through Travails," ESPN.com, 2017, http://www.espn.com/nba/playoffs/2014/story/_/id/11090861/kawhi-leonard-trip-finals-mvp-dad.

45. Ibid.

Chapter 9: How to Practice—Keeping It Real

1. "Iverson Practice!" *YouTube*, 2017, https://www.youtube.com/watch?v=eGDBR2L5kzI.

2. "Gary Payton and Allen Iverson Practice," *YouTube*, 2017, https://www.youtube.com/watch?v=16WiMRgnKOE.

3. "Allen Iverson's Infamous 'Practice' Press Conference (Longest Version)," *YouTube*, 2017, https://youtu.be/YeLUhD9s6FQ.

4. Palmer, Chris, "An Icon at 40: The Untold Story of Allen Iverson," *Bleacher Report,* 2017, http://bleacherreport.com/articles/2476540-an-icon-at-40-the-untold-story-of-allen-iverson.

5. Haberstroh, Tom, "Lebron: Iverson Is Pound-for-Pound Champ," ESPN.com, 2017, http://www.espn.com/nba/truehoop/miamiheat/story/_/id/9894693/lebron-james-miami-heat-says-allen-iverson-was-nba-best-player-pound-pound.

6. Palmer, Chris, "An Icon at 40: The Untold Story of Allen Iverson."

7. "Hi, I'm Malcolm Gladwell, Author of *The Tipping Point, Blink, Outliers* and—Most Recently—*David and Goliath: Underdogs, Misfits and the Art of Battling Giants.* Ask Me Anything!" Reddit, 2017, https://www.reddit.com/r/IAmA/comments/2740ct/hi_im_malcolm_gladwell_author_of_the_tipping/chx6ku3/.

8. Gladwell, Malcolm, "Complexity and the Ten-Thousand-Hour Rule," *New Yorker,* August 21, 2013.

9. Ericsson, K. Anders, Ralf T. Krampe, and Clemens Tesch-Römer, "The Role of Deliberate Practice in the Acquisition of Expert Performance," *Psychological Review* 100 (3) 1993: 363–406.

10. Ericsson, Anders, and Robert Pool, "Malcolm Gladwell Got Us Wrong: Our Research Was Key to the 10,000-Hour Rule, But Here's What Got Oversimplified," *Salon,* 2017, http://www.salon.com/2016/04/10/malcolm_gladwell_got_us_wrong_our_research_was_key_to_the_10000_hour_rule_but_heres_what_got_oversimplified/.

11. Ibid.

12. Ericsson, K. Anders, Ralf T. Krampe, and Clemens Tesch-Römer, "The Role of Deliberate Practice in the Acquisition of Expert Performance."

13. Author interview with K. Anders Ericsson, 7/5/2017.

14. Ibid.

15. Ibid.

16. Monroe, Mike, "How an NBA 'Shot Whisperer' Transformed Kawhi Leonard into a 3-Point Fire Hazard," *Bleacher Report,* 2017, http://bleacherreport.com/articles/2634107-how-an-nba-shot-whisperer-transformed-kawhi-leonard-into-a-3-point-fire-hazard.

17. Barnwell, Bill, "The Shot Doctor," *Grantland*, 2017, http://grantland .com/features/the-shot-doctor/.

18. Bailey, Stephen, "Spurs Assistant Chip Engelland Is Shooting Up the Ranks in NBA," *Los Angeles Times,* June 12, 2013.

19. Barnwell, Bill, "The Shot Doctor."

20. Monroe, Mike, "How an NBA 'Shot Whisperer' Transformed Kawhi Leonard into a 3-Point Fire Hazard."

21. Author interview with K. Anders Ericsson, 7/5/2017.

22. Bailey, Stephen, "Spurs Assistant Chip Engelland Is Shooting Up the Ranks in NBA."

23. Vergano, Dan, "Are Malcolm Gladwell's 10,000 Hours of Practice Really All You Need?" News.Nationalgeographic.com, 2017, http://news .nationalgeographic.com/news/2014/03/140310-gladwell-expertise-prac tice-debate-intelligence/.

24. Macnamara, Brooke N., David Z. Hambrick, and Frederick L. Oswald, "Deliberate Practice and Performance in Music, Games, Sports, Education, and Professions," *Psychological Science* 25 (8) 2014: 1608–18.

25. Ibid.

26. "It Takes More Than Practice to Excel," *Sciencedaily,* 2017, https:// www.sciencedaily.com/releases/2014/07/140728094258.htm.

27. Macnamara, Brooke N., David Moreau, and David Z. Hambrick, "The Relationship Between Deliberate Practice and Performance in Sports," *Perspectives on Psychological Science* 11 (3) 2016: 333–50.

28. Ibid.

29. Güllich, Arne, "The Efficacy of Early TID Programs in Sport. Prof. Dr. Arne Güllich #Nysitalks," *YouTube,* 2017, https://youtu.be/Nd4r TUCpOAE.

30. Hornig, Manuel, Friedhelm Aust, and Arne Güllich, "Practice and Play in the Development of German Top-Level Professional Football Players," *European Journal of Sport Science* 16 (1) 2014: 96–105.

31. Güllich, Arne, "International Medallists' and Non-Medallists' Developmental Sport Activities—A Matched-Pairs Analysis," *Journal of Sports Sciences* 35 (23) 2016: 2281–88.

32. Güllich, Arne, "The Efficacy of Early TID Programs in Sport. Prof. Dr. Arne Güllich #Nysitalks."

33. Ibid.

34. Author interview with Peter Vint, 7/3/2017.

35. Bruyninckx, Michel, "Interview with Michel Bruyninckx (Cogi Training) at BMO Centre London—Mon Mar 6Th 2017," *YouTube,* 2017, https:// youtu.be/4_DK2i4HjzQ.

36. Sinnott, John, "BBC Sport—Football—Cracking Coaching's Final Frontier," News.bbc.co.uk, 2017, http://news.bbc.co.uk/sport2/hi/football/9421702.stm.

37. Sinnott, John, "AC Milan Focuses on Brain Power to Develop Young Players," Worldsport.Blogs.Cnn.com, 2017, http://worldsport.blogs.cnn.com/2013/10/22/ac-milan-focuses-on-brain-power-to-develop-young-players/.

38. Sinnott, John, "Standard Liege's Bruyninckx Leads Way in Developing Mental Capacity," SI.com, 2017, https://www.si.com/soccer/2011/12/23/blizzard-sinnottmental.

39. Ibid.

40. Sinnott, John, "BBC Sport—Football—Cracking Coaching's Final Frontier."

41. Smith, Rory, "Cybernetics, Cesarean Sections and Soccer's Most Magnificent Mind," *New York Times*, April 26, 2017.

42. Oliveira, Bruno, *Mourinho* (Lisboa: Gradiva, 2016).

43. Gendelman, David, "Coaching, Portuguese Style," *The Paris Review*, https://www.theparisreview.org/blog/2014/05/29/coaching-portuguese-style/.

44. Connolly, Fergus, and John Weatherly, "Changing the Game With Dr. Fergus Connolly—Simplifaster," Simplifaster Blog, 2017, https://simplifaster.com/articles/changing-game-dr-fergus-connolly/.

45. Oliveira, Bruno, *Mourinho*.

46. Ibid.

47. Author interview with Valter Di Salvo, 6/5/2017.

48. Ibid.

49. Hamilton, Tom, "England's Late Tries Down to Eddie Jones' Adaptation of Mourinho's Tactics," ESPN.com, 2017, http://www.espn.co.uk/rugby/story/_/id/18670839/england-late-tries-eddie-jones-adaptation-jose-mourinho-tactical-periodisation.

50. Meagher, Gerard, "Eddie Jones' Tactical Periodisation Stirs Up Perfect Brew for England," *The Guardian*, 2017, https://www.theguardian.com/sport/blog/2017/feb/20/eddie-jones-tactical-periodisation-stirs-up-perfect-brew-england-six-nations.

51. Ibid.

52. Author interview with Dave Hadfield, 5/17/2017.

53. "A Quote from All of Grace," Goodreads, 2017, https://www.goodreads.com/quotes/744825-begin-as-you-mean-to-go-on-and-go-on.

Chapter 10: How to Compete: The Clutch and Choke of the Performance Engine

1. Author interview with Mark Newman, 6/16/2017.
2. McCarron, Anthony, "Derek Jeter Moments: The Flip Play from the Daily News Archives," *New York Daily News,* 2017, http://www.nydaily news.com/sports/baseball/yankees/derek-jeter-moments-flip-play-daily -news-archives-article-1.1952399.
3. Ibid.
4. Ibid.
5. Author interview with Mark Newman, 6/16/2017.
6. "NFL Films Presents: Super Bowl LI, the Greatest Comeback in Super Bowl History," NFL Films, *YouTube,* February 13, 2017, https://youtu .be/aV5l1G_1hxY
7. King, Peter, "Peter King's Monday Morning QB: Brady in Montana," SI.com, 2017, http://mmqb.si.com/mmqb/2017/02/13/tom-brady-mon tana-super-bowl-51-nfl-patriots-peter-king.
8. "New England Patriots Super Bowl Postgame Transcripts 2/5," New England Patriots, 2017, http://www.patriots.com/news/2017/02/05/new-en gland-patriots-super-bowl-postgame-transcripts-25.
9. King, Peter, "Peter King: Tom Brady in Montana, Part 2," SI.com, 2017, http://mmqb.si.com/mmqb/2017/02/15/tom-brady-montana-part-2-nfl -patriots-peter-king.
10. "Atlanta Falcons Super Bowl Postgame Transcripts 2/5," New England Patriots, 2017 http://www.patriots.com/news/2017/02/05/atlanta-fal cons-super-bowl-postgame-transcripts-25.
11. Swann, Christian, "In the Mind of an Elite Athlete: What Do Sports-people Think When They Excel?" *The Conversation,* 2017, http://the conversation.com/in-the-mind-of-an-elite-athlete-what-do-sportspeople -think-when-they-excel-62624.
12. Ibid.
13. Ibid.
14. Kimiecik, Jay C., and Gary L. Stein, "Examining Flow Experiences in Sport Contexts: Conceptual Issues and Methodological Concerns," *Journal of Applied Sport Psychology* 4 (2) 1992: 144–60.
15. Swann, Christian, Richard J. Keegan, David Piggott, and Lee Crust, "A Systematic Review of the Experience, Occurrence, and Controllability of Flow States in Elite Sport," *Psychology of Sport and Exercise* 13 (6) 2012: 807–19.
16. "Kobe Bryant Explains 'Being in the Zone,'" *YouTube,* 2017, https:// youtu.be/wl49zc8g3DY.

17. Swann, Christian, Richard Keegan, Lee Crust, and David Piggott, "Psychological States Underlying Excellent Performance in Professional Golfers: 'Letting It Happen' vs. 'Making It Happen,' " *Psychology of Sport and Exercise* 23 (2016): 101–113.

18. Swann, Christian, Lee Crust, Patricia Jackman, Stewart A. Vella, Mark S. Allen, and Richard Keegan, "Psychological States Underlying Excellent Performance in Sport: Toward an Integrated Model of Flow and Clutch States," *Journal of Applied Sport Psychology* 2017, 1–27.

19. Swann, Christian, "In the Mind of an Elite Athlete: What Do Sportspeople Think When They Excel?"

20. Author interview with Christian Swann, PhD, 7/5/2017.

21. Ibid.

22. Ibid.

23. Kotler, Steven, *The Rise of Superman* (Boston, MA: New Harvest, 2014).

24. Author interview with Steven Kotler, 7/4/2017.

25. Ibid.

26. Kotler, Steven, and Wheal Jamie, *Stealing Fire: How Silicon Valley, the Navy SEALS, and Maverick Scientists Are Revolutionizing the Way We Live and Work* (New York: HarperCollins, 2017).

27. Myers, Gary, "After Super Bowl Choke Job, Falcons' Quinn Leans on Kerr, Others," *New York Daily News*, June 3, 2017.

28. "Human Performance Lab, The University of Chicago," Human Performance Lab, University of Chicago, https://hpl.uchicago.edu/.

29. Beilock, Sian L., and Thomas H. Carr, "On the Fragility of Skilled Performance: What Governs Choking Under Pressure?" *Journal of Experimental Psychology: General* 130 (4) 2001: 701–25.

30. Author interview with Christian Swann, PhD, 7/5/2017.

31. Beilock, Sian L., and Rob Gray, "Why Do Athletes Choke Under Pressure?" *Handbook of Sport Psychology*, 425–44, doi:10.1002/9781118270011.ch192012.

32. Ibid.

33. Beilock, Sian L., Thomas H. Carr, Clare MacMahon, and Janet L. Starkes, "When Paying Attention Becomes Counterproductive: Impact of Divided Versus Skill-Focused Attention on Novice and Experienced Performance of Sensorimotor Skills," *Journal of Experimental Psychology: Applied* 8 (1) 2002: 6–16.

34. Gray, Rob, "Attending to the Execution of a Complex Sensorimotor Skill: Expertise Differences, Choking, and Slumps," *Journal of Experimental Psychology: Applied* 10 (1) 2004: 42–54.

35. Ibid.

36. Gray, Rob, "The Perception and Action Podcast—Talking Sports Science and Psychology," Perceptionaction.com, 2017, http://perceptionaction.com/.

37. "New England Patriots Super Bowl Postgame Transcripts 2/5," New England Patriots, 2017, http://www.patriots.com/news/2017/02/05/new-england-patriots-super-bowl-postgame-transcripts-25.

38. Stonkus, Mark, "The Development and Validation of the Inventory of Mental Toughness Factors in Sport (IMTF-S)," unpublished doctoral dissertation, Boston University.

39. "No Shortcuts to the Top: Climbing the World's 14 Highest Peaks" (October 2006), http://a.co/4Iqkbwc.

40. Blatherwick, Jack, *Over-Speed: Skill Training for Hockey*, USA Hockey, 1994.

41. Zaichkowsky, L. B., and L. D. Zaichkowsky, "The Effects of a School-based Relaxation Training Program on Fourth-grade Children," *Journal of Clinical Child Psychology* 13 (1) 1984: 81–85.

42. Zaichkowsky, L. D., "Psychophysiology and Neuroscience in Sport: Introduction to the Special Issue," *Journal of Clinical Sport Psychology* 6 (1) 2012: 1–5.

43. Davis, Henry, M. Liotti, E. T. Ngan, T. S. Woodward, J. X. Van Snellenberg, S. M. van Anders, A. Smith, H. S. Mayberg, "Signal Changes in Elite Swimmers While Viewing Videos of Personal Failure," *Brain Imaging and Behavior* 2 (2) 2008.

44. Hammond, T. H. Davis, and L. Zaichkowsky, "The Effects of Self-focus on Affect and Vertical Jump Performance of NCAA Athletes," *International Journal of Kinesiology and Sports Science* 3 (2) 2015, 9–16.

45. Ibid.

46. Y. Pitsiladis and G. Wang, "Genomics of Elite Sporting Performance," in J. Baker and D. Farrow (eds.), *Routledge Handbook of Sport Expertise* (New York: Routledge, 2015), 295–304.

Epilogue: Preparing Future Players

1. Hamm, Mia, and Aaron Heifetz, *Go for the Goal: A Champion's Guide to Winning in Soccer and Life* (New York: Quill, 2000).

2. Anderson, Kelli, "16 Mia Hamm," SI.com, February 9, 1995, https://www.si.com/vault/1995/02/09/133250/16-mia-hamm.

3. "Anson Dorrance—UNC Tar Heels Athletics," 2017, Goheels.com .http://goheels.com/staff.aspx?staff=219.

4. "The Vision of a Champion: What Drives Winning," Whatdriveswinning.com, 2017, http://whatdriveswinning.com/video/anson-dorrance-mia-hamm/.

5. "Jordan, Hamm Named ACC's Greatest Athletes," WRAL.com, 2017, http://www.wral.com/news/local/story/104512/.

6. "Pele's List of Soccer's Best Includes Hamm, Akers," USAToday.com, 2004, https://usatoday30.usatoday.com/sports/soccer/2004-03-04-pele -list_x.htm.

7. "Records," Ussoccer.com, 2017, https://www.ussoccer.com/womens -national-team/records.

8. "The Essence of Mia Hamm," *EspnW*, 2017, http://www.espn.com /espnw/title-ix/article/8078671/the-essence-mia-hamm.

9. "Wambach: Mia's Still My Idol," FIFA.com, July 15, 2013, http://www .fifa.com/womensworldcup/news/y=2013/m=7/news=wambach-can-wait -for-record-broken-2135505.html.

10. "Home," Team First Soccer Academy, 2017, http://teamfirstsocceracad emy.com/.

11. Ramsey, David, "David Ramsey: Soccer Great Mia Hamm Asks Sports Parents to Stop Being So Childish," *Colorado Springs Gazette*, November 8, 2016.

12. Ibid.

13. Woitalla, Mike, "Mallory Pugh: The Teen Star's Amazing Rise and How It All Started," *Youth Soccer Insider* (blog), 2016, https://www.soccer america.com/publications/article/68353/mallory-pugh-the-teen-stars -amazing-rise-and-how.html.

14. Ackerman, Jon, "National Phenomenon: Mallory Pugh and Her Mother Karen," milehighsports.com, 2016, https://milehighsports.com/national -phenomenon-mallory-pugh-and-her-mother-karen/.

15. Ibid.

16. Woitalla, Mike, "Mallory Pugh: The Teen Star's Amazing Rise and How It All Started."

17. Panduro, Jimena, "First Cap, First Goal: Mallory Pugh," U.S. Soccer Federation, ussoccer.com, February 12, 2016, https://www.ussoccer.com /stories/2016/02/12/16/49/160212-wnt-mallory-pugh-earns-first-goal-in -debut-game.

18. Kennedy, Paul, "Jill Ellis Hails the US Newbies on Olympic Roster," *Soccer America Daily* (blog), socceramerica.com, July 12, 2016, https:// www.socceramerica.com/publications/article/69545/jill-ellis-hails-the-us -newbies-on-olympic-roste.html.

19. Panduro, Jimena, "First Cap, First Goal: Mallory Pugh."

20. Schaerlackens, Leander, "Mallory Pugh, the USWNT's Next Big Thing, Has No Use for Your Hype," *Yahoo!Sports*, 2017, https://sports.yahoo

.com/news/mallory-pugh-the-uswnts-next-big-thing-has-no-use-for-your
-hype-090549575.html.

21. *Twitter*, https://twitter.com/MiaHamm/status/756664136814108672.

22. Kassouf, Jeff, "The Next Who? Spirit's Star Can Be the Next Mallory
Pugh," *FourFourTwo*, May 2017, https://www.fourfourtwo.com/us/fea
tures/mallory-pugh-interview-profile-nwsl-washington-spirit-debut-pre
view.

23. Floyd, Thomas, "USWNT Star Mallory Pugh Forging Unprecedented
Path Through NWSL," *Goal USA Podcast*, 2017, http://www.goal.com
/en-us/news/goal-usa-podcast-uswnt-star-mallory-pugh-forging/kbvvxtt
21yqi1kbyqq998tklt.

24. Wright, Nick, "Luka Modric Is Still Key for Real Madrid Under Zinedine Zidane," skysports.com, 2017, http://www.skysports.com/football
/news/11835/10842948/luka-modric-is-still-key-for-real-madrid-under
-zinedine-zidane.

25. "The World's Best Playmaker 2017: One More for Lionel Messi," IFFHS,
2017, https://iffhs.de/worlds-best-playmaker-2017-one-lionel-messi/.

26. Baxter, Kevin, "Christian Pulisic May Be the Perfect 10 for Aging U.S.
National Team," Latimes.com, 2016. http://www.latimes.com/sports
/soccer/la-sp-soccer-baxter-20160903-snap-story.html.

27. " 'Just a Natural': Christian Pulisic Shines in Playmaker Role as USA
Routs Honduras," *Sporting News* (blog), *Yahoo!Sports*, 2017, https://
uk.sports.yahoo.com/news/christian-pulisic-shines-usa-playmaker
-050740327.html.

28. Alfonsi, Sharyn, "Will Christian Pulisic Be the Next Big Name in Soccer?" *CBS News*, 2017, https://www.cbsnews.com/news/will-christian
-pulisic-be-the-next-big-name-in-soccer/.

29. Tanenwald, Jonathan, "Christian Pulisic, Just 18, Is Already Becoming a
U.S. Soccer Leader," *The Inquirer Daily News*, philly.com, September 5,
2017, http://www.philly.com/philly/sports/soccer/christian-pulisic-amer
ican-soccer-star-borussia-dortmund-usmnt-hershey-liverpool-20170905
.html.

30. Alfonsi, Sharyn, "Will Christian Pulisic Be the Next Big Name in Soccer?"

31. Ibid.

32. Wahl, Grant, "The Education of Christian Pulisic: Inside the Dortmund,
USA Rising Star's Rapid Growth," SI.com, 2016, https://www.si.com
/planet-futbol/2016/11/09/christian-pulisic-borussia-dortmund-usmnt
-usa.

33. Kwesi O'Mard, Marcus, "How Christian Pulisic Compares to Lionel Messi, Cristiano Ronaldo at 19," *NESN*, 2017, https://nesn.com/2017/09/how-christian-pulisic-compares-to-lionel-messi-cristiano-ronaldo-at-19/.

34. Caley, Michael, "The Great American Soccer Hope Is Here (for Real, This Time)," *FiveThirtyEight*, 2017, https://fivethirtyeight.com/features/the-great-american-soccer-hope-is-here-for-real-this-time/.

35. Alfonsi, Sharyn, "Will Christian Pulisic Be the Next Big Name in Soccer?"

36. "Anson Dorrance: Grading Character," *YouTube*, 2015, https://youtu.be/IpHFVu3dPGs.